Learn TensorFlow Enterprise

Build, manage, and scale machine learning workloads seamlessly using Google's TensorFlow Enterprise

KC Tung

BIRMINGHAM—MUMBAI

Learn TensorFlow Enterprise

Commissioning Editor: Sunith Shetty
Acquisition Editor: Hiral Dhorda
Senior Editor: Mohammed Imaratwale
Content Development Editor: Nazia Shaikh
Technical Editor: Manikandan Kurup
Copy Editor: Safis Editing
Project Coordinator: Aishwarya Mohan
Proofreader: Safis Editing
Indexer: Priyanka Dhadke
Production Designer: Joshua Misquitta

First published: November 2020
Production reference: 2050121

Published by Packt Publishing Ltd.
Livery Place
35 Livery Street
Birmingham
B3 2PB, UK.

ISBN 978-1-80020-914-5

www.packt.com

To my beloved wife Katy, whose support and encouragement keep me going every day.

To all my passionate and driven readers, whose growth mindset inspires me to write this book.

Packt.com

Subscribe to our online digital library for full access to over 7,000 books and videos, as well as industry leading tools to help you plan your personal development and advance your career. For more information, please visit our website.

Why subscribe?

- Spend less time learning and more time coding with practical eBooks and videos from over 4,000 industry professionals

- Improve your learning with Skill Plans built especially for you

- Get a free eBook or video every month

- Fully searchable for easy access to vital information

- Copy and paste, print, and bookmark content

Did you know that Packt offers eBook versions of every book published, with PDF and ePub files available? You can upgrade to the eBook version at packt.com and, as a print book customer, you are entitled to a discount on the eBook copy. Get in touch with us at customercare@packtpub.com for more details.

At www.packt.com, you can also read a collection of free technical articles, sign up for a range of free newsletters, and receive exclusive discounts and offers on Packt books and eBooks.

Contributors

About the author

KC Tung is a cloud solution architect at **Microsoft** and specializes in machine learning, as well as AI model development and deployment. He has a Ph.D. in biophysics from the **University of Texas Southwestern Medical Center** in **Dallas** and has spoken at the 2018 O'Reilly AI Conference in San Francisco and the 2019 O'Reilly TensorFlow World Conference in San Jose. He has worked on building data ingestion and feature engineering pipelines for custom datasets in cloud environments. He has also delivered machine learning models for scalable deployment. He is a Microsoft certified AI engineer and data engineer.

I would like to express my gratitude to the entire Packt team of very thoughtful, thorough and professional editors: Ayaan Hoda, Nazia Shaikh, Gebin George, Kirti Pisat, Yusuf Imaratwale, Manikandan Kurup. Also, I really appreciate reviewers' feedback and suggestions. Finally, a special thank for the acquisition editor Hiral Dhorda for giving me an opportunity to write this book.

About the reviewers

Hanchao Liu achieved his Ph.D. in computational chemistry. He has 10 years' experience in developing machine learning applications and infrastructures in domains ranging from chemistry, to marketing technology, to cloud computing. He currently works at Google where he focuses on building machine learning infrastructures for Google Cloud Platform.

Viacheslav Kovalevskyi is a Senior Engineering Manager. He focuses on helping big enterprises with building MLOps solutions, teaches Java courses, and actively creates content on YouTube.

Viacheslav has also created his own unique management execution framework: UODP. Blogger, podcaster.

Packt is searching for authors like you

If you're interested in becoming an author for Packt, please visit `authors.packtpub.com` and apply today. We have worked with thousands of developers and tech professionals, just like you, to help them share their insight with the global tech community. You can make a general application, apply for a specific hot topic that we are recruiting an author for, or submit your own idea.

Table of Contents

Section 2 – Data Preprocessing and Modeling

3
Data Preparation and Manipulation Techniques

4
Reusable Models and Scalable Data Pipelines

Section 3 – Scaling and Tuning ML Works

8

Best Practices for Model Training and Performance

9

Serving a TensorFlow Model

Other Books You May Enjoy

Index

Preface

TensorFlow as a **machine learning** (**ML**) library has matured into a production-ready ecosystem. This beginner's book uses practical examples to enable you to build and deploy TensorFlow models using optimal settings that ensure long-term support without having to worry about library deprecation or being left behind when it comes to bug fixes or workarounds.

The book begins by showing you how to refine your TensorFlow project and set it up for enterprise-level deployment. You'll then learn to choose the version of TensorFlow. As you advance, you'll find out how to build and deploy models in a robust and stable environment by following recommended practices made available in TensorFlow Enterprise. This book also teaches you how to manage your services better and enhance the performance and reliability of your **artificial intelligence** (**AI**) applications. You'll discover how to use various enterprise-ready services to accelerate your ML and AI workflows on Google Cloud. Finally, you'll scale your ML models and handle heavy workloads across CPUs, GPUs, and cloud TPUs.

By the end of this TensorFlow book, you'll have learned the patterns needed for TensorFlow Enterprise model development, data pipelines, training, and deployment.

Who this book is for

This book is for data scientists, ML developers or engineers, and cloud practitioners who want to learn and implement various services and features offered by TensorFlow Enterprise from scratch. Basic knowledge of the ML development process will be useful.

What this book covers

Chapter 1, Overview of TensorFlow Enterprise, illustrates how to set up and run TensorFlow Enterprise in a **Google Cloud Platform** (**GCP**) environment. This will give you initial hands-on experience in seeing how TensorFlow Enterprise integrates with other data services in GCP.

Chapter 2, Running TensorFlow Enterprise in Google AI Platform, describes how to use GCP to set up and run TensorFlow Enterprise. As a differentiated TensorFlow distribution, TensorFlow Enterprise can be found on several (but not all) GCP platforms. It is important to use these platforms in order to ensure that the correct distribution is provisioned.

Chapter 3, Data Preparation and Manipulation Techniques, illustrates how to deal with raw data and format it to uniquely suit consumption by a TensorFlow model training process. We will look at a number of essential TensorFlow Enterprise APIs that convert raw data into Protobuf format for efficient streaming, which is a recommended workflow for feeding data into a training process.

Chapter 4, Reusable Models and Scalable Data Pipelines, describes the different ways in which a TensorFlow Enterprise model may be built or reused. These options provide the flexibility to suit different situational requirements for building, training, and deploying TensorFlow models. Equipped with this knowledge, you will be able to make informed choices and understand the trade-offs among different model development strategies.

Chapter 5, Training at Scale, illustrates the use of TensorFlow Enterprise distributed training strategies to scale your model training to a cluster (either GPU or TPU). This will enable you to build a model development and training process that is robust and take advantage of all the hardware at your disposal.

Chapter 6, Hyperparameter Tuning, focuses on hyperparameter tuning as this is a necessary part of model training, especially when building your own model. TensorFlow Enterprise now provides high-level APIs for advanced hyperparameter space search algorithms. Through this chapter, you will learn how to leverage the distributed computing power at your disposal to reduce the training time required for hyperparameter tuning.

Chapter 7, Model Optimization, explores the concept of how lean and mean your model is. Does your model run as efficiently as possible? If your use case requires the model to run with limited resources (memory, model size, or data type), such as in the case of edge or mobile devices, then it's time to consider model runtime optimization. This chapter discusses the latest means of model optimization through the TensorFlow Lite framework. After this chapter, you will be able to optimize a trained TensorFlow Enterprise model to be as lightweight as possible for inferencing.

Chapter 8, Best Practices for Model Training and Performance, focuses on two aspects of model training that are universal: data ingestion and overfitting. First, it is necessary to build a data ingestion pipeline that works regardless of the size and complexity of the training data. In this chapter, best practices and recommendations for using TensorFlow Enterprise data preprocessing pipelines are explained and demonstrated. Second, in dealing with overfitting, standard practices of regularization as well as some recently released regularizations by the TensorFlow team are discussed.

Chapter 9, Serving a TensorFlow Model, describes the fundamentals of model inferencing as a web service. You will learn how to serve a TensorFlow model using TensorFlow Serving by building a Docker image of the model. In this chapter, you will begin by learning how to make use of saved models in your local environment first. Then you will build a Docker image of the model using TensorFlow Serving as the base image. Finally, you will serve this model as a web service through the RESTful API exposed by your Docker container.

To get the most out of this book

It would be very helpful to have a fundamental understanding of, and experience with, the Keras API, as this book pivots on a TensorFlow version beyond 2.x, in which the Keras API is officially supported and adopted as the `tf.keras` API. In addition, having a basic understanding of image classification techniques (convolution, and multiclass classification) would be helpful, as this book reuses the image classification problem as a vehicle to introduce and explain new features in TensorFlow Enterprise 2. Another helpful tool is GitHub. Basic experience with cloning GitHub repositories and navigating file structures would be very helpful for downloading the source code in this book.

From the ML perspective, having a basic understanding of model architectures, feature engineering processes, and hyperparameter optimization would be helpful. It is also assumed that you are familiar with fundamental Python data structures, including NumPy arrays, tuples, and dictionaries.

If you are using the digital version of this book, we advise you to type the code in yourself or access the code via the GitHub repository (link available in the next section). Doing so will help you avoid any potential errors related to the copying/ pasting of code.

Download the example code files

You can download the example code files for this book from GitHub at `https://github.com/PacktPublishing/learn-tensorflow-enterprise/`. In case there's an update to the code, it will be updated on the existing GitHub repository.

We also have other code bundles from our rich catalog of books and videos available at `https://github.com/PacktPublishing/`. Check them out!

Download the color images

We also provide a PDF file that has color images of the screenshots/diagrams used in this book. You can download it here: `https://static.packt-cdn.com/downloads/9781800209145_ColorImages.pdf`

Conventions used

There are a number of text conventions used throughout this book.

`Code in text`: Indicates code words in text, database table names, folder names, filenames, file extensions, pathnames, dummy URLs, user input, and Twitter handles. Here is an example: 'Just like `lxterminal`, we can run Linux commands from here too.'

A block of code is set as follows:

```
p2 = Person()
p2.name = 'Jane'
p2.age = 20
print(p2.name)
print(p2.age)
```

Any command-line input or output is written as follows:

```
sudo apt-get install xrdp -y
```

Bold: Indicates a new term, an important word, or words that you see on screen. For example, words in menus or dialog boxes appear in the text like this. Here is an example: 'Open the **Remote Desktop Connection** application on your Windows PC.'

> **Tips or important notes**
> Appear like this.

Get in touch

Feedback from our readers is always welcome.

General feedback: If you have questions about any aspect of this book, mention the book title in the subject of your message and email us at customercare@packtpub.com.

Errata: Although we have taken every care to ensure the accuracy of our content, mistakes do happen. If you have found a mistake in this book, we would be grateful if you would report this to us. Please visit www.packtpub.com/support/errata, selecting your book, clicking on the Errata Submission Form link, and entering the details.

Piracy: If you come across any illegal copies of our works in any form on the internet, we would be grateful if you would provide us with the location address or website name. Please contact us at copyright@packt.com with a link to the material.

If you are interested in becoming an author: If there is a topic that you have expertise in, and you are interested in either writing or contributing to a book, please visit authors.packtpub.com.

Reviews

Please leave a review. Once you have read and used this book, why not leave a review on the site that you purchased it from? Potential readers can then see and use your unbiased opinion to make purchase decisions, we at Packt can understand what you think about our products, and our authors can see your feedback on their book. Thank you!

For more information about Packt, please visit packt.com.

Section 1 – TensorFlow Enterprise Services and Features

Welcome to TensorFlow Enterprise! This is a TensorFlow distribution that includes all the building blocks and APIs that enable more optimizations, better monitoring, more high-level APIs, and long-term support. In this part, you will learn about how to get started with using TensorFlow Enterprise in Google Cloud-native platforms and services.

This section comprises the following chapters:

- *Chapter 1, Overview of TensorFlow Enterprise*
- *Chapter 2, Running TensorFlow Enterprise in Google AI Platform*

1
Overview of TensorFlow Enterprise

In this introductory chapter, you will learn how to set up and run TensorFlow Enterprise in a **Google Cloud Platform** (**GCP**) environment. This will enable you to get some initial hands-on experience of how TensorFlow Enterprise integrates with other services in GCP. One of the most important improvements in TensorFlow Enterprise is the integration with the data storage options in Google Cloud, such as Google Cloud Storage and BigQuery.

This chapter starts by covering how to complete a one-time setup for the cloud environment and enable the necessary cloud service APIs. Then we will see how easy it is to work with these data storage systems at scale.

In this chapter, we'll cover the following topics:

- Understanding TensorFlow Enterprise
- Configuring cloud environments for TensorFlow Enterprise
- Accessing the data sources

Understanding TensorFlow Enterprise

TensorFlow has become an ecosystem consisting of many valuable assets. At the core of its popularity and versatility is a comprehensive machine learning library and model templates that evolve quickly with new features and capabilities. This popularity comes at a cost, and that cost is expressed as complexity, intricate dependencies, and API updates or deprecation timelines that can easily break the models and workflow that were laboriously built not too long ago. It is one thing to learn and use the latest improvement in your code as you build a model to experiment with your ideas and hypotheses, but it is quite another if your job is to build a model for long-term production use, maintenance, and support.

Another problem associated with early TensorFlow in general concerned its code debugging process. In TensorFlow 1, lazy execution makes it rather tricky to test or debug your code because the code is not executed unless it is wrapped in a *session*, AKA a graph. Starting with TensorFlow 2, eager execution finally becomes a first-class citizen. Also, another welcome addition to TensorFlow 2 is the adoption of the Keras high-level API. This makes it much easier to code, experiment with, and maintain your model. It also improves the readability of your code and its training flow.

For enterprise adoption, there are typically these three major challenges that are of concern for stakeholders:

- The first challenge is **scale**. A production-grade model has to be trained with large amounts of data, and often it is not practical or possible to fit into a single-node computer's memory. This also can be thought of as another problem: how do you pass training data to the model? It seems the natural and instinctive way is to declare and involve the entire dataset as a Pythonic structure such as a **NumPy array** or a **pandas DataFrame**, as we have seen in so many open source examples. But if the data is too large, then it seems reasonable to use another way of passing data into a model instance, similar to the Python iterator. In fact, **TensorFlow.io** and **TensorFlow dataset libraries** are specifically provided to address this issue. We will see how they ingest data in batches to a model training process in the subsequent chapters.

- The second challenge that typically arises in consideration of enterprise adoption of TensorFlow is the **manageability** of the development environment. Backward compatibility is not a strength of TensorFlow, because there are historically very quick updates to and new releases of APIs that replace or deprecate old ones. This includes but is not limited to library version, API signature, and usage style deprecation. As you can imagine by now, this is a deal-breaker for development, debugging, and maintenance of the codebase; it also doesn't help with managing the stability and reproducibility of a production environment and its scoring results. It can easily become a nightmare for someone who manages and controls a machine learning development infrastructure and the standard practices in an enterprise project.

- The third challenge is the efforts for API improvements, patch releases, and bug fixes. To address this, TensorFlow rolls these efforts into **long-term support**. Typically, for any TensorFlow release, Google's TensorFlow team is committed to providing these fixes for up to a year only. However, for an enterprise, this is too short for them to get a proper return on investment from the development cycle. Therefore, for enterprises' mission-critical performance, a longer commitment to TensorFlow releases is essential.

TensorFlow Enterprise was created to address these challenges. TensorFlow Enterprise is a special distribution of TensorFlow that is exclusively available through Google Cloud's various services. TensorFlow Enterprise is available through the following:

- Google Cloud AI Notebooks
- Google Cloud AI Deep Learning VMs
- Google Cloud AI Deep Learning Containers
- Partially available on Google Cloud AI Training

The dependencies such as drivers and library version compatibility are managed by Google Cloud. It also provides optimized connectivity with other Google Cloud services, such as Cloud Storage and the data warehouse (**BigQuery**). Currently, TensorFlow Enterprise supports versions 1.15, 2.1, and 2.3 of Google Cloud, and the GCP and TensorFlow teams will provide long-term support for up to three years, including bug fixes and updates.

In addition to these exclusive services and managed features, the TensorFlow team also takes enterprise support to another level by offering a **white-glove service**. This is a separate service from Google Cloud Support. In this case, TensorFlow engineers in Google will work with qualified enterprise customers to solve problems or provide bug fixes in cutting edge AI applications.

TensorFlow Enterprise packages

At the time of writing this book, TensorFlow Enterprise includes the following packages:

Package	Version
TensorFlow	1.15, 2.1, 2.2, 2.3
TensorFlow-io	0.8, 0.11
TensorFlow-estimator	1.15, 2.1.0
TensorFlow-probability	0.8, 0.9
TensorFlow-datasets	1.12, 2.0.0
TensorFlow-hub	0.6, 0.7

Figure 1.1 – TensorFlow packages

We will have more to say about how to launch JupyterLab in Google AI Platform in *Chapter 2, Running TensorFlow Enterprise in Google AI Platform*, but for now, as a demonstration, the following command can be executed as a CLI command in a **JupyterLab** cell. It will provide the version for each package in your instance so that you can be sure of version consistency:

```
!pip list | grep tensorflow
```

Here's the output:

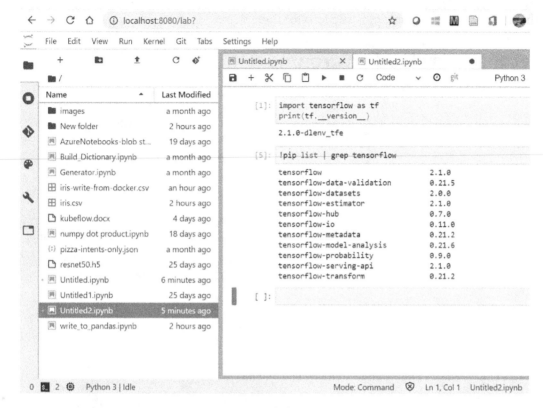

Figure 1.2 – Google Cloud AI Platform JupyterLab environment

We confirmed the environment is running a TensorFlow Enterprise distribution and all the library versions. Knowing this would help in future debugging and collaboration efforts.

Configuring cloud environments for TensorFlow Enterprise

Assuming you have a Google Cloud account already set up with a billing method, before you can start using TensorFlow Enterprise, there are some one-time setup steps that you must complete in Google Cloud. This setup consists of the following steps:

1. Create a cloud project and enable billing.

2. Create a Google Cloud Storage bucket.

3. Enable the necessary APIs.

The following are some quick instructions for these steps.

Setting up a cloud environment

Now we are going to take a look at what we need to set up in **Google Cloud** before we can start using TensorFlow Enterprise. These setups are needed so that essential Google Cloud services can integrate seamlessly into the user tenant. For example, the **project ID** is used to enable resource creation credentials and access for different services when working with data in the TensorFlow workflow. And by virtue of the project ID, you can read and write data into your Cloud Storage and data warehouse.

Creating a project

This is the first step. It is needed in order to enable billing so you can use nearly all Google Cloud resources. Most resources will ask for a project ID. It also helps you organize and track your spending by knowing which services contribute to each workload. Let's get started:

1. The URL for the page to create a project ID is `https://console.cloud.google.com/cloud-resource-manager`.

    After you have signed into the GCP portal, you will see a panel similar to this:

Figure 1.3 – Google Cloud's project creation panel

2. Click on **CREATE PROJECT**:

Figure 1.4 – Creating a new project

3. Then provide a project name, and the platform will instantly generate a project ID for you. You can either accept it or edit it. It may give you a warning regarding how many projects you can create if you already have a few active projects:

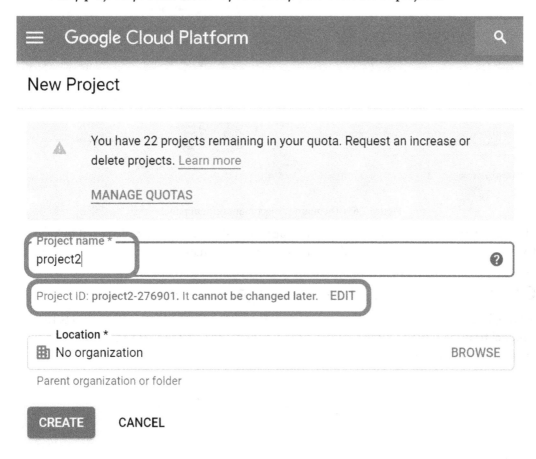

Figure 1.5 – Project name and project ID assignment

4.   Make a note of the project name and project ID. Keep these handy for future use. Hit **CREATE** and soon you will see the platform dashboard for this project:

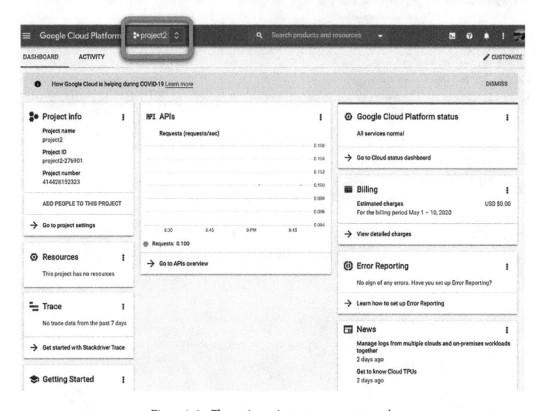

Figure 1.6 – The main project management panel

The project ID will frequently be used when accessing data storage. It is also used to keep track of resource consumption and allocation in a cloud tenant.

Creating a Google Cloud Storage bucket

A **Google Cloud Storage bucket** is a common way to store models and model assets from a model training job. Creating a storage bucket is very easy. Just look for **Storage** in the left panel and select **Browser**:

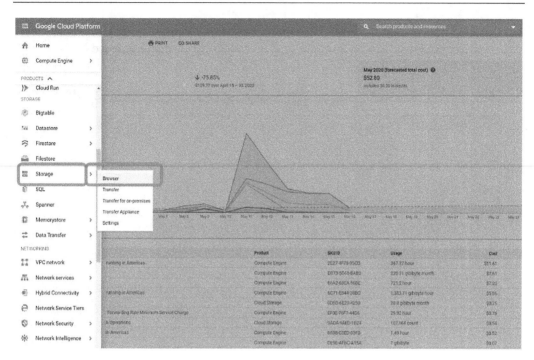

Figure 1.7 – Google Cloud's Storage options

Click **CREATE BUCKET**, and follow the instructions as indicated in the panel. In all cases, there are default options selected for you:

1. **Choose where to store your data**. This is a trade-off between cost and availability as measured by performance. The default is multi-region to ensure the highest availability.

2. **Choose a default storage class for your data**. This choice lets you decide on costs related to retrieval operations. The default is the standard level for frequently accessed data.

3. **Choose how to control access to objects**. This offers two different access levels for the bucket. The default is **object-level permissions (ACLs)** in addition to **bucket level permission (IAM)**.

4. **Advanced settings (optional)**. Here, you can choose the encryption type, bucket retention policy, and any bucket labels. The default is a Google-managed key and no retention policy nor labels:

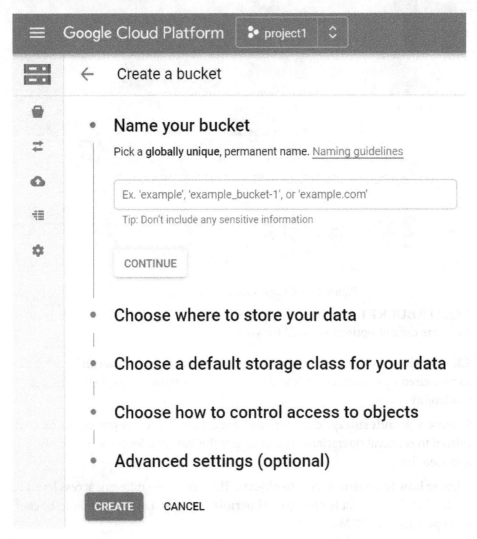

Figure 1.8 – Storage bucket creation process and choices

Enabling APIs

Now we have a project, but before we start consuming Google Cloud services, we need to enable some APIs. This process needs to be done only once, usually as the project ID is created:

1. For now, let's enable the Compute Engine API for the project of your choice:

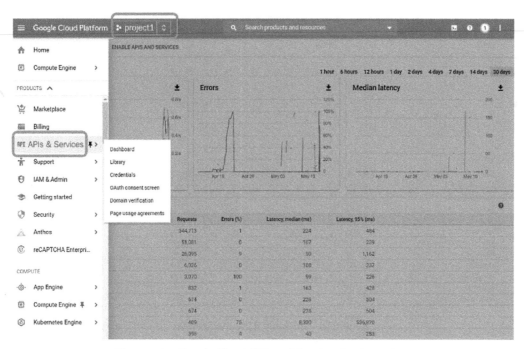

Figure 1.9 – Google Cloud APIs and Services for the project

Optional: Then select **ENABLE APIS AND SERVICES.**

You may do it here now, or as you go through the exercises in this book. If you need to use a particular cloud service for the first time, you can enable the API as you go along:

Figure 1.10 – Enabling APIs and Services

2. In the search box, type `Compute Engine API`:

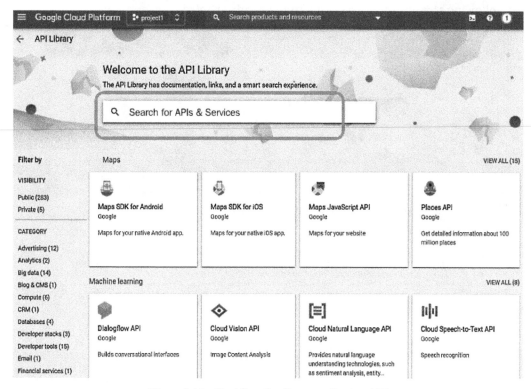

Figure 1.11 – Enabling the Compute Engine API

3. You will see the status of the **Compute Engine API** in your project as shown in the following screenshot. Enable it if it's not already enabled:

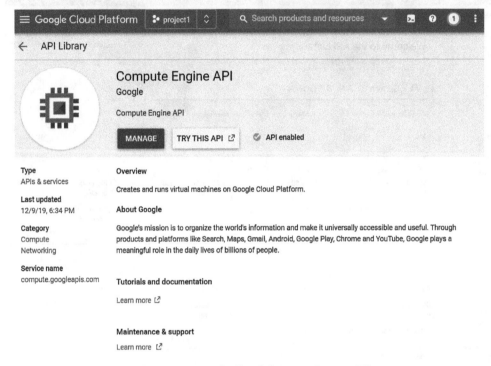

Figure 1.12 – Google Cloud Compute Engine API

For now, this is good enough. There are more APIs that you'll need as you go through the examples in this book; GCP will ask you to enable the API when relevant. You can do so at that time.

If you wish, you may repeat the preceding procedure to enable several other APIs as well: specifically, the *BigQuery API*, *BigQuery Data Transfer API*, *BigQuery Connection API*, *Service Usage API*, *Cloud Storage*, and the *Storage Transfer API*.

Next, let's take a look at how to move data in a storage bucket into a table inside a BigQuery data warehouse.

Creating a data warehouse

We will use a simple example of putting data stored in a Google Cloud bucket into a table that can be queried by BigQuery. The easiest way to do so is to use the BigQuery UI. Make sure it is in the right project. We will use this example to create a dataset that contains one table.

You can navigate to BigQuery by searching for it in the search bar of the GCP portal, as in the following screenshot:

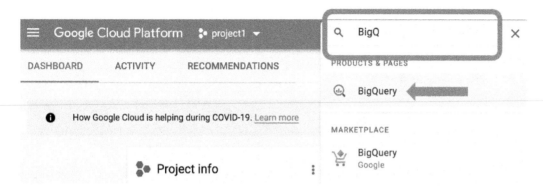

Figure 1.13 – Searching for BigQuery

You will see **BigQuery** being suggested. Click on it and it will take you to the BigQuery portal:

Figure 1.14 – BigQuery and the data warehouse query portal

Here are the steps to create a persistent table in the BigQuery data warehouse:

1. Select **Create dataset**:

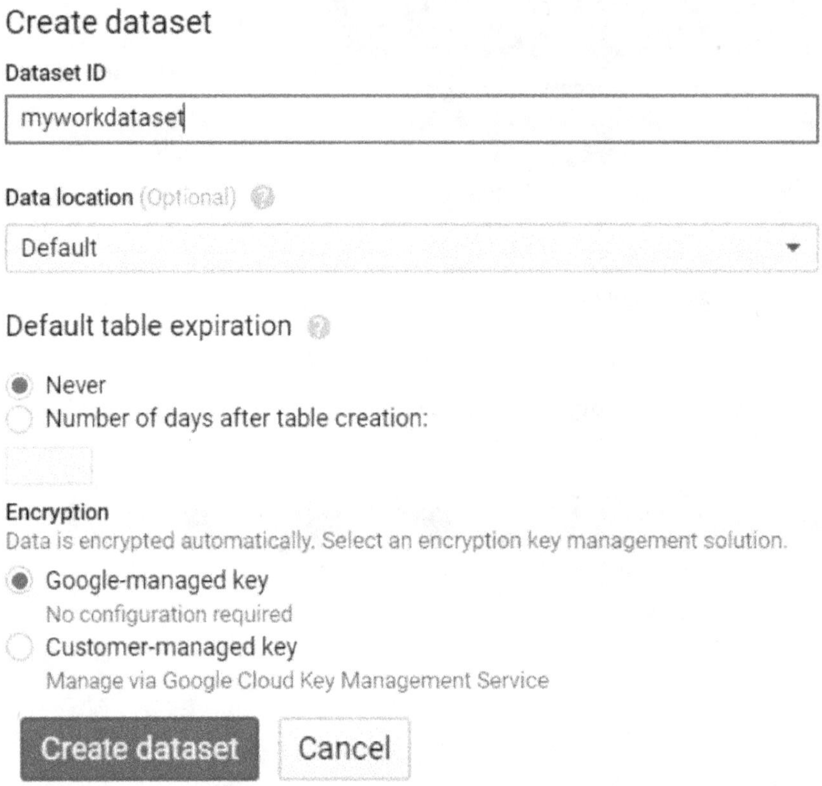

Create dataset

Dataset ID

myworkdataset

Data location (Optional)

Default ▼

Default table expiration

◉ Never
◯ Number of days after table creation:

Encryption
Data is encrypted automatically. Select an encryption key management solution.

◉ Google-managed key
No configuration required
◯ Customer-managed key
Manage via Google Cloud Key Management Service

[Create dataset] [Cancel]

Figure 1.15 – Creating a dataset for the project

2. Make sure you are in the dataset that you just created. Now click **CREATE TABLE**:

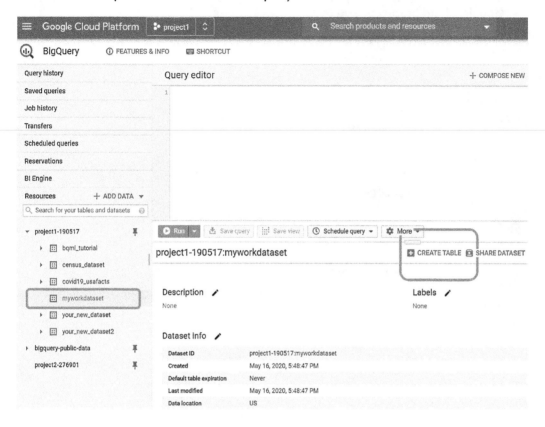

Figure 1.16 – Creating a table for the dataset

In the **Source** section, under **Source**, in the **Create table from** section, select **Google Cloud Storage**:

Create table

Source

Create table from:

Empty table
Empty table
Google Cloud Storage
Upload
Drive
Google Cloud Bigtable

Destination

Project name	Dataset name	Table type ⓘ
project1 ▾	myworkdataset ▾	Native table ▾

Table name

Letters, numbers, and underscores allowed

Schema

⬤▭ Edit as text

➕ Add field

Partition and cluster settings

Partitioning: ⓘ

No partitioning ▾

Clustering order (optional): ⓘ
Clustering order determines the sort order of the data. Clustering can only be used on a partitioned table, and works with tables partitioned either by column or ingestion time.

Comma-separated list of fields to define clustering order (up to 4)

Advanced options ⌄

Figure 1.17 – Populating the table by specifying a data source

3. Then it will transition to another dialog box. You may enter the name of the file or use the **Browse** option to find the file stored in the bucket. In this case, a CSV file has already been put in my Google Cloud Storage bucket. You may either put your own CSV file into the storage bucket, or download the one I used from `https://data.mendeley.com/datasets/7xwsksdpy3/1`. Also, enter the column names and datatypes as the schema:

Create table

Source

Create table from:	Select file from GCS bucket: ⓘ		File format:
Google Cloud Storage ▾	☑ myworkdataset/iris-write-from-docker.csv	Browse	CSV ▾
☐ Source Data Partitioning			

Destination

Project name	Dataset name	Table type ⓘ
project1 ▾	myworkdataset ▾	Native table ▾

Table name

iris

Figure 1.18 – An example of populating a table using an existing CSV file stored in the bucket

4. In the **Schema** section, use **Auto-detect**, and in the **Advanced options**, since the first row is an array of column names, we need to tell it to skip the first row:

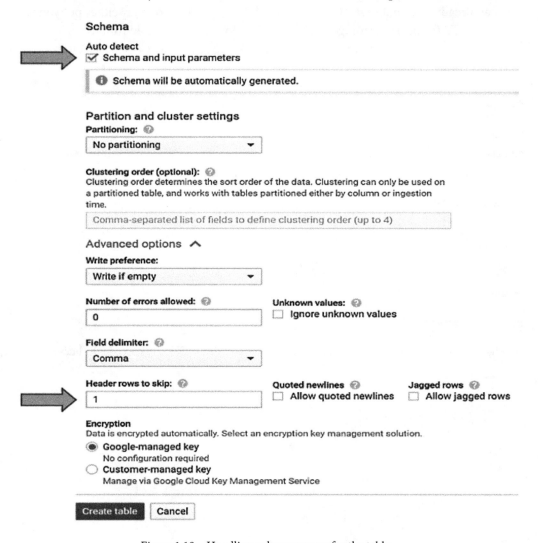

Figure 1.19 – Handling column names for the table

5. Once the table is created, you can click **QUERY TABLE** to update the SQL query syntax, or just enter this query:

```
SELECT * FROM `project1-190517.myworkdataset.iris` LIMIT
1000
```

6. Execute the preceding query and now click on **Run**:

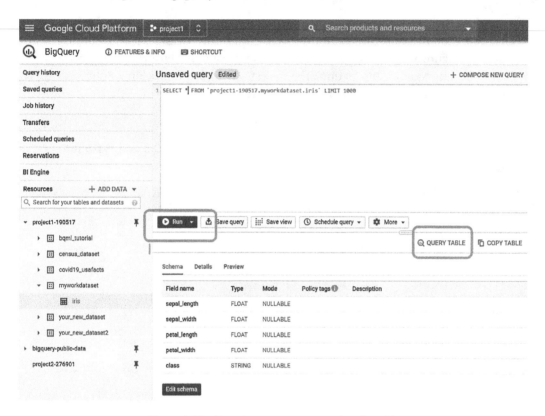

Figure 1.20 – Running a query to examine the table

There are many different data source types, as well as many different ways to create a data warehouse from raw data. This is just a simple example for structured data. For more information on other data sources and types, please refer to the BigQuery documentation at https://cloud.google.com/bigquery/docs/loading-data-cloud-storage-csv#console.

Now you have learned how to create a persistent table in your BigQuery data warehouse using the raw data in your storage bucket.

We used a CSV file as an example and added it to BigQuery as a table. In the next section, we are going to see how to connect TensorFlow to our data stored in BigQuery and the Cloud Storage bucket. Now we are ready to launch an instance of TensorFlow Enterprise running on AI Platform.

Using TensorFlow Enterprise in AI Platform

In this section, we are going to see firsthand how easy it is to access data stored in one of the Google Cloud Storage options, such as a storage bucket or BigQuery. To do so, we need to configure an environment to execute some example TensorFlow API code and command-line tools in this section. The easiest way to use TensorFlow Enterprise is through the AI Platform Notebook in Google Cloud:

1. In the GCP portal, search for AI Platform.
2. Then select **NEW INSTANCE**, with **TensorFlow Enterprise 2.3** and **Without GPUs**. Then click **OPEN JUPYTERLAB**:

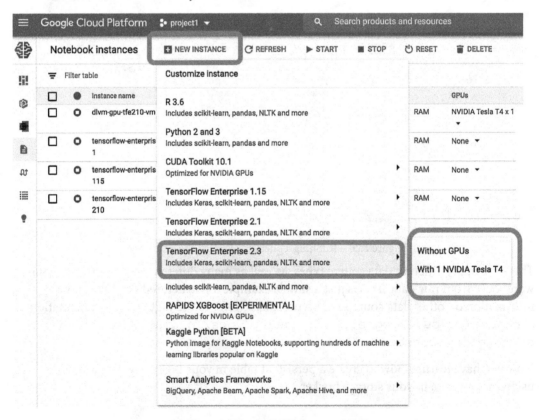

Figure 1.21 – The Google Cloud AI Platform and instance creation

3. Click on **Python 3**, and it will provide a new notebook to execute the remainder of this chapter's examples:

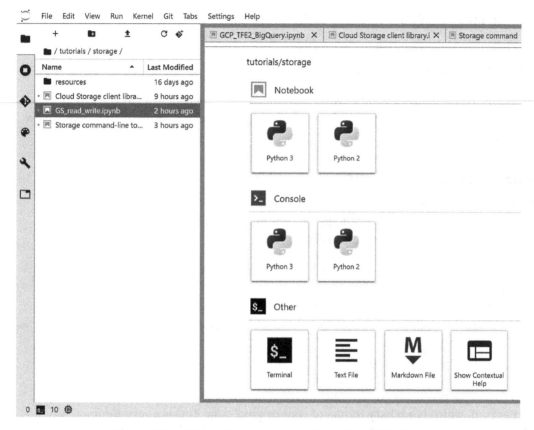

Figure 1.22 – A JupyterLab environment hosted by AI Platform

An instance of TensorFlow Enterprise running on AI Platform is now ready for use. Next, we are going to use this platform to perform some data I/O.

Accessing the data sources

TensorFlow Enterprise can easily access data sources in Google Cloud Storage as well as BigQuery. Either of these data sources can easily host gigabytes to terabytes of data. Reading training data into the JupyterLab runtime at this magnitude of size is definitely out of question, however. Therefore, streaming data as batches through training is the way to handle data ingestion. The `tf.data` API is the way to build a data ingestion pipeline that aggregates data from files in a distributed system. After this step, the data object can go through transformation steps and evolve into a new data object for training.

In this section, we are going to learn basic coding patterns for the following tasks:

- Reading data from a Cloud Storage bucket

- Reading data from a BigQuery table

- Writing data into a Cloud Storage bucket

- Writing data into BigQuery table

After this, you will have a good grasp of reading and writing data to a Google Cloud Storage option and persisting your data or objects produced as a result of your TensorFlow runtime.

Cloud Storage Reader

Cloud Storage Reader is integrated with `tf.data`, so a `tf.data` object can easily access data in Google Cloud Storage. For example, the following code snippet demonstrates how to read a `tfrecord` dataset:

```
my_train_dataset = tf.data.TFRecordDataset('gs://<BUCKET_
NAME>/<FILE_NAME>*.tfrecord')
my_train_dataset = my_train_dataset.repeat()
my_train_dataset = my_train_dataset.batch()
...
model.fit(my_train_dataset, ...)
```

In the example preceding pattern, the file stored in the bucket is serialized into `tfrecord`, which is a binary format of your original data. This is a very common way of storing and serializing large amounts of data or files in the cloud for TensorFlow consumption. This format enables a more efficient read for data being streamed over a network. We will discuss `tfrecord` in more detail in a future chapter.

BigQuery Reader

Likewise, **BigQuery Reader** is also integrated into the TensorFlow Enterprise environment, so training data or derived datasets stored in BigQuery can be consumed by TensorFlow Enterprise.

There are three commonly used methods to read a table stored in a BigQuery data warehouse. The first way is the %%bigquery *magic command*. The second way is using the *BigQuery API in a general Python runtime*, and the third way is to *use TensorFlow I/O*. Each has its advantages.

The BigQuery magic command

This method is perfect for running SQL statements directly in a JupyterLab cell. This is equivalent to switching the cell's command interpreter. The %%bigquery interpreter executes a standard SQL query and the results are returned as a pandas DataFrame.

The following code snippet shows how to use the %%bigquery interpreter and assign a pandas DataFrame name to the result. Each step is a JupyterLab cell:

1. Specify a project ID. This JupyterLab cell uses a default interpreter. Therefore, this is a Python variable. If the BigQuery table is in the same project, then you don't need to specify the project ID:

    ```
    project_id = '<PROJECT-XXXXX>'
    ```

2. Invoke the %%bigquery magic command, and assign the project ID and a DataFrame name to hold the result:

    ```
    %%bigquery --project $project_id mydataframe
    SELECT * from `bigquery-public-data.covid19_jhu_csse.
    summary` limit 5
    ```

    If the table is in the same project as you currently running from, you don't need --project argument.

3. Verify the result is a pandas DataFrame:

    ```
    type(mydataframe)
    ```

4. Show the DataFrame:

    ```
    mydataframe
    ```

The complete code snippet for this example is as follows:

```
project_id = 'project1-190517'
```

```
%%bigquery --project $project_id mydataframe
SELECT * from `bigquery-public-data.covid19_jhu_csse.summary` limit 5
```

```
type(mydataframe)
```

```
pandas.core.frame.DataFrame
```

```
mydataframe
```

	province_state	country_region	date	latitude	longitude	location_geom	confirmed	deaths	recovered	active	fips
0	None	UK	2020-02-20	NaN	NaN	None	9	0	8	NaN	None
1	None	UK	2020-02-11	NaN	NaN	None	8	0	0	NaN	None
2	None	UK	2020-02-18	NaN	NaN	None	9	0	8	NaN	None
3	None	UK	2020-02-12	NaN	NaN	None	9	0	1	NaN	None
4	None	UK	2020-02-01	NaN	NaN	None	2	0	0	NaN	None

Figure 1.23 – Code snippet for BigQuery and Python runtime integration

Here are the key takeaways:

- It is required to have a project ID in order to use the BigQuery API.

- You may pass a Python variable such as the project ID as a value into the cell that runs the `%%bigquery` interpreter using the `$` prefix.

- In order for the result to be reusable further by the Python preprocessing functionality or for TensorFlow consumption, you need to specify a name for the DataFrame that will hold the query result.

The Python BigQuery API

The second method by which we can invoke the BigQuery API is through Google Cloud's BigQuery client. This will give us direct access to the data, execute the query, and allow us to receive the results right away. This method does not require the user to know about the table schema. In fact, it simply wraps a SQL statement inside the BigQuery client instantiated through a library call.

This code snippet demonstrates how to invoke the BigQuery API and use it to return the results in a pandas DataFrame:

```
from google.cloud import bigquery
project_id ='project-xxxxx'
client = bigquery.Client(project=project_id)
sample_count = 1000
row_count = client.query('''
   SELECT
     COUNT(*) as total
   FROM `bigquery-public-data.covid19_jhu_csse.summary`''').
to_dataframe().total[0]

df = client.query('''
   SELECT
      *
   FROM
      `bigquery-public-data.covid19_jhu_csse.summary`
   WHERE RAND() < %d/%d
''' % (sample_count, row_count)).to_dataframe()

print('Full dataset has %d rows' % row_count)
```

The output of the preceding code is as follows:

```
 ⌐→  Full dataset has 195097 rows
```

Figure 1.24 – Code output

Let's take a closer look at the preceding code:

- An import of the BigQuery library is required to create a BigQuery client.
- The project ID is required for using this API to create a BigQuery client.
- This client wraps a SQL statement and executes it.
- The returned data can be easily converted to a pandas DataFrame right away.

The pandas DataFrame rendition of the BigQuery table has the following columns:

df													
	province_state	country_region	date	latitude	longitude	location_geom	confirmed	deaths	recovered	active	fips	admin2	combined_key
0	None	South Korea	2020-02-15	NaN	NaN	None	28	0.0	9.0	NaN	None	None	None
1	None	Russia	2020-02-20	NaN	NaN	None	2	0.0	2.0	NaN	None	None	None
2	None	South Korea	2020-01-31	NaN	NaN	None	11	NaN	NaN	NaN	None	None	None
3	None	France	2020-02-24	NaN	NaN	None	12	1.0	4.0	NaN	None	None	None
4	None	South Korea	2020-02-11	NaN	NaN	None	28	0.0	3.0	NaN	None	None	None
...	...	...	...	...	...	...	...	...	...	...	...	...	...
1990	None	Paraguay	2020-03-31	-23.442500	-58.443800	POINT(-58.4438 -23.4425)	65	3.0	1.0	61.0	None	None	Paraguay
1991	Aruba	Netherlands	2020-03-30	12.521100	-69.968300	POINT(-69.9683 12.5211)	50	0.0	1.0	49.0	None	None	Aruba, Netherlands
1992	Arizona	US	2020-03-13	33.729759	-111.431221	POINT(-111.431221 33.729759)	9	0.0	1.0	NaN	None	None	None
1993	Anguilla	United Kingdom	2020-04-23	18.220600	-63.068600	POINT(-63.0686 18.2206)	3	0.0	1.0	2.0	None	None	Anguilla, United Kingdom
1994	Madison, WI	US	2020-03-06	43.073100	-89.401200	POINT(-89.4012 43.0731)	1	0.0	1.0	NaN	None	None	None

Figure 1.25 – The pandas DataFrame rendition of the BigQuery table

This is ready for further consumption. It is now a pandas DataFrame that occupies memory space in your Python runtime.

This method is very straightforward, as it can help you explore the data schema and do simple aggregation and filtering, and since it is basically a SQL statement wrapper, it is very easy to just get the data out of the warehouse and start using it. You didn't have to know much about the table schema to do this.

However, the problem with this approach is when the table is big enough to overflow your memory. TensorFlow I/O can help solve this problem.

TensorFlow I/O

For TensorFlow consumption of BigQuery data, it is better if we use TensorFlow I/O to invoke the BigQuery API. This is because TensorFlow I/O will provide us with a dataset object that represents the query results, rather than the entire results, as in the previous method. A dataset object is the means to stream training data for a model during training. Therefore not all training data has to be in memory at once. This complements mini-batch training, which is arguably the most common implementation of gradient descent optimization used in deep learning. However, this is a bit more complicated than the previous method. It requires you to know the schema of the table. This example uses a public dataset hosted by Google Cloud.

We need to start with the columns of our interest from the table. We can use the previous method to examine the column names and datatypes, and create a session definition:

1. Load the required libraries and set up the variables as follows:

```
import tensorflow as tf
from tensorflow_io.bigquery import BigQueryClient
```

```
PROJECT_ID = 'project-xxxxx' # This is from what you
created in your Google Cloud Account.
DATASET_GCP_PROJECT_ID = 'bigquery-public-data'
DATASET_ID = 'covid19_jhu_csse'
TABLE_ID = 'summary'
```

2. Instantiate a BigQuery client and specify the batch size:

```
batch_size = 2048
client = BigQueryClient()
```

3. Use the client to create a read session and specify the columns and datatypes of
    interest. Notice that when using the BigQuery client, you need to know the correct
    column names and their respective datatypes:

```
read_session = client.read_session(
    'projects/' + PROJECT_ID,
    DATASET_GCP_PROJECT_ID, TABLE_ID, DATASET_ID,
    ['province_state',
        'country_region',
        'confirmed',
        'deaths',
        'date',
        'recovered'
        ],
    [tf.string,
        tf.string,
        tf.int64,
        tf.int64,
        tf.int32,
        tf.int64],
        requested_streams=10
)
```

4. Now we can use the session object created to execute a read operation:

```
dataset = read_session.parallel_read_rows(sloppy=True).
batch(batch_size)
```

5. Let's take a look at the dataset with `type()`:

```
type(dataset)
```

Here's the output:

```
tensorflow.python.data.ops.dataset_ops.BatchDataset
```

Figure 1.26 – Output

6. In order to actually see the data, we need to convert the dataset ops to a Python iterator and use `next()` to see the content of the first batch:

```
itr = tf.compat.v1.data.make_one_shot_iterator(
    dataset
)
next(itr)
```

The output of the preceding command shows it is organized as an ordered dictionary, where the keys are column names and the values are Tensors:

```
OrderedDict([('confirmed',
  <tf.Tensor: shape=(2048,), dtype=int64, numpy=array([  3,   9,   2, ..., 109, 239,   3])>),
 ('country_region',
  <tf.Tensor: shape=(2048,), dtype=string, numpy=array([b'UK', b'UK', b'UK', ..., b'US', b'US', b'US'], dtype=object)>),
 ('date',
  <tf.Tensor: shape=(2048,), dtype=int32, numpy=array([18299, 18308, 18293, ..., 18380, 18394, 18349], dtype=int32)>),
 ('deaths',
  <tf.Tensor: shape=(2048,), dtype=int64, numpy=array([0, 0, 0, ..., 0, 8, 0])>),
 ('province_state',
  <tf.Tensor: shape=(2048,), dtype=string, numpy=array([b'', b'', b'', ..., b'Iowa', b'Iowa', b'Iowa'], dtype=object)>),
 ('recovered',
  <tf.Tensor: shape=(2048,), dtype=int64, numpy=array([0, 8, 0, ..., 0, 0, 0])>)])
```

Figure 1.27 – Raw data as an iterator

Here are the key takeaways:

- TensorFlow I/O's BigQuery Client requires setting up a read session, which consists of column names from your table of interest.

- This client then executes a read operation that also includes data batching.

- The output of the read operation is a TensorFlow ops.

- This ops may be converted to a Python iterator, so it can output the actual data read by the ops.

- This improves the efficiency of memory use during training, as data is sent for training in batches.

Persisting data in BigQuery

We have looked at how to read data stored in Google Storage solutions, such as Cloud Storage buckets or a BigQuery data warehouse, and how to enable the data for consumption by AI Platform's TensorFlow Enterprise instance running in JupyterLab. Now let's take a look at some ways to write data back, or persist our working data, into our cloud Storage.

Our first example concerns writing a file stored in JupyterLab runtime's directory (in some TensorFlow Enterprise documentations, this is also referred to as a *local* file). The process in general is as follows:

1. For convenience, execute a BigQuery SQL read command on a table from a public dataset.

2. Store the result locally as a **comma-separated file** (CSV).

3. Write the CSV file to a table in our BigQuery dataset.

Each step is a code cell. The following step-by-step code snippet applies to JupyterLab in any of the three AI platforms (AI Notebook, AI Deep Learning VM, and Deep Learning Container):

1. Designate a project ID:

```
project_id = 'project1-190517'
```

2. Execute the BigQuery SQL command and assign the result to a pandas DataFrame:

```
%%bigquery --project $project_id mydataframe
SELECT * from `bigquery-public-data.covid19_jhu_csse.
summary`
```

The BigQuery results come back as a pandas DataFrame by default. In this case, we designate the DataFrame name to be mydataframe.

3. Write the pandas DataFrame to a CSV file in a local directory. In this case, we used the /home directory of this JupyterLab runtime:

```
import pandas as pd
mydataframe.to_csv('my_new_data.csv')
```

4. Designate a dataset name:

```
dataset_id = 'my_new_dataset'
```

5. Use the BigQuery command-line tool to create an empty table in this project's dataset. This command starts with !bq:

```
!bq --location=US mk --dataset $dataset_id
```

This command creates a new dataset. This dataset doesn't have any tables yet. We are going to write a new table into this dataset in the next step.

6. Write the local CSV file to a new table:

```
!bq \
    --location=US \
    load \
    --autodetect \
    --skip_leading_rows=1 \
    --source_format=CSV \
    {dataset_id}.my_new_data_table \
    'my_new_data.csv'
```

In this command, since the CSV file is stored in the current directory, its filename of 'my_new_data.csv' will suffice. Otherwise, a full path is required. Also, {dataset_id}.my_new_data_table indicates that we want to write the CSV file into this particular dataset and the table name.

7. Now you can navigate to the BigQuery portal, and you will find the dataset and the table:

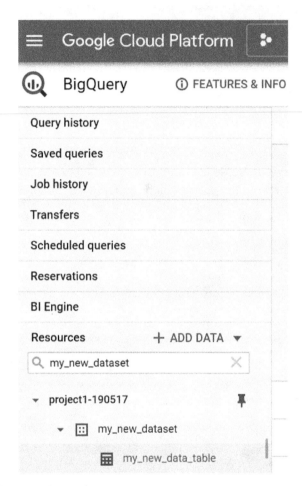

Figure 1.28 – The BigQuery portal and navigation to the dataset

In this case, we have one dataset, which contains one table.

8. Then, execute a simple query, as follows:

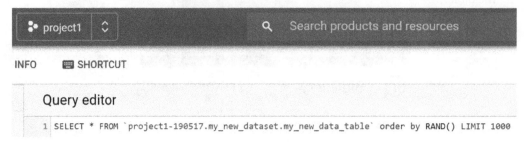

Figure 1.29 – A query for examining the table

This is a very simple query where we just want to show 1,000 randomly selected rows. You can now execute this query and the output will be as shown in the following screenshot.

The following query output shows the data from the BigQuery table we just created:

Row	province_state	country_region	date	latitude	longitude	location_geom	confirmed	deaths	recovered	active
1	Mississippi	US	2020-05-22	34.61810501	-88.51986294	POINT(-88.51986294 34.61810501)	37	3	0	34.0
2	Michigan	US	2020-05-11	43.03197711	-85.54934642	POINT(-85.54934642 43.03197711)	2332	42	0	2290.0
3	Tennessee	US	2020-05-03	36.28590426	-83.83651902	POINT(-83.83651902 36.28590426)	3	0	0	3.0
4	Texas	US	2020-03-29	29.18757369	-95.44563172	POINT(-95.44563172 29.18757369)	61	0	0	0.0
5	null	Brunei	2020-05-12	4.5353	114.7277	POINT(114.7277 4.5353)	141	1	134	6.0
6	Georgia	US	2020-04-12	31.92289565	-83.76811843	POINT(-83.76811843 31.92289565)	70	0	0	70.0

Figure 1.30 – Example table output

Here are the key takeaways:

- Data generated during the TensorFlow workflow in the AI Platform's JupyterLab runtime can be seamlessly persisted as a table in BigQuery.

- Persisting data in a structured format, such as a pandas DataFrame or a CSV file, in BigQuery can easily be done using the BigQuery command-line tool.

- When you need to move a data object (such as a table) between the JupyterLab runtime and BigQuery, use the BigQuery command-line tool with !bq to save time and effort.

Persisting data in a storage bucket

In the previous *Persisting data in BigQuery* section, we saw how a structured data source such as a CSV file or a pandas DataFrame can be persisted in a BigQuery dataset as a table. In this section, we are going to see how to persist working data such as a NumPy array. In this case, the suitable target storage is a Google Cloud Storage bucket.

The workflow for this demonstration is as follows:

1. For convenience, read a NumPy array from `tf.keras.dataset.`

2. Save the NumPy array as a pickle (`pkl`) file. (FYI: The pickle file format, while convenient and easy to use for serializing Python objects, also has its downsides. For one, it may be slow and creates a larger object than the original. Second, a pickle file may contain bugs or security risks for any process that opens it. It is used only for convenience here.)

3. Use the `!gsutil` storage command-line tool to transfer files from JupyterLab's / home directory (in some documentation, this is referred to as the *local directory*) to the storage bucket.

4. Use `!gsutil` to transfer the content in the bucket back to the JupyterLab runtime. Since we will use Python with `!gsutil`, we need to keep the content in separate cells.

Follow these steps to complete the workflow:

1. Let's use the IMDB dataset because it is already provided in NumPy format:

```python
import tensorflow as tf
import pickle as pkl


(x_train, y_train), (x_test, y_test) = tf.keras.datasets.
imdb.load_data(
    path='imdb.npz',
    num_words=None,
    skip_top=0,
    maxlen=None,
    seed=113,
    start_char=1,
    oov_char=2,
    index_from=3
)
```

```
with open('/home/jupyter/x_train.pkl','wb') as f:
    pkl.dump(x_train, f)
```

x_train, y_train, x_test, and y_test are returned as NumPy arrays. Let's use x_train for the purposes of this demonstration. The x_train array is going to be saved as a pkl file in the JupyterLab runtime.

The preceding code opens the IMDB movie review dataset that is distributed as a part of TensorFlow. This dataset is formatted as tuples of NumPy arrays and separated as training and test partitions. Then we proceed to save the x_train array as a pickle file in the runtime's /home directory. This pickle file will then be persisted in a storage bucket in the next step.

2. Designate a name for the new storage bucket:

```
bucket_name = 'ai-platform-bucket'
```

3. Create a new bucket with the designated name:

```
!gsutil mb gs://{bucket_name}/
```

Use !gsutil to move the pkl file from the runtime to the storage bucket:

```
!gsutil cp /home/jupyter/x_train.pkl gs://{bucket_name}/
```

4. Read the pkl file back:

```
!gsutil cp gs://{bucket_name}/x_train.pkl /home/
jupyter/x_train_readback.pkl
```

5. Now let's inspect the Cloud Storage bucket:

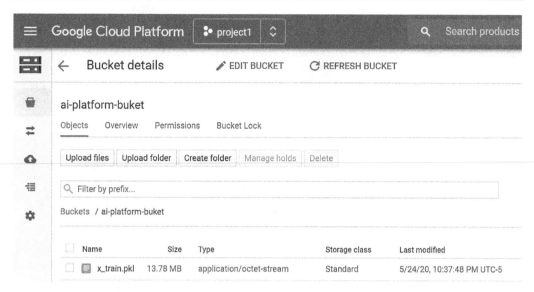

Figure 1.31 – Serializing an object in a bucket from the workflow in AI Platform

Here are the key takeaways:

- Working data generated during the TensorFlow workflow can be persisted as a serialized object in the storage bucket.

- Google AI Platform's JupyterLab environment provides seamless integration between the TensorFlow runtime and the Cloud Storage command-line tool, `gsutil`.

- When you need to transfer content between Google Cloud Storage and AI Platform, use the `!gsutil` command-line tool.

Summary

This chapter provided a broad overview of the TensorFlow Enterprise environment hosted by Google Cloud AI Platform. We also saw how this platform seamlessly integrates specific tools such as command-line APIs to facilitate the easy transfer of data or objects between the JupyterLab environment and our storage solutions. These tools make it easy to access data stored in BigQuery or in storage buckets, which are the two most commonly used data sources in TensorFlow.

In the next chapter, we will take a closer look at the three ways available in AI Platform to use TensorFlow Enterprise: the Notebook, Deep Learning VM, and Deep Learning Containers.

2
Running TensorFlow Enterprise in Google AI Platform

Currently, the TensorFlow Enterprise distribution is only available through Google Cloud AI Platform. This chapter will demonstrate how to launch AI Platform for use with TensorFlow Enterprise. In AI Platform, TensorFlow Enterprise can interact with Cloud Storage and BigQuery via their respective command-line tools as well as simple APIs to load data from the source. In this chapter, we are going to take a look at how to launch AI Platform and how easy it is to start using the TensorFlow Enterprise distribution.

We'll cover the following main topics:

- Setting up a notebook environment
- Easy parameterized data extraction from BigQuery

Setting up a notebook environment

TensorFlow Enterprise is exclusively available in the JupyterLab environment hosted by Google Cloud. There are three ways to consume the JupyterLab with this TensorFlow distribution: **Google Cloud AI Platform Notebook**, **Google Cloud Deep Learning Virtual Machine Images (DLVM)**, and **Google Cloud Deep Learning Containers (Docker image)** running on your local machine. No matter which one you choose, you will see the same interface of a standard JupyterLab environment like this:

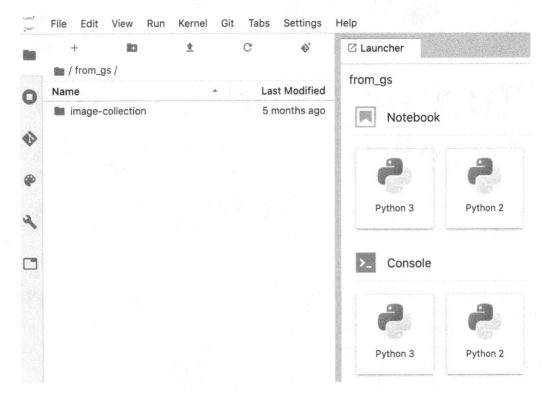

Figure 2.1 – JupyterLab portal

So let's take a look at how to get started.

AI Platform Notebook

This is the easiest and least complicated way to start using TensorFlow Enterprise and get it running in Google Cloud:

1. Simply go to the Google Cloud portal, select **AI Platform** in the left panel, then select the **Notebooks** option:

Figure 2.2 – AI Platform starting portal

2. Then click on **NEW INSTANCE**, and you'll be offered choices for TensorFlow Enterprise, which is available for **1.15** as well as **2.1** and **2.3**. You also have the option to use one **Tesla K4** GPU:

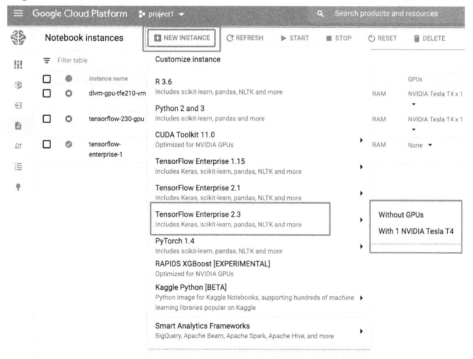

Figure 2.3 – Creating a new notebook instance in AI Platform

For our examples in this chapter, we don't need to use a GPU. Selecting **Without GPUs** will suffice.

3. Then click on **CREATE** to accept the default node choice, or **CUSTOMIZE** to see all the setup options available:

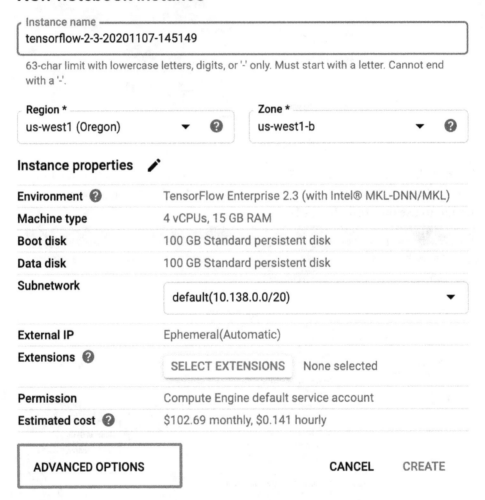

Figure 2.4 – Customizing a compute instance

These are the available machine configuration choices when using the notebook option in AI Platform:

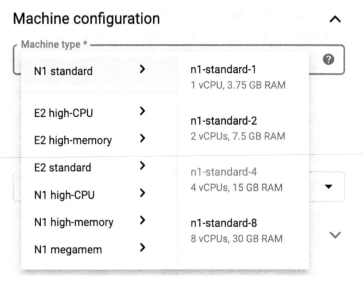

Figure 2.5 – Available options for the machine instance

The Notebook instance will be available within a few minutes after clicking **CREATE:**

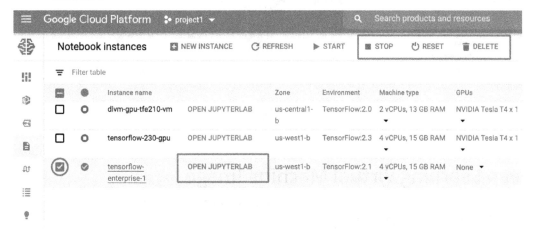

Figure 2.6 – Instance going live and ready

4. When the instance is ready, **OPEN JUPYTERLAB** will be activated and you may click on it. Clicking on it will lead you to a JupyterLab notebook:

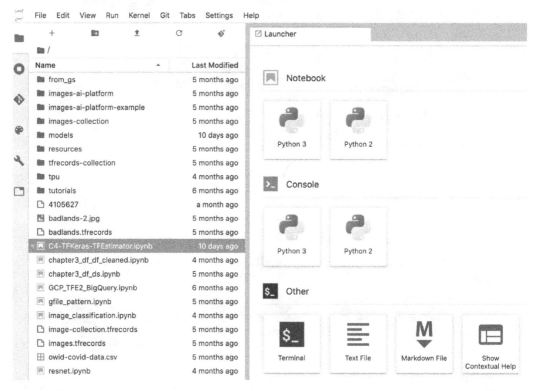

Figure 2.7 – JupyterLab environment

We will use Python 3 for all our examples.

Deep Learning Virtual Machine Image

If you wish to have more options, such as different GPU choices, then DLVM is a better choice. You may find these references helpful:

- `https://cloud.google.com/ai-platform/deep-learning-vm/docs/quickstart-cli`

- `https://cloud.google.com/ai-platform/deep-learning-vm/docs/quickstart-marketplace`

Follow these steps to choose DLVM:

1. Click **Marketplace** in the left panel:

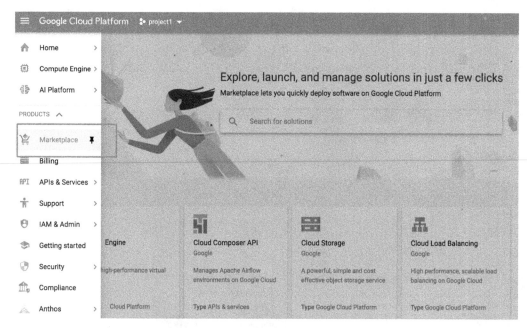

Figure 2.8 – Google Cloud Platform Marketplace

2. Search for Deep Learning VM in the query box and you will see the following:

Figure 2.9 – Enabling DLVM

This is where you can launch a DLVM deployment.

3. Click on **LAUNCH**, and you will see many options available, including **Machine Type**, **GPU type**, and **Number of GPUs**:

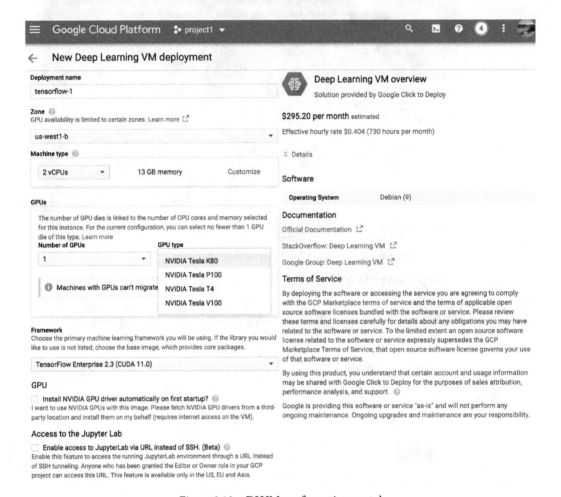

Figure 2.10 – DLVM configuration portal

Also, DLVM has many more frameworks besides TensorFlow Enterprise:

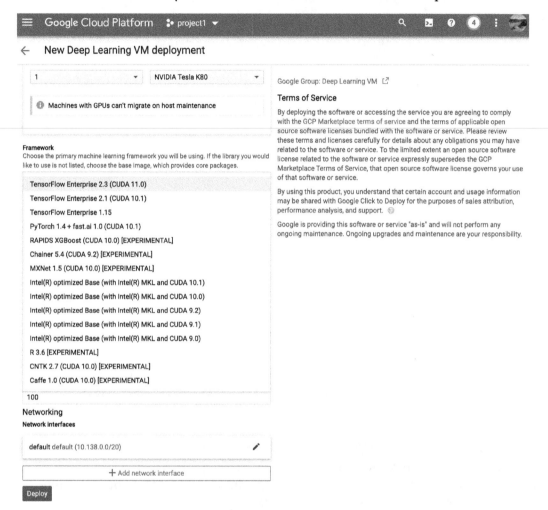

Figure 2.11 – DLVM and options for frameworks

4. If you choose one of the two TensorFlow Enterprise frameworks, then click

CREATE, you will be able to reach JupyterLab as you did previously:

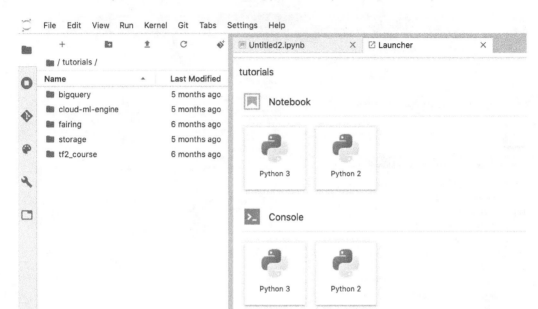

Figure 2.12 – JupyterLab entry point

Here's a suggestion. In order to minimize your cost, it is important to stop your instances after you are done. The quickest way to see what you have running is to choose **Compute Engine** in the left panel, and then select **VM instances**:

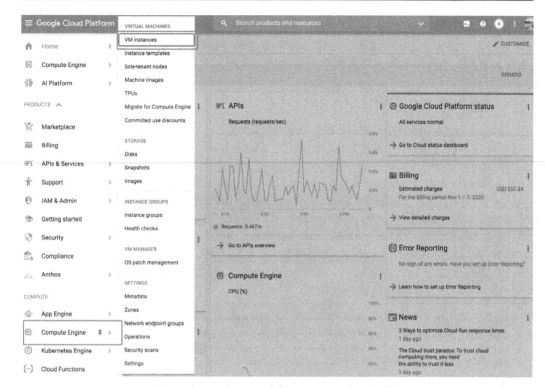

Figure 2.13 – Compute instances in a subscription

From there you will see all the instances you have created. Stop them when you are done:

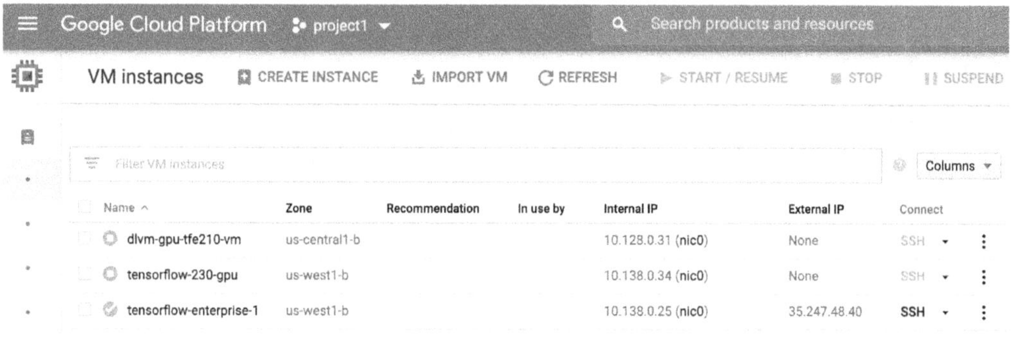

Figure 2.14 – Listing VM instances and managing their use

It is the user's responsibility to be aware of the instances that are running. As a good practice, when you are finished with your work, download or check in your notebook to save your work, and delete the instance when not in use.

Deep Learning Container (DLC)

This is a relatively more complicated way of using TensorFlow Enterprise. An important reason for using this approach is for cases where data is not stored in Google Cloud, and you wish to run TensorFlow Enterprise on-premises or in your local machine. Another reason is that for enterprise use, you may want to use DLC as a base Docker image to build your own Docker image for a specific use or distribution amongst your team. This is the way to run TensorFlow Enterprise outside of Google Cloud. Since it is a Docker image, it requires the Docker Engine installed, and the daemon running. It would be extremely helpful to have some basic understanding of Docker. You will find a full list of currently available DLCs at `https://console.cloud.google.com/gcr/images/deeplearning-platform-release`.

The goal is running a TensorFlow Enterprise JupyterLab. But since it is in a local machine, the URL to the JupyterLab is in the following format:

`localhost:<LOCAL_PORT>`

Here's how we can accomplish this (for reference, see `https://cloud.google.com/ai-platform/deep-learning-containers/docs/getting-started-local`):

1. Assuming a Docker daemon is running, we will execute the following command to run the TensorFlow Enterprise container:

    ```
    docker run -d -p <LOCAL_PORT>:8080 -v <LOCAL_DIR>:/home
    <CONTAINER_REGISTRY>
    ```

    Let's understand the parts of the preceding command with the following table:

Variable	Meaning	Example
<LOCAL_PORT>	Port number in the local machine to host this Docker image instance.	8080, or any other port number available if 8080 is in use.
<LOCAL_DIR>	Path to top directory where the training data and assets can be found.	Windows: `C:\Users\xxxx\Documents` Linux or Mac: `/home/xxxx/Documents`
<CONTAINER_REGISTRY>	Where the Docker image can be found.	`gcr.io/deeplearning-platform-release/tf2-cpu.2-1`

Figure 2.15 – Explaining the objects of the command to run the TensorFlow Enterprise container

In the preceding table, note the following:

- `<LOCAL_PORT>` refers to the port number in the local machine to host this Docker image instance. It may be `8080`, or any other available port number that you wish to use, should `8080` be in use by another program or process already.

- `<LOCAL_DIR>` is the path to the top-level directory where the training data and assets can be found. For a Windows machine, it may be `C:\Users\XXXX\Documents`. For Linux or Mac machine, it may be `/home/XXXX/Documents`.

- `<CONTAINER_REGISTRY>` is where the Docker image can be found on the internet, and for the Docker container of our interest, it is in `gcr.io/deeplearning-platform-release/tf2-cpu.2-1`.

2. Put these together in a command and run it from a terminal of a local machine (such as Windows Command Prompt):

```
docker run -d -p 8080:8080 -v C:\Users\xxxx\Documents:/
home/jupyter gcr.io/deeplearning-platform-release/
tf2-cpu.2-3
```

```
C:\Users\xxxx>docker run -d -p 8080:8080 -v    C:\
Users\xxxx\Documents:/home/jupyter gcr.io/deeplearning-
platform-release/tf2-cpu.2-3
```

A local port must be mapped to the Docker image's JupyterLab port. JupyterLab uses port 8080 inside the Docker image. Notice that the preceding command maps local port 8080 to the Docker image's port 8080. The first 8080 is your local port, the second 8080 is the port number used by JupyterLab inside the Docker image environment. Again, the local port number doesn't have to be 8080.

3. Now you may access the local port through your browser:

    localhost:8080

    And you will see the JupyterLab running as a Docker container, as follows:

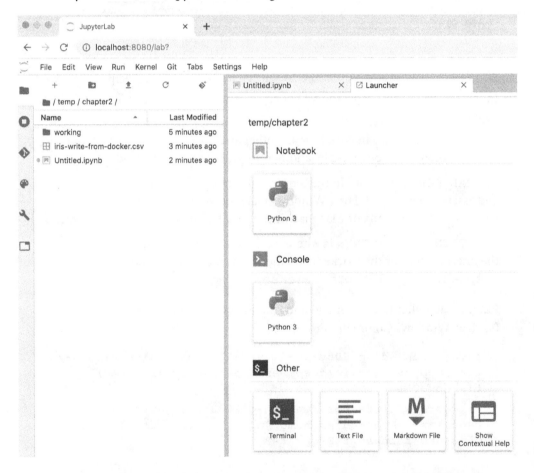

Figure 2.16 – Docker image of JupyterLab running in a local or on-premises environment

Let's take a look at the left panel first. The left panel shows all the local files and folders that you designated as <LOCAL_DIR>. In this case, it is /temp/chapter2

The -v (or --volume) option maps the local directory to the /home directory of your Docker container instance. This is how local contents become accessible to your Docker container.

4. You can click on the **Python 3** icon in launcher to start using JupyterLab to read any file in /home:

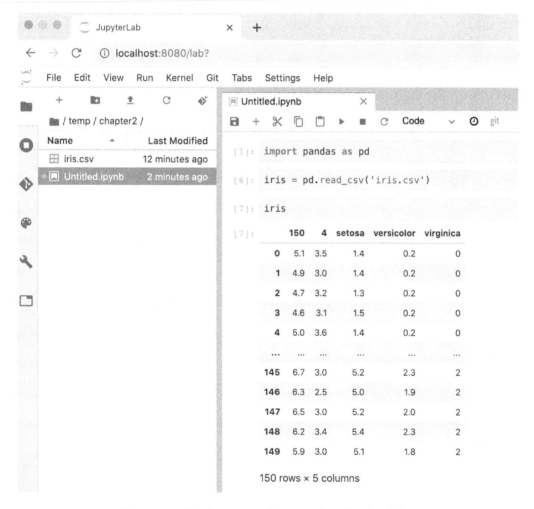

Figure 2.17 – Docker image of JupyterLab reading local data

5.   You can also write data to the local directory:

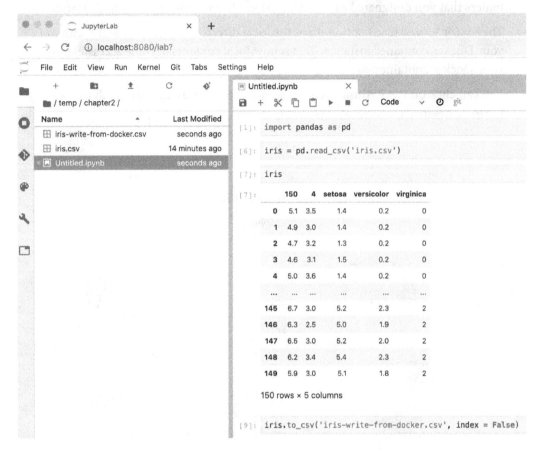

Figure 2.18 – Docker image of JupyterLab writing data locally

The following command uses /home as the file path:

```
iris.to_csv('/home/iris-write-from-docker.csv',
index=False)
```

Since you mapped /home with a local directory, you will also find the file in the local file explorer:

Figure 2.19 – Local data written by JupyterLab running in a Docker image

6. Once you are done, in order to shut down the Docker image, you need to know the container ID assigned to this instance by your local Docker daemon. The command is as follows:

```
docker ps
```

And it will return an output similar to this:

```
CONTAINER ID          IMAGE
COMMAND                   CREATED              STATUS
PORTS                     NAMES
553cfd198067          gcr.io/deeplearning-platform-release/
tf2-cpu.2-1    '/entrypoint.sh /run…'    44 minutes ago
Up 44 minutes          0.0.0.0:8080->8080/tcp    intelligent_
goldwasser
```

7. Make a note of the CONTAINER ID value. Then use the following command to shut it down:

```
docker stop 553cfd198067
```

Suggestions for selecting workspaces

All three methods discussed in the previous section lead you to a JupyterLab that runs TensorFlow Enterprise. There are some differences and consequences to consider for each method:

- The Docker image running locally is preferred for local data access.
- The DLC can serve as a base image for creating a new enterprise-specific image.

  With the Docker image running locally, its advantage lies in its direct access to the local environment or data sources. We have seen how it can easily read and write data on a local node. This obviously cannot be easily achieved with the AI Platform environment. Therefore, if the training data and output are to stay on-premises or in the local environment, then this is the most sensible choice. The downside of this method is the overhead of setting up and managing your own Docker environment. Another reason for using the DLC is that big enterprises often need to have customizable environments. They may want to create their own Docker container on top of the DLC and later ask everyone in the company to use that container with Cloud AI Platform Notebook. Notebook supports the custom container mode, as long as that container is based on the DLC.

- Use DLVM if you want to customize compute instance cores, memory, and disk resources.

  If you want to configure the CPU, GPU, memory, or disk resources for the workload, then DLVM is the method of choice.

- Use the default notebook environment for most general needs.

  With AI Platform, the notebook environment obviously has direct access to cloud storage such as bucket containers or BigQuery tables. If it is not essential to pick and choose your CPU or GPU configurations, then the AI Platform Notebook would definitely suffice.

What we have learned so far are the three different environments for users to start using Google's AI Platform and consume the TensorFlow Enterprise distribution. By and large, these methods all provide a consistent user experience and runtime distribution of the TensorFlow Enterprise library. The rationale for choosing a method is grounded in your need for data access and compute resource configurations. If the training data is on-premises or on your local disks, then the Docker image is the preferred method. If compute resources and speed are the primary concerns, then DLVM is the preferred choice.

Now, having arrived at AI Platform and its notebook environment, as a starter, we are going to take a closer look at a common example of using AI Platform to access data in BigQuery and build your own training data.

Easy parameterized data extraction from BigQuery

Very often, your enterprise data warehouse contains the sources for you to build your own training data, and simple SQL query commands would meet your requirements for row and column selection and feature transformation. So let's take a look at a convenient, flexible, and fast way of selecting and manipulating original data through SQL queries, where the result of the query is a pandas DataFrame. We have already seen how to use the `%%bigquery` interpreter to execute a query and return the result as a pandas DataFrame. We now will look at how to pass in query parameters so users may explore and select data suitable for model training. The following example uses one of the public datasets, `covid19_juh_csse`, and its `summary` table.

This table has the following structure:

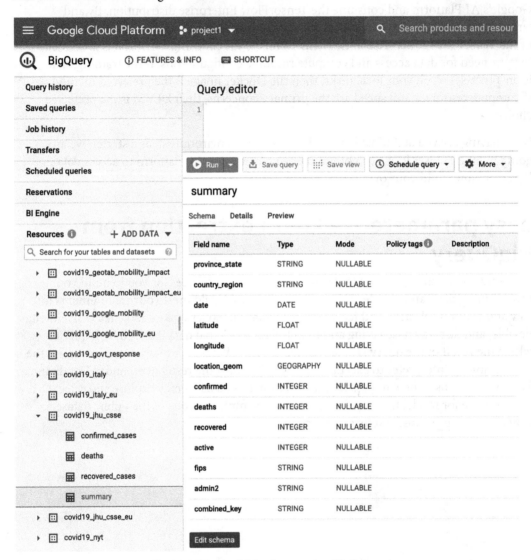

Figure 2.20 – A table's schema using BigQuery

In the JupyterLab provided by any of the three methods discussed earlier, you may execute the following steps to perform parameterized queries:

1. Define a set of parameters in a JSON-compatible format, that is, a key-value pair as in a Python dictionary:

```
params = {'min_death': 1000,
                  'topn': 10}
```

2. Construct the query and assign it to a DataFrame by name. Notice how each key in the parameter is referenced in the query with a preceding @:

```
%%bigquery myderiveddata   --params $params
SELECT country_region,   MAX(confirmed) as total_
confirmed, MAX(deaths) AS total_deaths
FROM `bigquery-public-data.covid19_jhu_csse.summary`
GROUP BY country_region
HAVING (total_deaths > @min_death)
ORDER BY total_deaths DESC
LIMIT @topn
```

3. Examine the data:

```
myderiveddata
```

And the following is the output of the aggregation command, which demonstrates the total results by country:

	country_region	total_confirmed	total_deaths
0	India	1710314	44965
1	United Kingdom	975504	42736
2	Brazil	1125936	39717
3	France	1665403	39557
4	Iran	663800	37409
5	Argentina	1228814	33136
6	Italy	242947	31106
7	Spain	319651	27104
8	US	317656	23689
9	South Africa	734175	19749

Figure 2.21 – Output of the aggregation command from the notebook

We may confirm the data structure of our data object using Python's `type` command:

```
type(myderiveddata)
```

And it confirms the object being a pandas DataFrame:

```
pandas.core.frame.DataFrame
```

Figure 2.22 – Output from type(myderiveddata)

The DataFrame may be serialized as a pickle file for future use. Once converted to the pickle format, you may persist it in the cloud storage as demonstrated in the previous chapter.

Here are the key takeaways:

- Parameterized querying enables quick and easy data selection and manipulation for building training data as a pandas DataFrame.
- Parameters are wrapped in a Python dictionary and can be passed into the query string during execution.
- The query string can refer to the parameter with the @ operator.

Putting it together

The following is the complete code snippet for the quick example we just worked with:

```
params = {'min_death': 1000,
          'topn': 10}


%%bigquery myderiveddata --params $params
SELECT country_region,  MAX(confirmed) as total_confirmed,
MAX(deaths) AS total_deaths
FROM `bigquery-public-data.covid19_jhu_csse.summary`
GROUP BY country_region
HAVING (total_deaths > @min_death)
ORDER BY total_deaths DESC
LIMIT @topn


print(myderiveddata)
```

The output is shown in *Figure 2.23*:

```
    Untitled1.ipynb                  ●
    🖫  +  ✂  🗐  📋  ▶  ■  C   Code        ∨   ⊙   git

    [1]:  params = {"min_death": 1000,
                    "topn": 10}

    [2]:  %%bigquery myderiveddata --params $params
          SELECT country_region, MAX(confirmed) as total_confirmed, MAX(deaths) as total_deaths
          FROM `bigquery-public-data.covid19_jhu_csse.summary`
          GROUP BY country_region
          HAVING (total_deaths > @min_death)
          ORDER BY total_deaths DESC
          limit @topn

    [3]:  myderiveddata
```

[3]:		country_region	total_confirmed	total_deaths
	0	India	1710314	44965
	1	United Kingdom	975504	42736
	2	Brazil	1125936	39717
	3	France	1665403	39557
	4	Iran	663800	37409
	5	Argentina	1228814	33136
	6	Italy	242947	31106
	7	Spain	319651	27104
	8	US	317656	23689
	9	South Africa	734175	19749

```
    [5]:  type(myderiveddata)

    [5]:  pandas.core.frame.DataFrame
```

Figure 2.23 – Output from BigQuery and compatibility with pandas DataFrame format

As the preceding steps demonstrate, the notebook environment is integrated closely with BigQuery. As a result, an inline query with SQL produces a DataFrame that is ready for use in Python. This further demonstrates the flexibility of the Google Cloud AI Platform Notebook environment.

Summary

In this chapter, you have learned how to launch the JupyterLab environment to run TensorFlow Enterprise. TensorFlow Enterprise is available in three different forms: AI Platform Notebook, DLVM, and a Docker container. The computing resources used by these methods can be found in the Google Cloud Compute Engine panel. These compute nodes do not shut down on their own, therefore it is important to stop or delete them once you are done using them.

The BigQuery command tool is seamlessly integrated with the TensorFlow Enterprise environment. Parameterized data extraction via the use of a SQL query string enables the quick and easy creation of a derived dataset and feature selection.

TensorFlow Enterprise works even when your data is not yet in Google Cloud storage. By pulling and running the TensorFlow Enterprise Docker container, you can use it with on-premises or local data sources.

Now that you have seen how to leverage data availability and accessibility for TensorFlow Enterprise consumption, in the next chapter, we are going to examine some common data transformation, serialization, and storage techniques optimized for TensorFlow Enterprise consumption and model training pipelines.

Section 2 – Data Preprocessing and Modeling

In this part, you will learn how to preprocess and set up raw data for efficient TensorFlow consumption, and you will also learn how to build several different models using the TensorFlow Enterprise API. We will also discuss how to build custom models as well as leverage prebuilt models in TensorFlow Hub.

This section comprises the following chapters:

- *Chapter 3, Data Preparation and Manipulation Techniques*
- *Chapter 4, Reusable Models and Scalable Data Pipelines*

3
Data Preparation and Manipulation Techniques

In this chapter, you will learn how to convert the two common data types into structures suitable for ingestion pipelines—structured CSVs or pandas DataFrames into a dataset, and unstructured data such as images into **TFRecords**.

Along the way, there will be some tips and utility functions that are reusable in many situations. You will also understand the rationale of the conversion process.

As demonstrated in the previous chapter, TensorFlow Enterprise takes advantage of the flexibility offered by the Google Cloud AI platform to access training data. Once access to the training data is resolved, our next task is to develop a workflow to let the model consume the data efficiently. In this chapter, we will learn how to examine and manipulate commonly used data structures.

While TensorFlow can consume Pythonic data structures such as pandas or numpy directly, for resource throughput and ingestion efficiency, TensorFlow built the dataset API to convert data from its native Pythonic structure into TensorFlow's specific structure. The dataset API can handle and parse many commonly used types of data. For instance, structured or tabular data with defined schemas are typically presented as a pandas DataFrame. The dataset API converts this data structure into a Tensorflow dataset. Image data is typically presented as a numpy array. In TensorFlow, it is preferred to convert it into `TFRecord`.

In working with these data structures, it is important to be certain that the conversion process is performed correctly and that the data can be verified. This chapter will demonstrate some techniques that help to ensure that data structure conversions are done correctly; for example, decoding a byte stream into an image. It is always helpful to decode these data structures into a readable format just for the purpose of a quick check of the data quality.

We will start with the TensorFlow dataset as applied to structured data. In particular, we'll cover the following main topics:

- Converting tabular data to a TensorFlow dataset
- Converting distributed CSV files to a TensorFlow dataset
- Handling image data for input pipelines
- Decoding `TFRecord` and reconstructing the image
- Handling image data at scale

Converting tabular data to a TensorFlow dataset

Tabular or **comma separated values (CSV)** data with fixed schemas and data types are commonly encountered. We typically work it into a pandas DataFrame. We have seen in the previous chapter how this can be easily done when the data is hosted in a **BigQuery table** (the BigQuery magic command that returns a query result to a pandas DataFrame by default).

Let's take a look at how to handle data that can fit into the memory. In this example, we are going to read a public dataset using the BigQuery magic command, so we can easily obtain the data in a pandas DataFrame. Then we are going to convert it to a TensorFlow dataset. A TensorFlow dataset is the data structure for streaming training data in batches without using up the compute node's runtime memory.

Converting a BigQuery table to a TensorFlow dataset

Each of the following steps is executed in a cell. Again, use any of the AI platforms you prefer (AI Notebook, Deep Learning VM, Deep Learning Container). An AI notebook is the simplest and cheapest choice:

> **Note**
>
> The table in this example is selected for demonstration purposes only. We are going to treat `daily_deaths` as if it is the target for machine learning model training. While we are going to treat it as if it is our training data (in other words, containing features and target columns), in actual training data engineering practices, there are other steps involved, such as feature engineering, aggregation, and normalization.

1. Let's look at the data from BigQuery, so we can be sure of its data structure and the data type of each column, and then take a preview of the table:

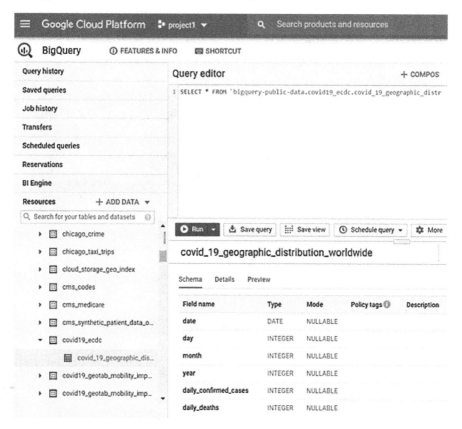

Figure 3.1 – Using BigQuery to examine the data structure

Once the preceding query is run, you will see output as shown in the following screenshot:

| covid_19_geographic_distribution_worldwide | | | | | | | | | |

Row	date	day	month	year	daily_confirmed_cases	daily_deaths	confirmed_cases	deaths	countries_and_territories
1	2019-12-31	31	12	2019	0	0	0	0	United_Arab_Emirates
2	2019-12-31	31	12	2019	0	0	0	0	Afghanistan
3	2019-12-31	31	12	2019	0	0	0	0	Armenia
4	2019-12-31	31	12	2019	0	0	0	0	Austria

Figure 3.2 – Table preview

2. Load the library, define the variables, and define the project ID only if you are running in a different project:

```
PROJECT_ID = '<PROJECT_ID>'
import tensorflow as tf
import pandas as pd
```

3. Use the BigQuery magic command to read a table into a pandas DataFrame (`train_raw_df`):

```
%%bigquery train_raw_df
SELECT countries_and_territories, geo_id, country_
territory_code,
year, month, day, confirmed_cases, daily_deaths, pop_
data_2019
FROM bigquery-public-data.covid19_ecdc.covid_19_
geographic_distribution_worldwide
```

4. Take a look at a few sample rows:

```
train_raw_df.sample(n=5)
```

Here's the output:

	countries_and_territories	geo_id	country_territory_code	year	month	day	confirmed_cases	daily_deaths	pop_data_2019
46698	British_Virgin_Islands	VG	VGB	2020	6	25	8	0	30033.0
39758	Slovakia	SK	SVK	2020	6	20	1576	0	5450421.0
46706	British_Virgin_Islands	VG	VGB	2020	7	3	8	0	30033.0
36200	Puerto_Rico	PR	PRI	2020	7	13	9821	0	2933404.0
11314	Germany	DE	DEU	2020	7	6	196554	4	83019213.0

Figure 3.3 – Output of a few rows from the table

5. Some columns are categorical. We need to encode them as integers. First, we designate the column as a pandas categorical feature:

```
train_raw_df['countries_and_territories'] =
pd.Categorical(train_raw_df['countries_and_territories'])
```

6. Then we replace the column content with category code:

```
train_raw_df['countries_and_territories'] = train_raw_
df.countries_and_territories.cat.codes
```

7. Then we repeat this procedure for the other categorical columns:

```
train_raw_df['geo_id'] = pd.Categorical(train_raw_
df['geo_id'])
train_raw_df['geo_id'] = train_raw_df.geo_id.cat.codes


train_raw_df['country_territory_code'] =
pd.Categorical(train_raw_df['country_territory_code'])
train_raw_df['country_territory_code'] = train_raw_
df.country_territory_code.cat.codes
```

8. Make lists to hold column names according to data type. The reason is to ensure that the dataset can cast the columns in our DataFrame to the correct TensorFlow data type:

```
int32_features = ['confirmed_cases']
float32_features = ['pop_data_2019']
int16_features = ['year', 'month', 'day']
categorical_features = ['countries_and_territories',
'geo_id', 'country_territory_code']
int32_target = ['daily_deaths']
```

9. Creating a dataset from a pandas DataFrame requires us to specify the correct column names and the data type. Column names are held in the respective list based on their data type:

```
training_dataset = tf.data.Dataset.from_tensor_slices(
    (
        tf.cast(train_raw_df[int32_features].values,
        tf.int32),
        tf.cast(train_raw_df[float32_features].
        values, tf.float32),
        tf.cast(train_raw_df[int16_features].values,
        tf.int16),
        tf.cast(train_raw_df[categorical_features].
        values, tf.int32),
        tf.cast(train_raw_df[int32_target].values,
        tf.int32)
    )
)
```

10. Look at the structure of the dataset to make sure its metadata is as specified during the creation process in the previous step:

```
training_dataset
```

The output is as follows:

```
<TensorSliceDataset shapes: ((1,), (1,), (3,), (3,),
(1,)), types: (tf.int32, tf.float32, tf.int16, tf.int32,
tf.int32)>
```

The tensor shapes and data types are in the exact order as indicated in the previous step.

Now you have created a dataset from a pandas DataFrame. The dataset is now a part of the input pipeline. If this dataset's features and targets are properly normalized and selected (for example, having performed a normalization operation such as min-max scaling, or a standardization operation such as Z-score conversion if the distribution of the column data can be assumed to be Gaussian), then it is ready to be fed into a model for training as-is.

So far, from this exercise, you've learned the following points:

- Use BigQuery as much as possible to examine data schemas and data types first.
- For data that can fit into the memory, leverage the BigQuery magic command to output a pandas DataFrame.
- Bin the column names by their data types for clarity and organization.
- Encode categorical features to integers so they can be cast into a TensorFlow data type that is compatible with a TensorFlow dataset.

Converting distributed CSV files to a TensorFlow dataset

If you are not sure about the data size, or are unsure as to whether it can all fit in the Python runtime's memory, then reading the data into a pandas DataFrame is not a viable option. In this case, we may use a **TF dataset** to directly access the data without opening it.

Typically, when data is stored in a storage bucket as parts, the naming convention follows a general pattern. This pattern is similar to that of a **Hadoop Distributed File System (HDFS)**, where the data is stored in parts and the complete data can be inferred via a wildcard symbol, *.

When storing distributed files in a Google Cloud Storage bucket, a common pattern for filenames is as follows:

```
<FILE_NAME>-<pattern>-001.csv
...
<FILE_NAME>-<pattern>-00n.csv
```

Alternatively, there is the following pattern:

```
<FILE_NAME>-<pattern>-aa.csv

...

<FILE_NAME>-<pattern>-zz.csv
```

There is always a pattern in the filenames. The TensorFlow module `tf.io.gfile.glob` is a convenient API that encodes such filename patterns in a distributed filesystem. This is critical for inferring distributed files that are stored in a storage bucket. In this section, we will use this API to infer our structured data (multiple CSV files), which is distributed in a storage bucket. Once inferred, we will then convert it to a dataset (using `tf.data.experimental.make_csv_dataset`).

Preparing an example CSV

Since we need multiple CSV files of the same schema for this demonstration, we may use open source CSV data such as the **Pima Indians Diabetes** dataset (CSV) as our data source. This CSV is hosted in `https://raw.githubusercontent.com/jbrownlee/Datasets/master/pima-indians-diabetes.data.csv`.

You may simply run the following command on your local system (where you downloaded the aforementioned file):

```
wget https://raw.githubusercontent.com/jbrownlee/Datasets/
master/pima-indians-diabetes.data.csv
```

Again, for demonstration purposes only, we need to split this data into multiple smaller CSVs, and then upload these CSVs to a Google Cloud Storage bucket.

The column names for this file are as follows:

```
['Pregnancies', 'Glucose', 'BloodPressure', 'SkinThickness',
 'Insulin', 'BMI', 'DiabetesPedigree', 'Age', 'Outcome']
```

Column names are not included in the CSV thus we may split the file into multiple parts without extracting the header row. Let's start with steps below:

1. Split the file into multiple parts.

    Once you have downloaded the CSV, you may split it into multiple parts with the following awk command. This will split the file into multiple CSV parts at every 200 rows:

```
awk '{filename = 'pima_indian_diabetes_data_part0'
int((NR-1)/200) '.csv'; print >> filename}' pima-indians-
diabetes.data.csv
```

    The following CSV files are generated:

```
-rw-r--r--  1 mbp16   staff      6043 Jul 21 16:25 pima_
indian_diabetes_data_part00.csv
```

```
-rw-r--r--  1 mbp16   staff      6085 Jul 21 16:25 pima_
indian_diabetes_data_part01.csv
```

```
-rw-r--r--  1 mbp16   staff      6039 Jul 21 16:25 pima_
indian_diabetes_data_part02.csv
```

```
-rw-r--r--  1 mbp16   staff      5112 Jul 21 16:25 pima_
indian_diabetes_data_part03.csv
```

2. Upload the files to storage. After you have created multiple CSV files from the downloaded file, you may upload these files to a Google Cloud Storage bucket:

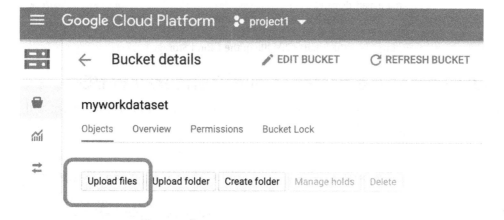

Figure 3.4 – Uploading CSV files to a Cloud Storage bucket

All the files are here:

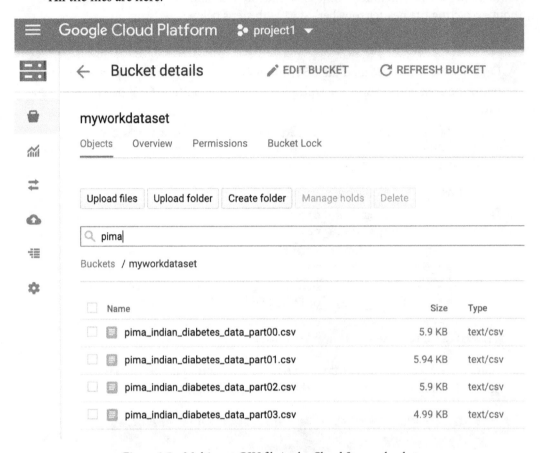

Figure 3.5 – Multi-part CSV file in the Cloud Storage bucket

Building filename patterns with TensorFlow I/O

Once the files are uploaded, let's now go to our AI Platform notebook environment and execute the following lines of code:

```
import tensorflow as tf
distributed_files_pattern = 'gs://myworkdataset/pima_indian_
diabetes_data_part*'
filenames = tf.io.gfile.glob(distributed_files_pattern)
```

`Tf.io.gfile.glob` takes a file pattern string as the input and creates a `filenames` list:

```
['gs://myworkdataset/pima_indian_diabetes_data_part00.csv',
 'gs://myworkdataset/pima_indian_diabetes_data_part01.csv',
 'gs://myworkdataset/pima_indian_diabetes_data_part02.csv',
 'gs://myworkdataset/pima_indian_diabetes_data_part03.csv']
```

Now that we have a list of filenames that match the pattern, we are ready to convert these files to a dataset.

Creating a dataset from CSV files

Typically, multiple CSV files are stored with either no header or all with a header. In this case, there is no header. We need to prepare the column names for the CSV before we convert it to dataset:

```
COLUMN_NAMES = ['Pregnancies', 'Glucose', 'BloodPressure',
                'SkinThickness', 'Insulin', 'BMI',
                'DiabetesPedigree', 'Age', 'Outcome']
```

Here's the source for column names: `https://data.world/data-society/pima-indians-diabetes-database`.

Then we need to specify that the first lines in these files are not headers as we convert the CSVs to a dataset:

```
ds = tf.data.experimental.make_csv_dataset(
      filenames,
      header = False,
      column_names = COLUMN_NAMES,
      batch_size=5, # Intentionally make it small for
      # convenience.
      label_name='Outcome',
      num_epochs=1,
      ignore_errors=True)
```

In `make_csv_dataset`, we use a list of filenames as the input and specify there is no header, and we then assign `COLUMN_NAMES`, make small batches for showing the result, select a column as the target column (`'Outcome'`), and set the number of epochs to `1` since we are not going to train a model with it at this point.

Inspecting the dataset

Now we may verify the content of the dataset. Recall that since we specified a column as the label, that means the rest of the columns are features. The output will be a tuple that contains features and targets.

Let's take the first batch of the dataset, which contains five observations, and print the data in features and target columns. In a dataset, the data is stored as arrays, and each column is now a key-value pair. Within `features` is another level of key-value pairs for each feature:

```
for features, target in ds.take(1):
    print(''Outcome': {}'.format(target))
    print(''Features:'')
    for k, v in features.items():
        print('  {!r:20s}: {}'.format(k, v))
```

The output is as follows:

```
'Outcome': [1 0 0 0 0]
'Features:'
  'Pregnancies'       : [ 7 12  1  0  2]
  'Glucose'           : [129  88 128  93  96]
  'BloodPressure'     : [ 68  74  82 100  68]
  'SkinThickness'     : [49 40 17 39 13]
  'Insulin'           : [125  54 183  72  49]
  'BMI'               : [38.5 35.3 27.5 43.4 21.1]
  'DiabetesPedigree'  : [0.439 0.378 0.115 1.021 0.647]
  'Age'               : [43 48 22 35 26]
```

During training, the data will be passed to the training process in batches, and not as a single file to be opened and possibly consume a large amount of runtime memory. In the preceding example, we see that as a good practice, distributed files stored in Cloud Storage follow a certain naming pattern. The `tf.io.gfile.glob` API can easily infer multiple files that are distributed in a Cloud Storage bucket. We may easily use `tf.data.experimental.make_csv_dataset` to create a dataset instance from the `gfile` instance. Overall, the `tf.io` and `tf.data` APIs together make it possible to build a data input pipeline without explicitly reading data into memory.

Handling image data for input pipelines

While there are many types of unstructured data, images are probably the most frequently encountered type. TensorFlow provided TFRecord as a type of dataset for image data. In this section, we are going to learn how to convert image data in Cloud Storage into a TFRecord object for input pipelines.

When working with image data in a TensorFlow pipeline, the raw image is typically converted to a TFRecord object for the same reason as for CSV or DataFrames. Compared to a raw numpy array, a TFRecord object is a more efficient and scalable representation of the image collections. Converting raw images to a TFRecord object is not a straightforward process. In TFRecord, the data is stored as a binary string. In this section, we are going to show how to do this step by step.

Let's start with the conversion process of converting a raw image to a TFRecord object. Feel free to upload your own images to the JupyterLab instance:

1. Upload images of your choice to the JupyterLab runtime. Create a folder for your images that we are going to upload. Give the folder a name, and this is the folder where the images will be uploaded:

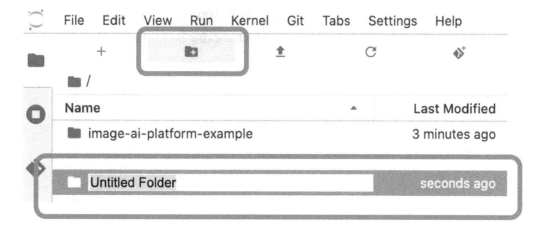

Figure 3.6 – Creating a folder in the notebook runtime

Now that the folder has a name, you may proceed to the next step.

2. Double-click on the folder you just named. Now you are inside this folder. In this example, I named this folder `image-ai-platform-examle`. Then, within this folder, I created another folder named `maldives`. Once inside, you may click the upload button to upload a few of your own images to this folder:

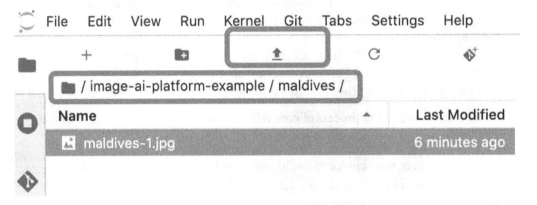

Figure 3.7 – Uploading an item to JupyterLab runtime

Here, I uploaded an image named `maldives-1.jpg`.

3. You may acquire the path to this image by right-clicking on the image file:

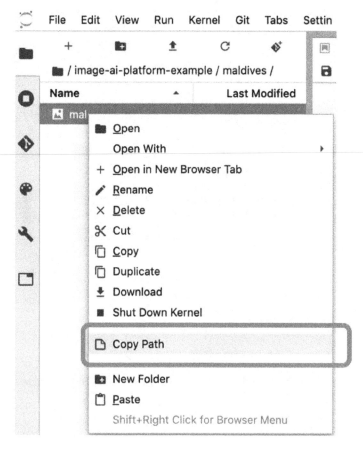

Figure 3.8 – Finding the path to images uploaded to the notebook

You may paste the file path to a notepad or editor for quick reference for the next step.

4. Select **Copy Path** to an editor. In this case, it is `images-ai-platform-example/maldives/maldives-1.jpg`:

5. Display the image for verification:

```
import IPython.display as display
my_image = 'images-ai-platform-example/maldives/
maldives-1.jpg'
display.display(display.Image(filename=my_image))
```

Here's the output:

Figure 3.9 – Displaying the image

6. Create a dictionary to map the filename with a label. We can use the `my_image` alias as the key and we may verify this dictionary:

```
image_labels = {
    my_image : 0
}
image_labels.items()
```

The output should be as follows:

```
dict_items([('images-ai-platform-example/maldives/
maldives-1.jpg', 0)])
```

Constructing a protobuf message

Now we have `image_labels` that map image files to their labels. The next thing we need to do is to convert this image to a `tf.Example` **protobuf** message. Protobuf is Google's language-neutral mechanism or structure for efficient serialization of data. When using this standard in formatting the image data, you effectively convert the raw image into a collection of key-value pairs, with most of the keys being the metadata of the image, including the filename, width, height, channels, label, and one key being the actual pixel values as a byte array. Similar to `image_label`, the `tf.Example` message consists of key-value pairs. The key-value pairs are the metadata of the image, including the three dimensions and their respective values, the label and its value, and finally the image itself in byte array format. The values are represented as `tf.Tensor`. Let's now construct this protobuf message.

At this time, the `tf.Example` protobuf message can only accept three types of `tf.Tensor`. These are as follows:

- `tf.train.ByteList` can handle `string` and `byte`.
- `tf.train.FloatList` can handle `float` `(float32)` and `double` `(float64)`.
- `tf.train.Int64List` can handle `bool`, `enum`, `int32`, `uint32`, `int64` and `uint64`.

Most other generic data types can be coerced into one of these three types as per TensorFlow's documentation, which is available at: `https://www.tensorflow.org/tutorials/load_data/tfrecord#tftrainexample`:

1. First, we may use these functions that are provided as per TensorFlow's documentation. These functions can convert values to types that are compatible with `tf.Example`:

```
def _bytes_feature(value):
    '''Returns a bytes_list from a string / byte.'''
    if isinstance(value, type(tf.constant(0))):
        value = value.numpy() # BytesList won't unpack a
        # string from an EagerTensor.
    return tf.train.Feature(bytes_list=
    tf.train.BytesList(value=[value]))


def _float_feature(value):
    '''Returns a float_list from a float / double.'''
```

```
    return tf.train.Feature(float_list=
tf.train.FloatList(value=[value]))


def _int64_feature(value):
    '''Returns an int64_list from a bool / enum / int /
    uint.'''
    return tf.train.Feature(int64_list=
tf.train.Int64List(value=[value]))
```

Generally speaking, from the pattern in the preceding function, we can see that the raw value from the data is first coerced into one of the three acceptable types and then it is converted to a feature.

2. Then, we can open the image as a byte string and extract its dimensions:

```
image_string = open(my_image, 'rb').read()
image_shape = tf.image.decode_jpeg(image_string).shape
image_shape
```

3. Let's now construct a dictionary that puts these key-value pairs together:

```
label = image_labels[my_image]


feature_dictionary = {
        'height': _int64_feature(image_shape[0]),
        'width': _int64_feature(image_shape[1]),
        'depth': _int64_feature(image_shape[2]),
        'label': _int64_feature(label),
        'image_raw': _bytes_feature(image_string),
}
```

Notice that the feature dictionary consists of key-value pairs of the metadata, where the values are one of the three coerced data types for tf.Example.

4. We will then convert this dictionary to tf.Train.Features:

```
features_msg = tf.train.Features(feature=feature_
dictionary)
```

5. Convert a tf.Features protobuf message to a tf.Example protobuf message:

```
example_msg = tf.train.Example(features=features_msg)
```

6. Now, create a directory for storing `tfrecords`:

```
!mkdir tfrecords-collection
```

7. Specify a target name, and then execute the write operation:

```
record_file = 'tfrecords-collection/maldives-1.tfrecord'
with tf.io.TFRecordWriter(record_file) as writer:
    writer.write(example_msg.SerializeToString())
```

The image is now written into a protobuf message, which is a collection of key-value pairs that store its dimensions, labels, and raw images (the image value is stored as a byte string).

Decoding TFRecord and reconstructing the image

In the previous section, we learned how to write a `.jpg` image into a TFRecord dataset. Now we are going to see how to read it back and display it. An important requirement is that you must know the feature structure of the TFRecord protobuf as indicated by its keys. The feature structure is the same as the feature description used to build the TFRecord in the previous section. In other words, in the same way as a raw image was structured into a `tf.Example` protobuf with a defined feature description, we can use that feature description to parse or reconstruct the image using the same knowledge stored in the feature description:

1. Read `TFRecord` back from the path where it is stored:

```
read_back_tfrecord = tf.data.TFRecordDataset('tfrecords-
collection/maldives-1.tfrecord')
```

2. Create a dictionary to specify the keys and values in `TFRecord`, and use it to parse all elements in the `TFRecord` dataset:

```
# Create a dictionary describing the features.
image_feature_description = {
    'height': tf.io.FixedLenFeature([], tf.int64),
    'width': tf.io.FixedLenFeature([], tf.int64),
    'depth': tf.io.FixedLenFeature([], tf.int64),
    'label': tf.io.FixedLenFeature([], tf.int64),
    'image_raw': tf.io.FixedLenFeature([], tf.string),
```

```
}

def _parse_image_function(example_proto):
    # Parse the input tf.Example proto using the dictionary
    # above.
    return tf.io.parse_single_example(example_proto,
    image_feature_description)


parsed_image_dataset = read_back_tfrecord.map(_parse_
image_function)
```

In the preceding code, _parse_image_function uses image_feature_ description to parse the tfrecord protobuf. We use the map function to apply _parse_iamge_function to each image in read_back_tfrecord.

3.   Next, we will show the image using the following code:

```
for image_features in parsed_image_dataset:
    image_raw = image_features['image_raw'].numpy()
    display.display(display.Image(data=image_raw))
```

Here's the output:

Figure 3.10 – Displaying a dataset as an image

In this section, you learned how to convert raw data (an image) to TFRecord format, and verify that the conversion was done correctly by reading the TFRecord back and displaying it as an image. From this example, we can also see that in order to decode and inspect TFRecord data, we need the feature dictionary as was used during the encoding process. It is important to bear this in mind when working with TFRecord.

Handling image data at scale

Handling data and their respective labels is simple if the everything can be loaded into Python engine's runtime memory. However, in the case of constructing a data pipeline for ingestion into a model training workflow, we want to ingest or stream data in batches so that we don't rely on the runtime memory to hold all the training data. In this case, maintaining the one-to-one relationship between the data (image) and label has to be preserved. We are going to see how to do this with TFRecord. We have already seen how to convert one image to a TFRecord. With multiple images, the conversion process is exactly the same for each image.

Let's take a look at how we can reuse and refactor the code from the previous section to apply to a batch of images. Since you have seen how it was done for a single image, you will have little to no problem understanding the code and rationale here.

Typically, when working with images for classification, we would organize images in the following directory structure, starting with a base directory (in other words, project name). The next level of directories are train, validation, and test. Within each of the three directories, there are image class directories. In other words, labels are the lowest directory name. For example, the directories may be organized into the following:

```
/home/<user_name>/Documents/<project_name>
```

Then, below this level, we would have the following:

```
/home/<user_name>/Documents/<project_name>train
/home/<user_name>/Documents/<project_name>train/<class_1_dir>
/home/<user_name>/Documents/<project_name>train/<class_2_dir>
/home/<user_name>/Documents/<project_name>train/<class_n_dir>
```

```
/home/<user_name>/Documents/<project_name>validation
/home/<user_name>/Documents/<project_name>/validation/<class_1_
dir>
/home/<user_name>/Documents/<project_name>/validation/<class_2_
dir>
```

```
/home/<user_name>/Documents/<project_name>/validation/<class_n_
dir>
```

```
/home/<user_name>/Documents/<project_name>test
/home/<user_name>/Documents/<project_name> /test /<class_1_dir>
/home/<user_name>/Documents/<project_name> test/<class_2_dir>
/home/<user_name>/Documents/<project_name> /test/<class_n_dir>
```

Another way of demonstrating the organization of images by classes is as follows:

```
-base_dir
      -train_dir
            -class_1_dir
            -class_2_dir
            -class_n_dir

      -validation_dir
            -class_1_dir
            -class_2_dir
            -class_n_dir

      -test
            -class_1_dir
            -class_2_dir
            -class_n_dir
```

Images are placed in a directory based on their class. In this section, the example is simplified to the following structure in Cloud Storage:

```
-bucket
    -badlands (Badlands national park)
    -kistefos (Kistefos Museum)
    -maldives (Maldives beaches)
```

You may find example jpg images in: `https://github.com/PacktPublishing/learn-tensorflow-enterprise/tree/master/chapter_03/from_gs`

Each folder name corresponds to the label of images. The general procedure is as follows:

1. Copy images stored in the Cloud Storage bucket to the JupyterLab runtime.

2. Map image filenames to their respective labels.

3. Write each image's dimension, label, and byte array to the `tf.Example` protobuf.

4. Store multiple protobufs together in a single `TFRecord`.

Executing the steps

Here are the detailed steps that need to be run in each cell for this example:

1. Copy images from a storage bucket to the notebook runtime:

```
!mkdir from_gs
!gsutil cp -r gs://image-collection from_gs
```

In this step, a folder, `from_gs`, is created, and the `image-collection` bucket is copied into it.

Consider the base directory to be `/from_gs/image-collection`:

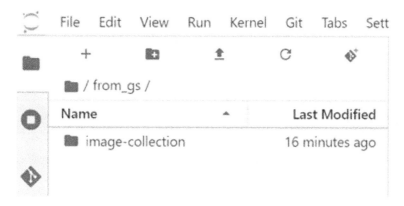

Figure 3.11 – Base directory

2. Since this example is for demonstrating how to create TFRecordDataset, and not about partitioning data into training, validation, and testing, we can go right to the image class directory level, as shown in the following screenshot:

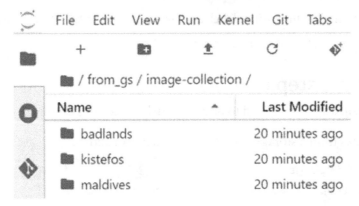

Figure 3.12 – Image class directory level

Upon inspecting one of the image class directories, we see the image files:

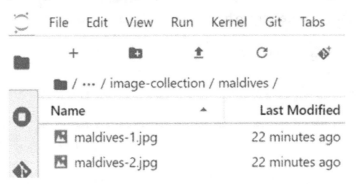

Figure 3.13 – Image files

3. Import libraries and designate the label names as CLASS_NAMES:

```
import tensorflow as tf
import numpy as np
import IPython.display as display
import pathlib


data_dir = pathlib.Path('from_gs/image-collection')
data_dir = pathlib.Path(data_dir)
```

```
CLASS_NAMES = np.array([item.name for item in data_dir.
glob('*')])
```

```
CLASS_NAMES
```

And CLASS_NAMES is captured properly as shown:

```
array(['kistefos', 'badlands', 'maldives'], dtype='<U8')
```

4. Now we need to construct a dictionary that maps filenames to their respective label from CLASS_NAMES. We can use glob to encode directory and filename patterns. A couple of empty lists are created so that we may iterate recursively through directories, and append the path-to-filename into the filename list, and the label (denoted by the directory name) into the class list:

```
import glob
file_name_list = []
class_list = []
for name in glob.glob('from_gs/image-collection/*/*.jpg',
recursive=True):
    file_name_list.append(name)
    # label is next to the last substring before the file
    # name.
    class_str = name.split('/')[-2]
    idx_tuple = np.where(CLASS_NAMES == class_str)
    idx = int(idx_tuple[0]) # first element of the idx
    # tuple is the index
    class_list.append(idx)
```

5. Once both lists are populated in exact order, we may zip these lists together and encode the result as key-value pairs (dictionary):

```
image_label_dict = dict(zip(file_name_list, class_list))


image_label_dict should look similar to:


{'from_gs/image-collection/kistefos/kistefos-1.jpg': 0,
 'from_gs/image-collection/kistefos/kistefos-3.jpg': 0,
 'from_gs/image-collection/kistefos/kistefos-2.jpg': 0,
 'from_gs/image-collection/badlands/badlands-1.jpg': 1,
 'from_gs/image-collection/badlands/badlands-2.jpg': 1,
```

```
'from_gs/image-collection/maldives/maldives-2.jpg': 2,
'from_gs/image-collection/maldives/maldives-1.jpg': 2}
```

As indicated, this is a dictionary, with the keys being the file path, and the values encoding respective labels (image classes).

6. We want to convert our data into a `tf.Example` protobuf message, which is the predecessor format for `TFRecord`. `tf.Example` requires us to specify features in the image (metadata such as the image width pixel count, height pixel count, or data such as decimal values expressed as a numpy array). The three data types designated by `tf.Example` are `tf.train.BytesList`, `tf.train.FloatList`, and `tf.train.Int64List`. Therefore, commonly observed Pythonic data types need to be coerced into one of these three types. These are what each `tf.Example` data type can accept and coerce:

- `tf.train.BytesList`: string, byte.

- `tf.train.FloatList`: float (float32, float64)

- `tf.train.Int64List`: bool, enum, int32, uint32, int64, uint64

In order to coerce common data types into the respective compatible `tf.Example` data type, the TensorFlow team provides the following helper functions:

If we want to convert a string of text (byte string) into a feature of the type `tf.train.ByteList`, the following function first converts the text (which is an eager tensor) into a numpy array, because `tf.train.BytesList` currently can only unpack numpy format into a byte list. After a protobuf message's value is casted to the `ByteList` type, then it is converted into a `feature` object with the `ByteList` data type:

```
def _bytes_feature(value):
  if not tf.is_tensor(value):
    value = tf.convert_to_tensor(value)
  value = value.numpy()
  bytes_list_msg = tf.train.BytesList(value = [value])
  coerced_list = tf.train.Feature(bytes_list =
  bytes_list_msg)
  return coerced_list
```

If we need to convert numbers with floating points into a feature of the `tf.train.FloatList` type, then the following function does the job:

```
def _float_feature(value):
    float_list_msg = tf.train.FloatList(value=[value])
    coerced_list = tf.train.Feature(float_list =
    float_list_msg)
    return coerced_list
```

7. And finally, for generating a feature of the `tf.train.Int64List` type, this can be done accordingly:

```
def _int64_feature(value):
    int64_list_msg = tf.train.Int64List(value=[value])
    coerced_list = tf.train.Feature(int64_list =
    int64_list_msg)
    return coerced_list
```

> **A note of caution**
>
> `tf.train.Feature` accepts one feature at a time. Each of these functions deals with converting and coercing one data feature at a time. This function is different from `tf.train.Features`, which accepts a dictionary of multiple features. In the next step, we are going to use `tf.train.Features`.

8. Consolidate the workflow of creating the `tf.Example` protobuf message into a wrapper function. This function takes two inputs: a byte string that represents the image, and the corresponding label of that image.

Inside this function, first, the image shape is specified through the output of decode_jpeg, which converts a byte array into a jpeg. Dimension values are held in image_shape as a numpy array, and we may pass these values into the feature dictionary. Inside the feature dictionary, keys are specified, and corresponding values are derived and type casted from the helper functions in the previous step. The feature dictionary is then used to specify schemas of the feature into a features protobuf. The feature protobuf is then converted to an example protobuf, which is the final format to be serialized into a TFRecord:

```python
def image_example(image_str, label):
    image_shape = tf.image.decode_jpeg(image_string).shape

    feature = {
        'height': _int64_feature(image_shape[0]),
        'width': _int64_feature(image_shape[1]),
        'depth': _int64_feature(image_shape[2]),
        'label': _int64_feature(label),
        'image_raw': _bytes_feature(image_string),
    }
    features_msg = tf.train.Features(feature=feature)
    example_msg = tf.train.Example(features=features_msg)
    return example_msg
```

9. Write multiple image files into TFRecords by looping through image_label_ dict:

```python
record_file = 'image-collection.tfrecords'
with tf.io.TFRecordWriter(record_file) as writer:
    for filename, label in image_image_label_dict.items():
        image_string = open(filename, 'rb').read()
        tf_example = image_example(image_string, label)
        writer.write(tf_example.SerializeToString())
```

In the preceding steps, we wrote all seven images in the three classes into a single TFRecord.

Reading TFRecord and displaying it as images

To be assured about the image data as presented by the TFRecord format, it would be helpful if we can read it back and display it, just to be sure everything was formatted correctly. Now, let's read TFRecord back and display it as images:

1. Use the same API as in the previous section to read tfrecords:

```
image_collection_dataset = tf.data.
TFRecordDataset('image-collection.tfrecords')
```

2. Define the specs for the dataset:

```
feature_specs = {
    'height': tf.io.FixedLenFeature([], tf.int64),
    'width': tf.io.FixedLenFeature([], tf.int64),
    'depth': tf.io.FixedLenFeature([], tf.int64),
    'label': tf.io.FixedLenFeature([], tf.int64),
    'image_raw': tf.io.FixedLenFeature([], tf.string),
}
```

3. Parse the protobuf. This is also exactly the same as shown in the previous section:

```
def parse_image(example):
  return tf.io.parse_single_example(example,
  feature_specs)


parsed_image_dataset = image_collection_dataset.
map(parse_image)
```

4. Display the images with the help of the following code:

```
import IPython.display as display
for image_features in parsed_image_dataset:
  image_raw = image_features['image_raw'].numpy()
  display.display(display.Image(data=image_raw))
```

And you should see all the images contained in this protobuf message. For brevity, we will show only two images, and notice that Figures 3.14 and 3.15 have different dimensions, which are preserved and retrieved correctly by the protobuf.

Here's the first image:

Figure 3.14 – Image of Maldives class (1)

And here's the second image:

Figure 3.15 – Image of Maldives class (2)

A few words about having multiple images in a single TFRecord

You have seen that whether it's one image or multiple images, everything can be written in a single TFRecord. There is no right or wrong way as to which one is preferred, as factors such as memory and I/O bandwidth all come into play. A rule of thumb is to distribute your training images to at least 32 - 128 shards (each shard is a TFRecord) to maintain a file-level parallelism in the I/O process whenever you have sufficient images to do so.

Summary

This chapter provided explanations and examples for dealing with commonly seen structured and unstructured data. We first looked at how to read and format a pandas DataFrame or CSV type of data structure and converted it to a dataset for efficient data ingestion pipelines. Then, as regards unstructured data, we used image files as examples. While dealing with image data, we have to organize these image files in a hierarchical pattern, such that labels can be easily mapped to each image file. TFRecord is the preferred format for handling image data, as it wraps the image dimension, label, and image raw bytes together in a format known as tf.Example.

In the next chapter, we are going to take a look at reusable models and patterns that can consume these data structures we have learned here.

4

Reusable Models and Scalable Data Pipelines

In this chapter, you will learn different ways of using scalable data ingestion pipelines with pre-made model elements in TensorFlow Enterprise's high-level API's. These options provide the flexibility to suit different requirements or styles for building, training, and deploying models. Armed with this knowledge, you will be able to make informed choices and understand trade-offs among different model development approaches. The three major approaches are TensorFlow Hub, the TensorFlow Estimators API, and the TensorFlow Keras API.

TensorFlow Hub is a library of open source machine learning models. TensorFlow Estimators and `tf.keras` APIs are wrappers that can be regarded as high-level elements that can be configured and reused as building blocks in a model. In terms of the amount of coding required, TensorFlow Hub models require the least amount of extra coding, while Estimator and Keras APIs are building blocks at a lower level, and therefore more coding is involved when using either Estimator or Keras APIs. But in any case, all three approaches really made TensorFlow much easier to learn and use. We are going to spend the next few sections of this chapter learning how these approaches work with scalable data ingestion pipelines from cloud storage.

With the help of an example, we will learn to use *TensorFlow datasets* and *TensorFlow I/O* as a means to ingest large amounts of data without reading it into the JupyterLab runtime memory. We will cover the following topics in this chapter:

- Using TensorFlow Hub
- Applying models from TensorFlow Hub
- Leveraging TensorFlow Keras API
- Working with TensorFlow Estimators

Using TensorFlow Hub

Of these three approaches (**TensorFlow Hub, the Estimators API, and the Keras API**), TensorFlow Hub stands out from the other two. It is a library for open source machine learning models. The main purpose of TensorFlow Hub is to enable model reusability through transfer learning. Transfer learning is a very practical and convenient technique in deep learning modeling development. The hypothesis is that as a well-designed model (peer reviewed and made famous by publications) learned patterns in features during the training process, the model learned to generalize these patterns, and such generalization can be applied to new data. Therefore, we do not need to retrain the model again when we have new training data.

Let's take human vision as an example. The content of what we see can be decomposed from simple to sophisticated patterns in the order of lines, edges, shapes, layers, and finally a pattern. As it turns out, this is how a computer vision model recognizes human faces. If we imagine a multilayer perceptron model, in the beginning, the layers learn patterns in lines, then shapes, and as we go into deep layers, we see that what's learned is the facial patterns.

Since the hierarchy of the same pattern can be used to classify other images, we can reuse the architecture of the model (from a repository such as TensorFlow Hub) and append a final classification layer for our own purposes. We will utilize this approach of transfer learning in this chapter.

Applying models from TensorFlow Hub

TensorFlow Hub contains many reusable models. For example, in image classification tasks, there are pretrained models such as Inception V3, ResNet of different versions, as well as feature vectors available. In this chapter, we will take a look at how to load and use a ResNet feature vector model for image classification of our own images. The images are five types of flowers: daisy, dandelion, roses, sunflowers, and tulips. We will use the `tf.keras` API to get these images for our use:

1. You may use Google Cloud AI Platform's JupyterLab environment for this work. Once you are in the AI Platform's JupyterLab environment, you may start by importing the necessary modules and download the images:

```
import tensorflow as tf
import tensorflow_hub as hub
import matplotlib.pyplot as plt
import numpy as np
data_dir = tf.keras.utils.get_file(
    'flower_photos',
    'https://storage.googleapis.com/download.tensorflow.
    org/example_images/flower_photos.tgz',
    untar=True)
print(data_dir)
```

You may find the flower images in the runtime instance of your JupyterLab at `/home/jupyter/.keras/datasets/flower_photos`.

2. In a new cell, we may run the following command to take a look at the directory structure for our data:

```
!ls -lrt {data_dir}
```

The preceding command will return the following structure:

```
-rw-r----- 1 jupyter jupyter 418049 Feb  9  2016 LICENSE.
txt
drwx------ 2 jupyter jupyter  45056 Feb 10  2016 tulips
drwx------ 2 jupyter jupyter  36864 Feb 10  2016
sunflowers
drwx------ 2 jupyter jupyter  36864 Feb 10  2016 roses
drwx------ 2 jupyter jupyter  45056 Feb 10  2016
dandelion
drwx------ 2 jupyter jupyter  36864 Feb 10  2016 daisy
```

Inside each folder, you will find colored images in .jpg format with different widths and heights. Before using any pre-built model, it is important to find out about the required data shape at the entry point of the model.

3. We are going to use the ResNet V2 feature vector that was pretrained with imagenet as our base model. The URL to this model is https://tfhub.dev/google/imagenet/resnet_v2_50/feature_vector/4.

    The documentation there indicates the expected height and width of the image at the entry point to be 224. Let's go ahead and specify these parameters as well as the batch size for training:

```
pixels =224
BATCH_SIZE = 32
IMAGE_SIZE = (pixels, pixels)
```

Now that we have understood the dimension of the image expected as model input, we are ready to deal with the next step, which is about how to ingest our training images.

Creating a generator to feed image data at scale

A convenient method to ingest data into the model is by a generator. A Pythonic generator is an iterator that goes through the data directory and passes batches of data to the model. When a generator is used to cycle through our training data, we do not have to load the entire image collection at one time and worry about memory constraints in our compute node. Rather, we send a batch of images at one time. Therefore, the use of the Python generator is more efficient for the compute node's memory than passing all the data as a huge NumPy array.

TensorFlow provides APIs and workflows to create such generators specific for the TensorFlow model's consumption. At a high level, it follows this process:

1. It creates an object with the ImageDataGenerator function.

2. It uses this object to invoke the flow_from_directory function to create a TensorFlow generator.

As a result, this generator knows the directory where the training data is stored.

When working with images, there are a few parameters about the data that we need to specify for the generator. The input images' color values are preferred to be between 0 and 1. Therefore, we have to normalize our image by dividing it by a rescale factor with a value of 255, which is the maximum pixel value in an RGB image of .jpg format. We may also hold on to 20% of the data for validation. This is known as the validation split factor. We also need to specify the standard image size that conforms to ResNet, an interpolation method that converts images of any size into this size, and the amount of data in a batch (batch size). The necessary steps are as follows:

1. Organize these factors as tuples. These factors are specified as input keywords for either `ImageDataGenerator` or `flow_from_directory`. We may pass these parameters and their values as tuples to these functions. The tuple will be unpacked when the function is executed. These parameters are held in these dictionaries:

```
datagen_kwargs = dict(rescale=1./255,
                      validation_split=.20)
dataflow_kwargs = dict(target_size=IMAGE_SIZE,
                       batch_size=BATCH_SIZE,
                       interpolation='bilinear')
```

As seen in the preceding lines of code, `datagen_kwargs` goes to `ImageDataGenerator`, while `dataflow_kwargs` goes to `flow_from_directory`.

2. Pass the tuples to `ImageGenerator`. These tuples encapsulate all these factors. Now we will pass these tuples into the generator, as shown in the following code:

```
valid_datagen = tf.keras.preprocessing.image.
ImageDataGenerator(
    **datagen_kwargs)
valid_generator = valid_datagen.flow_from_directory(
data_dir, subset='validation', shuffle=False, **dataflow_
kwargs)
```

And you will see the output with number of images and classes in the cross validation data:

```
Found 731 images belonging to 5 classes.
```

3. For training data, if you wish, you may consider the option for data augmentation. If so, then we may set these parameters in `ImageDataGenerator`:

```
rotation_range
horizontal_flip
Width_shift_range
height_shift_range
Shear_range
Zoom_range
```

These parameters help transform original images into different orientations. This is a typical technique to add more training data to improve accuracy.

4. For now, let's not bother with that, so we set `do_data_augmentation = False`, as shown in the following code. You may set it to `True` if you wish. Suggested augmentation parameters are provided:

```
do_data_augmentation = False
if do_data_augmentation:
   train_datagen = tf.keras.preprocessing.image.
ImageDataGenerator(
        rotation_range=40,
        horizontal_flip=True,
        width_shift_range=0.2, height_shift_range=0.2,
        shear_range=0.2, zoom_range=0.2,
        **datagen_kwargs)
else:
   train_datagen = valid_datagen
train_generator =
        train_datagen.flow_from_directory(
            data_dir, subset='training', shuffle=True,
            **dataflow_kwargs)
```

Upon executing the preceding code, you will receive the following output:

```
Found 731 images belonging to 5 classes.
Found 2939 images belonging to 5 classes.
```

Our generators for validation data and training data correctly identified the directory and were able to identify the number of classes.

5. As with all classification tasks, labels are converted to integer indices. The generator maps labels with `train_generator.class_indices`:

```
labels_idx = (train_generator.class_indices)
```

6. We can easily map indices back to labels by creating a reverse lookup, also in the form of a dictionary. This can be done by reversing the key-value pairs as we iterated `through labels_idx`, where the key is the index and the values are flower types:

```
idx_labels = dict((v,k) for k,v in labels_idx.items())
print(idx_labels)
{0: 'daisy', 1: 'dandelion', 2: 'roses', 3: 'sunflowers',
4: 'tulips'}
```

In this section, we learned how to implement `ImageGenerator` for both training and validation data. We leveraged optional input parameters to rescale and normalize our images. We also learned to retrieve the ground truth label mapping so that we may decode the model prediction.

Next, we will learn to implement transfer learning by reusing ResNet feature vectors for our own image classification task.

Reusing pretrained ResNet feature vectors

Now we are ready to construct the model. We will use the `tf.keras.sequential` API. It consists of three layers—input, ResNet, and a dense layer—as the classification output. We also have the choice between fine-tuning and retraining the ResNet (this requires longer training time). The code for defining the model architecture is as follows:

1. We'll begin by defining the parameters, as shown in the following lines of code:

```
FINE_TUNING_CHOICE = True
NUM_CLASSES = len(idx_labels)
```

2. Next, we will construct the model with the help of the following code:

```
mdl = tf.keras.Sequential([
    tf.keras.layers.InputLayer(input_shape=IMAGE_SIZE +
                               (3,)),
```

```
hub.KerasLayer('https://tfhub.dev/google/imagenet/
resnet_v2_50/feature_vector/4',
trainable = FINE_TUNING_CHOICE),
tf.keras.layers.Dense(NUM_CLASSES,
activation='softmax', name = 'custom_class')
])
```

3. Now, let's build the model with the following line of code:

```
mdl.build([None, 224, 224, 3])
```

ResNet requires RGB layers to be separated as a third dimension. Therefore, we need to add an input layer that takes on input_shape of [224, 224, 3]. Also, since we have five types of flowers, this is a multiclass classification. We need a dense layer with softmax activation for outputting probability for each label.

4. We may confirm the model architecture with the following line of code:

```
mdl.summary()
```

Upon executing the preceding line of code, you will see the sequence of the three layers and their expected output shape:

```
Model: 'sequential_1'
_____

_____
Layer (type)                  Output
Shape                 Param #
=============================================================
=========
keras_layer_1 (KerasLayer)    (None,
2048)              23564800


_____
custom_class (Dense)          (None,
5)                    10245
=============================================================
=========
Total params: 23,575,045
Trainable params: 23,529,605
Non-trainable params: 45,440
```

This shows the model is very simple in its structure. It consists of the ResNet feature vector layer that we downloaded from TensorFlow Hub, followed by a classification head with five nodes (there are five flower classes in our image collection).

Compiling the model

Now that we have wrapped the ResNet feature vector with proper input and output layers, we are ready to set up the training workflow. To begin, we need to compile the model, where we specify the optimizer (in this case, we select **stochastic gradient descent (SGD)** with hyperparameters such as learning rate and momentum). It also requires a `loss` function. The optimizer leverages the gradient decent algorithm to continuously seek weights and biases to minimize the `loss` function. Since this is a multiclass classification problem, it needs to be categorical cross-entropy.

For a deeper discussion, see *TensorFlow 2.0 Quick Start Guide*, by *Tony Holroyd*, published by *Packt Publishing*. You can refer to *Chapter 4 Supervised Machine Learning Using TensorFlow 2*, and the section entitled *Logistic regression*, concerning loss functions and optimizers. This is how we define an optimizer:

```
my_optimizer = tf.keras.optimizers.SGD(lr=0.005, momentum=0.9)
```

And since we want to output probability for each class, we set `from_logits = True,` We also would like the model not to become overconfident, so we set `label_smoothing = 0.1` as a regularization to penalize extremely high probability. We may define a `loss` function as follows:

```
my_loss_function = tf.keras.losses.
CategoricalCrossentropy(from_logits=True, label_smoothing=0.1)
```

We need to configure the model for training. This is accomplished by defining the `loss` function and optimizer as part of the model's training process, as the training process needs to know what the `loss` function is to optimize for, and what optimizer to use. To compile the model with the optimizer and `loss` function specified, execute the following code:

```
mdl.compile(
    optimizer=my_optimizer,
    loss=my_loss_function,
    metrics=['accuracy'])
```

The outcome is a model architecture that is ready to be used for training.

Training the model

For model training, we will use the `tf.keras.fit` function. We are only going to train for five epochs:

```
steps_per_epoch = train_generator.samples // train_generator.
batch_size
validation_steps = valid_generator.samples // valid_generator.
batch_size
hist = mdl.fit(
    train_generator,
    epochs=5, steps_per_epoch=steps_per_epoch,
    validation_data=valid_generator,
    validation_steps=validation_steps).history
```

And the training result should be similar to this:

```
Epoch 1/5
91/91 [==============================] - 404s 4s/step - loss:
1.4899 - accuracy: 0.7348 - val_loss: 1.3749 - val_accuracy:
0.8565
Epoch 2/5
91/91 [==============================] - 404s 4s/step - loss:
1.3083 - accuracy: 0.9309 - val_loss: 1.3359 - val_accuracy:
0.8963
Epoch 3/5
91/91 [==============================] - 405s 4s/step - loss:
1.2723 - accuracy: 0.9704 - val_loss: 1.3282 - val_accuracy:
0.9077
Epoch 4/5
91/91 [==============================] - 1259s 14s/step - loss:
1.2554 - accuracy: 0.9869 - val_loss: 1.3302 - val_accuracy:
0.9020
Epoch 5/5
91/91 [==============================] - 403s 4s/step - loss:
1.2487 - accuracy: 0.9935 - val_loss: 1.3307 - val_accuracy:
0.8963
```

At each epoch, the `loss` function value and accuracy on training data is provided. Since we have cross-validation data provided, the model is also tested with a validation dataset at the end of each training epoch. The `loss` function and accuracy measurement are provided at each epoch by the Fit API. This is the standard output for each training run.

It is also worth mentioning that when the preceding code is executed in AI Notebook using the Nvidia Tesla T4 Graphics Processing Unit (GPU) and a basic driver node of 4 CPUs at 15 GB RAM, the total training time is just a little over 2 minutes, whereas if this training process was executed in the same driver node without a GPU, it could take more than 30 minutes to complete the training process.

GPUs are well suited for deep learning model training because it can process multiple computations in parallel. A GPU achieves parallel processing through a large number of cores. This translates to large memory bandwidth and faster gradient computation of all trainable parameters in the deep learning architecture than otherwise would be the case in a CPU.

Scoring with test images

Now we may test the model using test (holdout) images. In this example, I uploaded five flower images, and we need to convert them all to the shape of [224, 224] and normalize pixel values to [0, 1]. As common practice, test images are stored separately from training and cross-validation images. Therefore, it is typical to have a different file path to test images:

1. We are going to download some test images for these types of flowers. The images are partitioned into training, validation, and test images at the following link:
    https://dataverse.harvard.edu/api/access/datafile/4159750

2. So, in the next cell, you may use `wget` to download it to your notebook:

    ```
    !wget https://dataverse.harvard.edu/api/access/
    datafile/4159750
    ```

3. Then, unzip it:

    ```
    !unzip 4159750
    ```

    You will have the`/flower_photos/small_test` directory available in the left panel of your notebook instance.

4. Create a data generator instance for test data. Since our `train_datagen` already knows how to do that, we may reuse this object. Make sure you specify the `working_dir` directory as a file path to where our test images reside:

```
working_dir = 'flower_photos/small_test'
test_generator =
    train_datagen.flow_from_directory
            (directory=working_dir,
            batch_size = 5,
            target_size = [224, 224],
            shuffle=False,
            classes = list(labels_idx))
```

5. Let's take a note of the label index:

```
print(test_generator.class_indices)
```

The output indicates the relative position of each label in the array of probability:

```
{'daisy': 0, 'dandelion': 1, 'roses': 2, 'sunflowers': 3,
'tulips': 4}
```

6. Let's also define a helper function that plots the images:

```
def plotImages(images_arr):
    fig, axes = plt.subplots(1, 5, figsize=(10,10))
    axes = axes.flatten()
    for img, ax in zip( images_arr, axes):
        ax.imshow(img)
        ax.axis('off')
    plt.tight_layout()
    plt.show()
```

7. Now, let's take a look at the test images and their corresponding labels (ground truth):

```
sample_test_images, ground_truth_labels = next(test_
generator)
print(ground_truth_labels)
```

The output for the test images is shown as follows. In the first three rows, one-hot encoding is 1 at the first position. This corresponds to `daisy` according to `test_generator.class_indices`, whereas for the last two rows, 1 is at the last position, indicating the last two images are of `tulips`:

```
[[1. 0. 0. 0. 0.]
 [1. 0. 0. 0. 0.]
 [1. 0. 0. 0. 0.]
 [0. 0. 0. 0. 1.]
 [0. 0. 0. 0. 1.]]
```

8. And we may plot these images:

```
plotImages(sample_test_images[:5])
```

Figure 4.1 – Test image examples; the first three are daisies, and the last two are tulips

9. For the model to make predictions on these images, execute the following code:

```
prediction = mdl.predict(sample_test_images[:5])
```

The output of the prediction is as follows:

```
array([[9.9985600e-01, 3.2907694e-05, 2.3326173e-05,
        6.8752386e-05, 1.8940274e-05],
       [9.9998152e-01, 7.6931758e-07, 9.4449973e-07,
        1.6520202e-05, 2.8859478e-07],
       [9.9977893e-01, 2.0959340e-05, 6.2238797e-07,
        1.8358800e-04, 1.6017557e-05],
       [6.7357789e-04, 5.8116650e-05, 3.0710772e-04,
        6.2863214e-04, 9.9833256e-01],
       [1.9417066e-04, 1.3316995e-04, 6.2624150e-04,
        1.4169540e-04, 9.9890471e-01]], dtype=float32)
```

This output is a NumPy array of probabilities for each class in each image. Each row corresponds to an image, and consists of five probabilities for each label. The first three rows have the highest probability in the first position, and the last two rows have the highest probability in the last position. This means the model predicted that the first three images would be daisies, and the last two images tulips, according to the mapping provided by `test_generator.class_indices`.

It would also be helpful if we could output these results in a more readable format such as a CSV file, with filenames of the test images and their respective predictions.

1. Let's map the probability magnitude with respect to the position and define a label reference:

```
labelings = tf.math.argmax(prediction, axis = -1)
label_reference = np.asarray(list(labels_idx))
```

2. Write a helper function to map position with respect to the actual label:

```
def find_label(idx):
    return label_reference[idx]
```

3. Now we can map the position of each observation's highest probability:

```
predicted_idx = tf.math.argmax(prediction, axis = -1)
```

4. And we can take a look at `predicted_idx`:

```
<tf.Tensor: shape=(5,), dtype=int64, numpy=array([0, 0,
0, 4, 4])>
```

This means that in the first three images, the maximum probability occurs at position 0, which corresponds to `daisy` according to `test_generator.class_indices`. By the same token, the last two images have the maximum probability occurring at position 4, which corresponds to `tulips`.

5. Then, apply the helper function to each row of the prediction output, and insert test image filenames (`test_generator.filenames`) alongside the prediction in a nicely formatted pandas DataFrame:

```
import pandas as pd
predicted_label = list(map(find_label, predicted_idx))
file_name = test_generator.filenames

results=pd.DataFrame({'File':file_name,
```

```
                          'Prediction':predicted_label})
  results
```

The results should look similar to the following diagram. Now you may save the pandas DataFrame to any format of your choice, such as a CSV file or a pickle:

	File	**Prediction**
0	daisy/2019064575_7656b9340f_m.jpg	daisy
1	daisy/3415180846_d7b5cced14_m.jpg	daisy
2	daisy/4144275653_7c02d47d9b.jpg	daisy
3	tulips/4612075317_91eefff68c_n.jpg	tulips
4	tulips/8690791226_b1f015259f_n.jpg	tulips

Figure 4.2 – Prediction output in a DataFrame format

This completes the demonstration of using a pretrained model from TensorFlow Hub, applying it to our own data, retraining the model, and making the prediction. We also saw how to leverage generators to ingest training data in batches to the model.

TensorFlow Hub sits at the highest level of model reusability. There, you will find many open source models already built for consumption via a technique known as transfer learning. In this chapter, we built a regression model using the tf.keras API. Building a model this way (custom) is actually not a straightforward task. Often, you will spend a lot of time experimenting with different model parameters and architectures. If your need falls into classification or regression problems that are compatible with pre-built open source models, then TensorFlow Hub is the one-stop shop for finding the classification or regression model for your data. However, for these pre-built models, you still need to investigate the data structure required for the input layer and provide a final output layer for your purpose. However, reusing these pre-built models in TensorFlow Hub will save time in building and debugging your own model architecture.

In the next section, we are going to see the TensorFlow Keras API, which is the newest high-level API that provides many reusable models.

Leveraging the TensorFlow Keras API

Keras is a deep learning API that wraps around machine learning libraries such as TensorFlow, Theano, and Microsoft Cognitive Toolkit (also known as CNTK). Its popularity as a standalone API stems from the succinct style of the model construction process. As of 2018, TensorFlow added Keras as a high-level API moving forward, and it is now known as `tf.keras`. Starting with the TensorFlow 2.0 distribution released in 2019, `tf.keras` has become the official high-level API.

`tf.keras` excels at modeling sophisticated deep learning architecture that contains **long short-term memory (LSTM)**, **gated recurring units (GRUs)**, and **convolutional neural network (CNN)** layers. These are considered to be workhorses in current **natural language processing (NLP)** and computer vision models. It also provides simple and straightforward architecture for simpler deep learning models, such as multilayer perceptrons. In the following example, we are going to use the `tf.keras` dense layer to build a regression model with tabular data from BigQuery.

Data acquisition

We are going to use a publicly available dataset from Google Cloud as the working data for this example:

1. This is our table of interest:

   ```
   DATASET_GCP_PROJECT_ID = 'bigquery-public-data'
   DATASET_ID = 'covid19_geotab_mobility_impact'
   TABLE_ID = 'us_border_volumes'
   ```

You may find it in BigQuery:

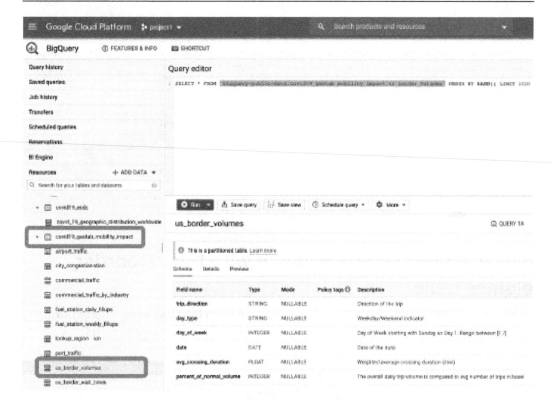

Figure 4.3 – BigQuery portal and table selection

2. Let's take a look at the data by running the following query:

```
SELECT * FROM `bigquery-public-data.covid19_geotab_
mobility_impact.us_border_volumes` ORDER BY RAND() LIMIT
1000
```

The preceding query helps us to retrieve 1,000 random rows of the table: `data.covid19_geotab_mobility_impact.us_border_volumes`.

And this is the output:

Row	trip_direction	day_type	day_of_week	date	avg_crossing_duration	percent_of_normal_volume	avg_crossing_duration_truck	percent_of_normal_volume_truck	version
1	Mexico to US	Weekdays	3	2020-07-07	30.1	97	28.2	102	1.4
2	Mexico to US	Weekdays	2	2020-06-08	30.9	110	29.5	117	1.4
3	US to Canada	Weekends	7	2020-04-18	8.3	56	8.1	61	1.4
4	US to Canada	Weekdays	4	2020-05-06	8.1	72	8.0	75	1.4
5	US to Mexico	Weekdays	3	2020-06-09	10.7	97	11.0	99	1.4
6	Canada to US	Weekdays	4	2020-03-25	8.6	77	8.3	79	1.4
7	US to Mexico	Weekends	7	2020-04-18	10.6	68	10.4	74	1.4
8	Canada to US	Weekdays	4	2020-05-27	8.2	84	8.3	87	1.4
9	Canada to US	Weekdays	2	2020-03-30	9.1	74	8.6	76	1.4
10	US to Canada	Weekdays	3	2020-03-17	10.5	101	10.4	103	1.4

Figure 4.4 – Table columns in us_border_volumes

Solving a data science problem with the us_border_volumes table

The output consists of rows that are randomly selected from the table being queried. Your output will consist of different values.

In the us_border_volumes table, each record represents a truck's entry or exit at a USA border point. The attributes in each record are trip_direction, day_type, day_of_week, date, avg_crossing_duration, percent_of_normal_volume, avg_crossing_duration_truck, and percent_of_nortal_volume_truck. We would like to build a model that predicts how long it would take for a truck to cross a border, given these features.

Selecting features and a target for model training

Here is an example problem that we will use to demonstrate how to leverage a TensorFlow I/O pipeline to provide training data to a model.

Let's set this problem up as a regression problem with this data. We are going to build a regression model to predict the average time it takes for a truck to cross the border (avg_crossing_duration_truck). Other columns (except date) are the features.

Streaming training data

For the rest of this example, we are going to use the Google AI Platform JupyterLab notebook with TensorFlow Enterprise 2.1 distribution. You may reuse the project ID from *Chapter 2, Running TensorFlow Enterprise in Google AI Platform*.

Having identified the data source, we are going to build a streaming workflow to feed training data to the model. This is different from reading the table as a pandas DataFrame in the Python runtime. We want to stream the training data by batches rather than using up all the memory allocated for the Python runtime. Therefore, we are going to use TensorFlow I/O for streaming the training data from BigQuery:

1. We will start with the following code to import the necessary libraries and set up environmental variables:

```
import tensorflow as tf
from tensorflow import feature_column
from tensorflow_io.bigquery import BigQueryClient
import numpy as np
from google.cloud import bigquery


client = BigQueryClient()


PROJECT_ID = 'project1-XXXXX'
# A project ID in your GCP subscription.
DATASET_GCP_PROJECT_ID = 'bigquery-public-data'
DATASET_ID = 'covid19_geotab_mobility_impact'
TABLE_ID = 'us_border_volumes'
```

2. Create a session to read from BigQuery:

```
read_session3 = client.read_session(
    'projects/' + PROJECT_ID,
    DATASET_GCP_PROJECT_ID, TABLE_ID, DATASET_ID,
    ['trip_direction',
     'day_type',
     'day_of_week',
     'avg_crossing_duration',
     'percent_of_normal_volume',
     'avg_crossing_duration_truck',
     'percent_of_normal_volume_truck'

    ],
    [tf.string,
     tf.string,
```

```
        tf.int64,
        tf.double,
        tf.int64,
        tf.double,
        tf.int64
        ],
        requested_streams=10
)
dataset3 = read_session3.parallel_read_rows()
```

3. We have just selected fields of interest from the table in BigQuery. Now that the table is read as a dataset, we need to designate each column as either features or target. Let's use this helper function:

```
def transfrom_row(row_dict):
    # Identify column names for features.
    feature_dict = { column:
        (tf.strings.strip(tensor) if tensor.dtype ==
            'string' else tensor)
                for (column,tensor) in row_dict.items()
            }
    # Remove target column from data
    target = feature_dict.pop
                        ('avg_crossing_duration_truck')
    # Return a tuple of features and target
    return (feature_dict, target)
```

4. Now we apply this function to each row of the training dataset. This is essentially a transformation of the dataset, because we are applying a function that splits a dataset into a tuple of two dictionaries—features and target:

```
transformed_ds = dataset3.map(transfrom_row)
```

5. And now we will shuffle the dataset and batch it:

```
BATCH_SIZE = 32
SHUFFLE_BUFFER = 1024
training_dataset3 = transformed_ds.shuffle
                    (SHUFFLE_BUFFER).batch(BATCH_SIZE)
```

In this section, we identified a table from BigQuery, identified the feature and target columns, convert the table to a TensorFlow dataset, shuffled it, and batched it. This is a common technique that is preferred when you are not sure if data size presents a problem in terms of memory usage.

For the next section, we are going to look at the tf.keras API and how to use it to build and train a model.

Input to a model

So far, we have taken care of specifying features and the target in the training dataset. Now, we need to specify each feature as either categorical or numeric. This requires us to set up TensorFlow's feature_columns object. The feature_columns object is the input to the model:

1. For each categorical column, we need to keep track of the possible categories. This is done through a helper function:

```
def get_categorical_feature_values(column):
    query = 'SELECT DISTINCT TRIM({}) FROM `{}`.{}.{}'.
        format(column, DATASET_GCP_PROJECT_ID,
                DATASET_ID, TABLE_ID)
    client = bigquery.Client(project=PROJECT_ID)
    dataset_ref = client.dataset(DATASET_ID)
    job_config = bigquery.QueryJobConfig()
    query_job = client.query(query,
                                job_config=job_config)
    result = query_job.to_dataframe()
    return result.values[:,0]
```

2. Then, we can create the feature_columns object (which is really a Python list) with the following code snippet:

```
feature_columns = []


# Numeric columns
for header in ['day_of_week',
                'avg_crossing_duration',
                'percent_of_normal_volume',
                'percent_of_normal_volume_truck']:
```

```
feature_columns.append
                   (feature_column.numeric_column(header))


# Categorical columns
for header in ['trip_direction', 'day_type']:
  categorical_feature = feature_column.categorical_column_
with_vocabulary_list(
      header, get_categorical_feature_values(header))
  categorical_feature_one_hot = feature_column.indicator_
column(categorical_feature)
  feature_columns.append(categorical_feature_one_hot)
```

Notice that the target column is not in the `feature_columns`.

3. Now all we have to do is create a layer that creates the input to the model. The first layer is the feature columns' input to the model, which is a multilayer perceptron as defined by a series of reusable `Dense` layers:

```
feature_layer = tf.keras.layers.DenseFeatures(feature_
columns)
Dense = tf.keras.layers.Dense


model = tf.keras.Sequential(
  [
    feature_layer,
    Dense(100, activation=tf.nn.relu,
    kernel_initializer='uniform'),
    Dense(75, activation=tf.nn.relu),
    Dense(50, activation=tf.nn.relu),
    Dense(25, activation=tf.nn.relu),
    Dense(1)
  ])
```

In this section, we created a flow to ingest our dataset into the model's feature layer. During this process, for categorical columns, we have to one-hot encode it as these columns are not numeric. We then build a model architecture with the `tf.keras` API.

Next, we are going to compile this model and launch the training process.

Model training

Before the model can be used, we need to compile it. Since this is a regression model, we may specify **mean-square-error** (**MSE**) as our `loss` function, and for training metrics, we will track MSE as well as **mean-absolute-error** (**MAE**):

1. Compile the model with the proper `loss` function and metrics used in the regression task:

    ```
    model.compile(
        loss='mse',
        metrics=['mae', 'mse'])
    ```

2. Train the model:

    ```
    model.fit(training_dataset3, epochs=5)
    ```

3. Once the model is trained, we may create a sample test dataset with two observations. The test data has to be in a dictionary format:

    ```
    test_samples = {
        'trip_direction' : np.array(['Mexico to US',
                                     'US to Canada']),
        'day_type' : np.array(['Weekdays', 'Weekends']),
        'day_of_week' : np.array([4, 7]),
        'avg_crossing_duration' : np.array([32.8, 10.4]),
        'percent_of_normal_volume' : np.array([102, 89]),
        'percent_of_normal_volume_truck' : np.array([106, 84])
    }
    ```

4. To score this test sample, execute the following code:

    ```
    model.predict(test_samples)
    ```

    The output of the preceding code is as follows:

    ```
    array([[29.453201],
           [10.395596]], dtype=float32)
    ```

    This indicates the predicted average number of waiting minutes for a truck to cross the border (`avg_crossing_duration_truck`).

We just learned how to reuse the `tf.keras` dense layer and the sequential API, and integrate it with a data input pipeline driven by the use of datasets for streaming, and `feature_column` objects for feature encoding.

`tf.keras` is a high-level API that provides another set of reusable elements specifically for deep learning problems. If your solution requires deep learning techniques, then `tf.keras` is the recommended starting point.

In the next section, we are going to take a look at another high-level API known as TensorFlow Estimators. Before the `tf.keras` API became a first-class citizen in TensorFlow and in the 1.x TensorFlow distribution, TensorFlow Estimators was the only high-level API available.

So, in the next section, we will take a look at how it works.

Working with TensorFlow Estimators

TensorFlow estimators are also reusable components. The Estimators are higher-level APIs that enable users to build, train, and deploy machine learning models. It has several pre-made models that can save users from the hassle of creating computational graphs or sessions. This makes it easier for users to try different model architectures quickly with limited code changes. The Estimators are not specifically dedicated to deep learning models in the same way as `tf.keras`. Therefore, you will not find a lot of pre-made deep learning models available. If you need to work with deep learning frameworks, then the `tf.keras` API is the right choice to get started.

For this example, we are going to set up the same regression problem and build a regression model. The source of data is the same one we used in streaming training data, which is available through Google Cloud's BigQuery:

```
DATASET_GCP_PROJECT_ID = 'bigquery-public-data'
DATASET_ID = 'covid19_geotab_mobility_impact'
TABLE_ID = 'us_border_volumes'
```

This is the same BigQuery table (*Figure 4.4*) that we used for the `tf.keras` section. See *Figure 4.4* for some randomly extracted rows of this table.

Just as we did in the previous section using the `tf.keras` API, here we want to build a linear regression model using TensorFlow Estimators to predict the average time it takes for a truck to cross the border (`avg_crossing_duration_truck`). Other columns (except `date`) are the features.

The pattern of using the TensorFlow Estimators API to build and train a model is as follows.

Create an estimator object by invoking an estimator (that is, for a pre-made estimator such as a linear regressor) and specify the feature_columns object, so the model knows what data types to expect in the feature data.

Use the estimator object to call .train() and pass an input function to it. This input function is responsible for parsing training data and the label. Since we are setting up a regression problem, let's use the pre-made linear regression estimator as an example. This is the common pattern for training:

```
linear_est = tf.estimator.LinearRegressor(feature_
columns=feature_columns, model_dir=MODEL_DIR)
linear_est.train(input_fn)
```

From the preceding code, the following is observed:

- First, an instance of a linear regressor, linear_est, is created with a feature_columns object. This object provides an annotation regarding each feature (numeric or categorical data types). model_dir is the specified directory to save the model by checkpoints.

- Next in the code is linear_est.train(input_fn). This instance invokes the train() method to start the training process. The train() method takes on a function, input_fn. This is responsible for streaming, formatting, and sending the training data by batches into the model. We will take a look at how to construct input_fn. In other words, TensorFlow Estimators separates data annotation from the data ingestion process for training workflows.

Data pipeline for TensorFlow Estimators

Like tf.keras, TensorFlow Estimators can leverage the streaming data pipeline when running in the TensorFlow Enterprise environment, such as the Google Cloud AI Platform. In this section, as an example, we are going to see how to stream training data (from a table in BigQuery) into a TensorFlow Estimator model.

Below are the steps to building a BigQuery data pipeline for TensorFlow Estimator's consumption.

1. As usual, we start with the import operations for the requisite libraries:

```
import tensorflow as tf
from tensorflow_io.bigquery import BigQueryClient
from tensorflow import feature_column
```

```
from google.cloud import bigquery
import pandas as pd
import numpy as np
import datetime, os
import itertools
```

2. Now we specify a few parameters for our table of interest in BigQuery. Make sure you specify your own `PROJECT_ID`:

```
PROJECT_ID = '<YOUR_PROJECT_ID>'
DATASET_GCP_PROJECT_ID = 'bigquery-public-data'
DATASET_ID = 'covid19_geotab_mobility_impact'
TABLE_ID = 'us_border_volumes'
```

3. Next, we will specify the input function for the training process. This input function will handle the read operation, data annotation, transformation, and separation of the target from features by means of the `transform_row` function. These are exactly the identical operations seen in the previously described `tf.keras` example in the *Leveraging TensorFlow Keras API* section. The only difference is that we now wrap all of the code as follows:

```
def input_fn():
  PROJECT_ID = 'project1-190517' # This is from what you
created in your Google Cloud Account.
  DATASET_GCP_PROJECT_ID = 'bigquery-public-data'
  TABLE_ID = 'us_border_volumes'
  DATASET_ID = 'covid19_geotab_mobility_impact'
  client = BigQueryClient()
  read_session = client.read_session(
    'projects/' + PROJECT_ID,
    DATASET_GCP_PROJECT_ID, TABLE_ID, DATASET_ID,
    ['trip_direction',
     'day_type',
     'day_of_week',
     'avg_crossing_duration',
     'percent_of_normal_volume',
     'avg_crossing_duration_truck',
     'percent_of_normal_volume_truck'
```

```
    ],
   [tf.string,
    tf.string,
    tf.int64,
    tf.double,
    tf.int64,
    tf.double,
    tf.int64
    ],
     requested_streams=10
   )
  dataset = read_session.parallel_read_rows()
```

We are still inside input_fn. Continue on with input_fn:

4. We also reorganized how we specify features and the target in our data with the
    transform_row function inside input_fn.

```
  def transform_row(row_dict):
    # Trim all string tensors
    feature_dict = { column:
        (tf.strings.strip(tensor) if tensor.dtype ==
            'string' else tensor)
        for (column,tensor) in row_dict.items()
    }
    # Extract target from features
    target = feature_dict.pop(
                        'avg_crossing_duration_truck')
    # return a tuple of features and target
    return (feature_dict, target)


  transformed_ds = dataset.map(transfrom_row)
  transformed_ds = transformed_ds.batch(32)


  return transformed_ds
```

This concludes the entire `input_fn`. At this point, `input_fn` returns a dataset read from `us_border_volumes`.

5. Just as we discussed in the `tf.keras` example in the *Leveraging TensorFlow Keras API* section, we also need to build a `feature_columns` object for feature annotation. We can reuse the same code:

```
feature_columns = []
# Numeric columns
for header in ['day_of_week',
               'avg_crossing_duration',
               'percent_of_normal_volume',
               'percent_of_normal_volume_truck']:
  feature_columns.append(
                  feature_column.numeric_column(header))
# Categorical columns
for header in ['trip_direction', 'day_type']:
  categorical_feature = feature_column.categorical_column_
with_vocabulary_list(
        header, get_categorical_feature_values(header))
  categorical_feature_one_hot = feature_column.indicator_
column(categorical_feature)
  feature_columns.append(categorical_feature_one_hot)
```

6. Now, let's set up a directory to save the model checkpoints:

```
MODEL_DIR = os.path.join('models', datetime.datetime.
now().strftime('%Y%m%d-%H%M%S'))
```

7. Use the following command to make the directory:

```
%mkdir models
%mkdir {MODEL_DIR}
```

8. Launch the training process:

```
linear_est = tf.estimator.LinearRegressor(feature_
columns=feature_columns, model_dir=MODEL_DIR)
linear_est.train(input_fn)
```

This completes the model training process.

Since the estimator model expects input to be a function, in order to use the estimator for scoring, I have to pass into it a function that takes the test data, formats it, and feeds it to the model just like the training data.

The input function for training basically did two things:

- It queried the table and got the dataset representation of the table.

- It transformed the data by separating the target from the features.

In terms of the scoring situation here, we do not need to worry about this. We just need to get a dataset representation of the test data:

1. We can reuse the same test data as shown in the *Model training* section:

```
test_samples = {
    'trip_direction' : np.array(['Mexico to US',
                                 'US to Canada']),
    'day_type' : np.array(['Weekdays', 'Weekends']),
    'day_of_week' : np.array([4, 7]),
    'avg_crossing_duration' : np.array([32.8, 10.4]),
    'percent_of_normal_volume' : np.array([102, 89]),
    'percent_of_normal_volume_truck' : np.array([106, 84])
}
```

2. Create a helper function to convert test_samples to a dataset with the following code:

```
def scoring_input_fn():
  return tf.data.Dataset.from_tensor_slices(test_samples).batch(2)
```

3. The next step involves scoring the test data with the following lines of code:

```
y = linear_est.predict(
        input_fn=scoring_input_fn)
```

4. Finally, let's print the prediction as shown in the following code:

```
predictions = list(p['predictions'] for p in itertools.
islice(y, 2))
```

```
print('Predictions: {}'.format(str(predictions)))
```

```
Above code prints the output:
```

```
Predictions: [array([23.875168], dtype=float32),
array([13.621282], dtype=float32)]
```

In the preceding code, we iterate through the model output, which is a dictionary. To refer to the values associated with the model output, we need to access it by the key named `prediction`. For readability, we convert it to a list and print it out as a string. It shows the first truck is predicted to cross the border in `23.87` minutes, while the second truck is predicted to cross the border in `13.62` minutes.

TensorFlow Estimators was the only high-level API before `tf.keras` became an official part of TensorFlow distribution. While it contains many pre-made modules, such as linear regressors and different flavors of classifiers, it lacks the support for some of the commonplace deep learning modules, including CNN, LSTM, and GRU. But if your need can be addressed with non-deep learning regressors or classifiers, then TensorFlow Estimators is a good starting point. It also integrates with the data ingestion pipeline.

Summary

In this chapter, you have seen how the three major sources of reusable model elements can integrate with the scalable data pipeline. Through TensorFlow datasets and TensorFlow I/O APIs, training data is streamed into the model training process. This enables models to be trained without having to deal with the compute node's memory.

TensorFlow Hub sits at the highest level of model reusability. There, you will find many open source models already built for consumption via a technique known as transfer learning. In this chapter, we built a regression model using the `tf.keras` API. Building a model this way (custom) is actually not a straightforward task. Often, you will spend a lot of time experimenting with different model parameters and architectures. If your need can be addressed by means of pre-built open source models, then TensorFlow Hub is the place. However, for these pre-built models, you still need to investigate the data structure required for the input layer, and provide a final output layer for your purpose. However, reusing these pre-built models in TensorFlow Hub will save time in building and debugging your own model architecture.

`tf.keras` is a high-level API that provides another set of reusable elements specifically for deep learning problems. If your solution requires deep learning techniques, then `tf.keras` is the recommended starting point. With the help of an example, we have seen how a multilayer perceptron can be built quickly with the `tf.keras` API and integrated with the TensorFlow I/O module that streams training data.

In the next chapter, we are going to take up what we learned about `tf.keras` and TensorFlow Hub here, and leverage Google Cloud AI Platform to run our model training routine as a cloud training job.

Section 3 – Scaling and Tuning ML Works

Having covered how to set up a training job through various means of TensorFlow Enterprise model development, now is the time to scale the training process by using a cluster of GPUs or TPUs. You will learn how to leverage distributed training strategies and implement hyperparameter tuning to scale and improve your model training experiment.

In this part, you will learn about how to set up GPUs and TPUs in a GCP environment for submitting a model training job in GCP. You also will learn about the latest hyperparameter tuning API and run it at scale using GCP resources.

This section comprises the following chapters:

- *Chapter 5, Training at Scale*
- *Chapter 6, Hyperparameter Tuning*

5
Training at Scale

When we build and train more complex models or use large amounts of data in an ingestion pipeline, we naturally want to make better use of all the compute time and memory resources at our disposal in a more efficient way. This is the major purpose of this chapter, as we are going to integrate what we learned in previous chapters with techniques for distributed training running in a cluster of compute nodes.

TensorFlow has developed a high-level API for distributed training. Furthermore, this API integrates with the Keras API very well. As it turns out, the Keras API is now a first-class citizen in the TensorFlow ecosystem. Compared to the estimator API, Keras receives the most support when it comes to a distributed training strategy. Therefore, this chapter will predominantly focus on using the Keras API with a distributed training strategy. We will leverage Google Cloud resources to demonstrate how to make minimal changes to the Keras API code we are already familiar with and integrate it with the distributed training strategy.

In this chapter, we will learn how to leverage Google Cloud's AI Platform and use the **Tensor Processing Unit (TPU)** or GPU to conduct transfer learning. Our goal is to use a prebuilt ResNet feature vector model as a base model to train with our own dataset, then store the model and assets in cloud storage. To do this, we will learn how to stream a training dataset as `TFRecordDataset` into the model training workflow, and designate a distributed training strategy for the TPU and GPU accelerators. All the code for this chapter can be found at `https://github.com/PacktPublishing/learn-tensorflow-enterprise/tree/master/chapter_05`.

In this chapter, we will cover the following topics:

- Using the Cloud TPU through AI Platform
- Using the Cloud GPU through AI Platform

Using the Cloud TPU through AI Platform

Before we begin, let's briefly discuss the possible costs you might incur in the **Google Cloud Platform** (**GCP**). All the scripts and examples here are catered to didactic purposes. Therefore, training epochs are usually set to minimally reasonable values. With that in mind, it is still worth noting that as we start to leverage cloud resources, we need to keep in mind the compute cluster's cost. You will find more information on AI Platform training charges here: `https://cloud.google.com/ai-platform/training/ pricing#examples_calculate_training_cost_using_price_per_hour`.

The examples in this book typically use the predefined scale tiers. In the predefined scale tiers listing at the preceding link, you will see the price per hour for different tiers. For example, `BASIC_TPU` is much more expensive than `BASIC_GPU`. We will use both in this chapter, as we will learn how to submit a training job to either the TPU or GPU. In my experience, each example in this book should complete its run between 20 to 60 minutes, with the parameters set either here in the book or in the GitHub repo. Your experience may vary, depending on your region and the availability of the compute resources.

This cost does not include the cost of cloud storage, where you will read and write data or model artifacts. Remember to delete cloud storage when you are not using it. FYI, the cloud storage cost for the content and work related to this book is a very small fraction of the overall cost.

> **Tip**
> Sometimes, when the GPU is in high demand, you may want to use the TPU, which is the fastest cluster that GCP offers. It may reduce the training time significantly, and likewise your expenses.

If you haven't done so already, go ahead and clone the repo:

```
git clone https://github.com/PacktPublishing/learn-tensorflow-
enterprise.git
```

As we have seen in previous chapters, Google's AI Platform offers a convenient development environment known as JupyterLab. It integrates with other Google Cloud services, such as BigQuery or cloud storage buckets, through SDKs. In this section, we are going to leverage Google Cloud's TPU for a distributed training workload.

The TPU is a custom-built ASIC per Google's specification and design. It is an accelerator that is specifically optimized to handle deep learning calculations and algorithms. For this reason, a TPU is ideally suited for training complex neural networks and machine learning models with a virtually unlimited amount of training data. It completes a training routine in minutes where it would have taken hours in a single node machine.

Currently, there are four types of TPU offerings: **V2**, **V2 Pod**, **V3**, and **V3 Pod**. For more details, refer to the official link, which includes Google Cloud's description of the benefits of the Cloud TPU: `https://cloud.google.com/tpu/?_ga=2.138028336.-1825888872.1592693180`). For AI Platform instances that run TensorFlow Enterprise 2.1 or above, V3 is the preferred choice. With either V2 or V3, a **TPU pod** consists of multiple TPUs. A pod is basically a cluster of TPUs. For more details about the TPU and TPU pods, the following link describes the different versions of TPU pods and their runtimes for different machine learning training jobs: `https://cloud.google.com/tpu/docs/system-architecture#configurations`. Each pod, whether it's V2 or V3, can perform up to 100 petaFLOPS. This performance is reported at this link: `https://techcrunch.com/2019/05/07/googles-newest-cloud-tpu-pods-feature-over-1000-tpus/`.

The benefit of a pod over a single TPU is the training speed and memory at your disposal for the training workflow. Compared to a V2 pod (512 cores = eight cores per TPU multiplied by 64 TPUs), each V2 TPU consists of eight cores, and each core is the basic unit for training data parallelism. At the core level, the TensorFlow distributed training strategy is executed. For demonstration and didactic purposes, all the examples in this section distribute a training strategy among eight cores within a TPU. The `tf.distribute.TPUStrategy` API is the means to distribute training in the TPU. This strategy implements synchronous distributed training coupled with the TPU's all-reduce operations across multiple TPU cores.

We will use a Cloud TPU and submit a training job. In this example, we are going to see how to submit such a training job using the **Google Cloud SDK** in a client node (this could be another VM, or even your local machine). The SDK is responsible for authenticating your credentials and project ID so that the data and compute consumptions in Google Cloud can be billed. We are going to train image classification models to classify five different types of flowers (daisies, dandelions, roses, sunflowers, and tulips). These flower images are obtained from the TensorFlow 2.1 distribution. The images are shuffled at random and split into training, validation, and test sets. Each set is converted into `tfrecord` format with the images' original dimensions. The `tfrecord` images are stored in a Google Cloud storage bucket (it is assumed that your `tfrecord` is ready; generating `tfrecord` formatted data from raw images is not covered in this chapter).

The training workflow will generate checkpoints and save model artifacts when the training is complete. These items are likewise saved in the storage bucket. Therefore, we will have to grant the TPU read and write access to our working storage bucket.

Before we begin using the TPU, there are a few administrative items in Google Cloud to take care of. Let's get started.

Installing the Cloud SDK

To install the Cloud SDK in the client node, download and install Google Cloud SDK. There is a good instruction page about how to install the Cloud SDK for different types of systems, be it Mac, Linux, or Windows. It is strongly recommended to follow the instructions at this link to install Google Cloud SDK: `https://cloud.google.com/sdk/docs#install_the_latest_cloud_sdk_version`. Once the installation is done, you can verify it with the following command:

```
gcloud --help
```

The preceding command will return the following output:

```
NAME
      gcloud - manage Google Cloud Platform resources and developer workflow
SYNOPSIS
      gcloud GROUP | COMMAND [--account=ACCOUNT]
          [--billing-project=BILLING_PROJECT] [--configuration=CONFIGURATION]
          [--flags-file=YAML_FILE] [--flatten=[KEY,...]] [--format=FORMAT]
          [--help] [--project=PROJECT_ID] [--quiet, -q]
          [--verbosity=VERBOSITY; default="warning"] [--version, -v] [-h]
          [--impersonate-service-account=SERVICE_ACCOUNT_EMAIL] [--log-http]
          [--trace-token=TRACE_TOKEN] [--no-user-output-enabled]

DESCRIPTION
      The gcloud CLI manages authentication, local configuration, developer
      workflow, and interactions with the Google Cloud Platform APIs.

      For a quick introduction to the gcloud command-line tool, a list of
      commonly used commands, and a look at how these commands are structured,
      refer to the gcloud command-line tool cheat sheet,
      https://cloud.google.com/sdk/docs/cheatsheet, or run gcloud cheat-sheet.

GLOBAL FLAGS
       --account=ACCOUNT
:
```

Figure 5.1 – gcloud SDK verification

Figure 5.1 shows the general format of the gcloud command. Use *Ctrl* + *C* to exit this mode and recover your Command Prompt.

Granting the Cloud TPU access to your project

From here, the setup instructions are from Google Cloud's own documentation site at this URL: https://cloud.google.com/ai-platform/training/docs/using-tpus#tpu-runtime-versions:

1. In this step, we are going to retrieve a cloud TPU service account name per our project ID. We can use the following command:

```
curl -H 'Authorization: Bearer $(gcloud auth print-
access-token)' \
  https://ml.googleapis.com/v1/projects/<your-project-
id>:getConfig
```

The preceding command will return the following output:

```
{
  "serviceAccount": "service-[redacted]@cloud-ml.google.com.iam.gserviceaccount.com",
  "serviceAccountProject": "[redacted]1",
  "config": {
    "tpuServiceAccount": "service-[redacted]1@cloud-tpu.iam.gserviceaccount.com"
  }
}
```

Figure 5.2 – TPU service account retrieval

2. Make a note of the `serviceAccountProject` and `tpuServiceAccount` details.
3. Once we know our TPU service account, we will have to initialize it as per the following command:

```
curl -H 'Authorization: Bearer $(gcloud auth print-
access-token)'  \
  -H 'Content-Type: application/json' -d '{}'  \
  https://serviceusage.googleapis.com/v1beta1/
projects/<serviceAccountProject>/services/tpu.googleapis.
com:generateServiceIdentity
```

The preceding command generates a Cloud TPU service account for you. Make sure you put your `<serviceAccountProject>` details in the URL.

Adding a TPU service account as a member of the project

The project we use must also know about the TPU service account. In *step 3* of the previous section, we passed our project's Bearer Token to our TPU service account so the TPU can access our project. Basically, it is similar to adding another member to this project, and in this case, the new member is the TPU service account:

1. We can use Google Cloud Console to achieve this, as shown in *Figure 5.3*:

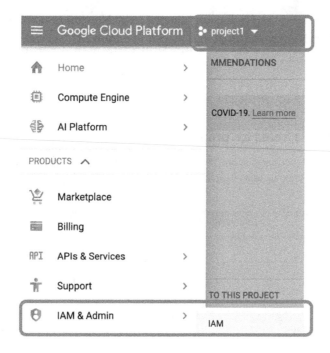

Figure 5.3 – The IAM & Admin entry

2. On the **IAM** screen, click the **ADD** button to add our TPU to this project, as in *Figure 5.4*:

Figure 5.4 – Adding a member to a project

3. Then, fill in the TPU service account details in the **New members** box. Under **Select a role**, find **Service Agent Roles**, and then find **Cloud ML Service Agent**. This is shown in *Figure 5.5*:

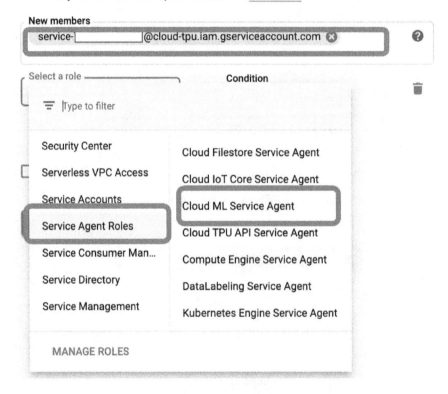

Add members to "project1"

Add members, roles to "project1" project

Enter one or more members below. Then select a role for these members to grant them access to your resources. Multiple roles allowed. Learn more

New members

service-[   ]@cloud-tpu.iam.gserviceaccount.com

Select a role   Condition

Type to filter

Security Center	Cloud Filestore Service Agent
Serverless VPC Access	Cloud IoT Core Service Agent
Service Accounts	Cloud ML Service Agent
Service Agent Roles	Cloud TPU API Service Agent
Service Consumer Man...	Compute Engine Service Agent
Service Directory	DataLabeling Service Agent
Service Management	Kubernetes Engine Service Agent

MANAGE ROLES

Figure 5.5 – Assigning the Cloud ML Service Agent role to the TPU service account

We are not done with the TPU service account yet. We also have to let it access our training data and our storage to write the training results to, such as checkpoints and model assets. This means adding a couple of new roles for our TPU service account.

4. Let's click **Add another role** and proceed to look for **Project**, as in *Figure 5.6*:

Figure 5.6 – Assigning the Project Viewer role to the TPU service account

5.   Likewise, we also add the **Cloud Storage Admin** role, as in *Figure 5.7*:

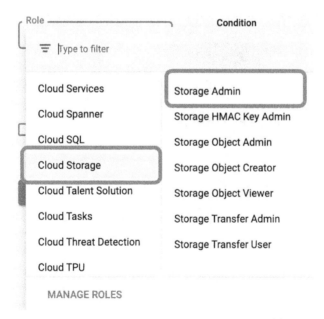

Figure 5.7 – Assigning the Storage Admin role to the TPU service account

6.   Once you have all three roles set up, click **Save**.

Whitelisting access for reading training data and writing artifacts (alternative)

The previous method grants rather broad permissions to the TPU service. It allows the TPU to have an admin credential to all of your storage buckets. If you'd prefer to limit the TPU service to only certain buckets, then you can put the TPU service account in each bucket's **access control list** (**ACL**). You can do this for your training data bucket and if you want the training job to write to another bucket, then do the same for that as well:

1. We can start by editing the bucket permissions, as shown in *Figure 5.8*. Select the **PERMISSIONS** tab:

Figure 5.8 – Editing the storage bucket permissions

2. Then, click on **ADD**, as shown in *Figure 5.9*:

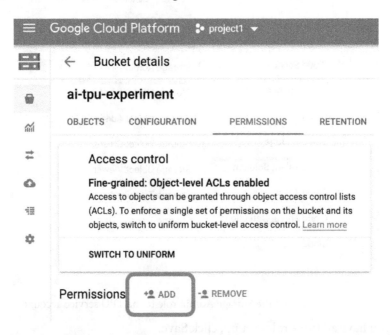

Figure 5.9 – Adding the TPU service account to the bucket ACL

3. Then, add two new roles to the TPU service account by filling in the service account name, as in *Figure 5.10*. In this example, we will use the same bucket for hosting training data and writing training artifacts. Therefore, we need to add two roles from **Cloud Storage Legacy**: **Storage Legacy Bucket Reader** and **Storage Legacy Bucket Writer**:

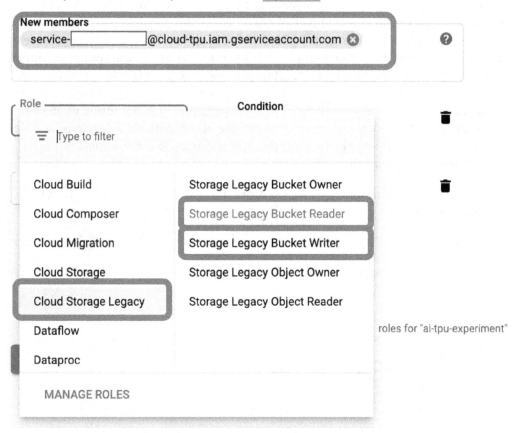

Figure 5.10 – Whitelisting the TPU service account for two roles in the storage bucket

4. Once these roles are added, click **Save**.

We have completed the minimum administrative work in order to use the Cloud TPU for our model training workflow. In the next section, we are going to see how to refactor our code and set up the distributed training strategy for the TPU.

Execution command and format

AI Platform also provides model training as a service. It enables users to submit a training job from their local environment's command line. The job will run on Google Cloud's compute cluster (with options for the CPU, TPU, or GPU in different pricing tiers). If you are new to the concept of training-as-a-service, refer to this link for details: `https://cloud.google.com/ai-platform/training/docs/training-jobs`.

Besides cloud training jobs, AI Platform can also do cloud inferencing jobs. The command we are going to run is for submitting a cloud training job. You can keep this link as a reference as you follow along with this chapter's exercises: `https://cloud.google.com/sdk/gcloud/reference/ai-platform/jobs/submit/training`. Since the approach is to keep the training script in a client node (that is, a local computer with Google Cloud SDK installed), we need to let the Google Cloud runtime know, when executing `gcloud ai-platform jobs submit training`, where all the training scripts are. Also, because there are libraries that will be imported in our script, we need to specify the information, such as their versions and the library names and versions, in a file named `setup.py`. In order to accomplish this, it is necessary to create a small `setup.py` file in your working directory:

1. In the command terminal (for Mac OS X or Linux) of your working directory, type the following:

```
cat << END > setup.py
from setuptools import find_packages
from setuptools import setup

setup(
    name='official',
    install_requires=['tensorflow-datasets~=3.1',
                      'tensorflow_hub>=0.6.0'],
    packages=find_packages()
)
END
```

The preceding code is generated according to *step 2* in this example. Alternatively, you can use a text editor to generate the following:

```
from setuptools import find_packages
from setuptools import setup
```

```
setup(
    name='official',
    install_requires=['tensorflow-datasets~=3.1',
                      'tensorflow_hub>=0.6.0'],
    packages=find_packages()
)
```

You should save the preceding code as setup.py. In install_requires, you will see a Python list that contains TensorFlow datasets or tensorflow_hub. This is where dependencies are added to the runtime in Google Cloud AI Platform.

2. Now that we are ready to set up the command for distributed training in the Cloud TPU, let's first take a look at the command and execution format. Recall that we stated earlier that this task will be executed using the Cloud SDK running in a client. In general, the client node will issue the gcloud command with input flags, such as this:

```
gcloud ai-platform jobs submit training cloudtpu \
--staging-bucket=gs://ai-tpu-experiment \
--package-path=python \
--module-name=python.ScriptProject.traincloudtpu_resnet_
cache \
--runtime-version=2.2 \
--python-version=3.7 \
--scale-tier=BASIC_TPU \
--region=us-central1 \
-- \
--distribution_strategy=tpu \
--model_dir=gs://ai-tpu-experiment/traincloudtpu_tfkd_
resnet_cache \
--train_epochs=10 \
--data_dir=gs://ai-tpu-experiment/tfrecord-flowers
```

There are many more flags (user input parameters) available than shown here. For detailed descriptions of all the possible input parameters, refer to the TensorFlow Google Cloud AI Platform reference (https://cloud.google.com/sdk/gcloud/reference/ai-platform/jobs/submit/training) and the Cloud SDK documentation (https://cloud.google.com/sdk/gcloud/reference/ai-platform).

Cloud command arguments

The example command (discussed ahead in this section), illustrates a directory structure as shown in *Figure 5.11*:

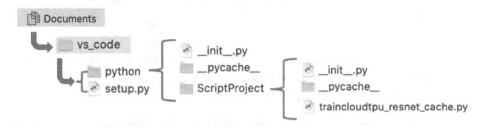

Figure 5.11 – Directory structure and file organization in a local client for an example training run

Some of the folder names in the preceding figure are personal choices: `vs_code`, `python`, `ScriptProject`. You can name these folders to your preference. The training script named `traincloudtpu_resnet_cache` is also a personal choice.

Let's take a look at this example command. This example command can be divided into two parts based on `--  \`. The first part of the command includes the following:

```
gcloud ai-platform jobs submit training cloudtpu \
--staging-bucket=gs://ai-tpu-experiment \
--package-path=python \
--module-name=python.ScriptProject.traincloudtpu_resnet_cache \
--runtime-version=2.1 \
--python-version=3.7 \
--scale-tier=BASIC_TPU \
--region=us-central1 \
```

This command is executed in the `vs_code` directory shown in *Figure 5.11*. In this directory, you will find `setup.py`. This is the file that tells the `gcloud` runtime about the dependencies or packages required for the training script. `cloudtpu` is just a name we provided for this training run. We also need to specify a staging bucket (a cloud storage bucket) for serialization of model artifacts during and after training.

`package-path` is the folder for organizing projects. In this case, within this package, we are interested in executing a training script, `traincloudtpu_resnet_cache.py`. In order for the `gcloud` runtime to find it, we need to specify the following:

```
module-name=python.ScriptProject.traincloudtpu_resnet_cache
```

We then specify the TensorFlow Enterprise version to be 2.1 and the Python interpreter version to be 3.7, and a scale tier of `BASIC_TPU` should suffice for this example. We also set the region to be `us-central1`. The `BASIC_TPU` scale tier provides us with a master VM and a TPU VM with eight TPU V2 cores.

As stated earlier, `--` \ separates the `gcloud` system flags from any other user-defined flags that are specified and serve as input parameters to the training script. This separation is necessary and by design. Do not mix system flags with user-defined flags. See the SDK reference (`https://cloud.google.com/sdk/gcloud/reference/ai-platform/jobs/submit/training`) for details about positional arguments.

Now, let's take a look at the second half of this command, which consists of user-defined flags:

```
--distribution_strategy=tpu \
--model_dir=gs://ai-tpu-experiment/traincloudtpu_tfkd_resnet_
cache \
--train_epochs=10 \--data_dir=gs://ai-tpu-experiment/tfrecord-
flowers
```

We specify `distribution_strategy=tpu` as a user-defined flag because we may use this value in conditional logic to select the proper distribution strategy. We also specify `model_dir`, which is a cloud storage path that we grant write permissions to the TPU service in order to serialize checkpoints and model assets. Then, for the remaining flags, we specify the number of epochs for training in `train_epochs`, and the path to the training data indicated by `data_dir`, which is also a cloud storage path that we grant read permissions to the TPU service. The TPU's distributed training strategy (`https://www.tensorflow.org/guide/distributed_training#tpustrategy`) implements all necessary operations across multiple cores.

Organizing the training script

The general structure of the training script for this example follows a minimalist style. In practice, it is common to organize Python code into multiple files and modules. Therefore, we will have everything we need in one Python script, `train.py`. Its pseudo-code is as follows:

```
def run( input parameters ):
    # specify distribute strategy (https://cloud.google.com/
    ai-platform/training/docs/using-tpus)
    import tensorflow as tf
    if distribution_strategy==TPU:
        resolver = tf.distribute.cluster_resolver.
        TPUClusterResolver()
    tf.config.experimental_connect_to_cluster(resolver)
    tf.tpu.experimental.initialize_tpu_system(resolver)
    strategy = tf.distribute.experimental.
TPUStrategy(resolver)
    # build data streaming pipeline with tf.io and tf.data.
TFRecordDataset
    # build model
    # train model
    # save results
def main():
run(input parameters)
if __name__ == '__main__'
app.run(main)
```

Once the `main()` routine is run, it will invoke `run()`, where a training strategy is defined, then a data pipeline is built, followed by building and training a model, then finally, it saves the results to cloud storage.

Next, we will dive into the actual code for `train.py`. Let's start with the data streaming pipeline.

Data streaming pipeline

Currently, the only way to stream a dataset when using Google Cloud AI Platform is through `tf.io` and `tf.dataTFRecordDataset`.

Our dataset (TFRecord) is already in a storage bucket. It is organized as shown in *Figure 5.12*:

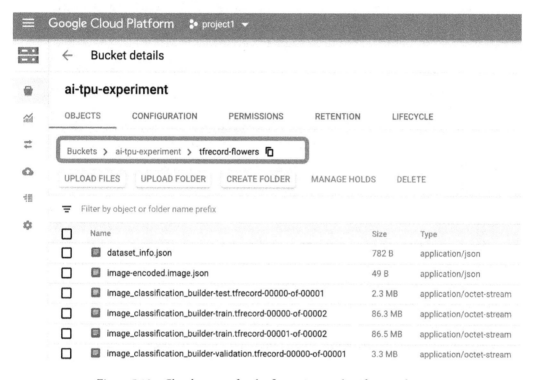

Figure 5.12 – Cloud storage for the flower image classification dataset

1. In our training script's `run` function, we need to specify the path to the cloud storage for the training data. We can leverage `tf.io.gfile` to encode the filename pattern for multiple parts. Then, we use `tf.data.TFRecordDataset` to instantiate a dataset object:

```
root_dir = flags_obj.data_dir # this is gs://<bucket>/
folder where tfrecord are stored

train_file_pattern = '{}/image_classification_builder-
train*.tfrecord*'.format(root_dir)

val_file_pattern = '{}/image_classification_builder-
validation*.tfrecord*'.format(root_dir)


train_all_files = tf.data.Dataset.list_files( tf.io.
gfile.glob(train_file_pattern))

val_all_files = tf.data.Dataset.list_files( tf.io.gfile.
glob(val_file_pattern))
```

```
train_all_ds = tf.data.TFRecordDataset(train_all_
files,num_parallel_reads=tf.data.experimental.AUTOTUNE)
val_all_ds = tf.data.TFRecordDataset(val_all_files,num_
parallel_reads=tf.data.experimental.AUTOTUNE)
```

As the preceding code indicates, after we encode the dataset name patterns, we then use `tf.data.Dataset.list_files` to encode a list of all the filenames that follow the pattern. Then, `tf.data.TFRecordDataset` instantiates a dataset reader object. Once these lines are executed during runtime, it effectively establishes the connection between the TPU and cloud storage. The dataset object streams the data into the model during the training workflow.

Why don't we use a `tf.keras` generator pattern, such as `ImageDataGenerator` or `flow_from_directory`? Well, it turns out this is not yet supported by the `gcloud ai-platform jobs submit training` command. This pattern is very convenient when the data is mounted or directly available in the filesystem, and it also easily takes care of the one-hot encoding of labels for classification problems, image normalization, and standardization processes via optional arguments through user input.

2. We have to handle image standardization (resampling to a different height and width) by writing our own function. Here is a function that performs these operations on `TFRecordDataset`:

```
def decode_and_resize(serialized_example):
    # resized image should be [224, 224, 3] and have
      value range [0, 255]
    # label is integer index of class.

    parsed_features = tf.io.parse_single_example(
    serialized_example,
    features = {
    'image/channels' :  tf.io.FixedLenFeature([],
                                      tf.int64),
    'image/class/label' :  tf.io.FixedLenFeature([],
                                        tf.int64),
    'image/class/text' : tf.io.FixedLenFeature([],
                                      tf.string),
    'image/colorspace' : tf.io.FixedLenFeature([],
                                      tf.string),
```

```
        'image/encoded' : tf.io.FixedLenFeature([],
                                    tf.string),
        'image/filename' : tf.io.FixedLenFeature([],
                                    tf.string),
        'image/format' : tf.io.FixedLenFeature([],
                                    tf.string),
        'image/height' : tf.io.FixedLenFeature([],
                                    tf.int64),
        'image/width' : tf.io.FixedLenFeature([],
                                    tf.int64)
    })
    image = tf.io.decode_jpeg(parsed_features[
                        'image/encoded'], channels=3)
    label = tf.cast(parsed_features[
                        'image/class/label'], tf.int32)
    label_txt = tf.cast(parsed_features[
                        'image/class/text'], tf.string)
    label_one_hot = tf.one_hot(label, depth = 5)
    resized_image = tf.image.resize(image,
                    [224, 224], method='nearest')
    return resized_image, label_one_hot
```

This decode_and_resize function parses the dataset to a JPEG image with the corresponding color value range, then parse the labels, one-hot encodes the image, and resizes the image using the nearest neighbor method in order to standardize it to 224 by 224 pixels for our model of choice (ResNet). This function also provides different ways to return the label, whether it is as plain text or an integer. If you wish, you can return labels in different notations and styles by simply adding the notations of your interest to the return tuple:

```
    return resized_image, label_one_hot, label_txt, label
```

Then, unpack the return tuple according to their position (the order as indicated in the preceding return statement) in the caller function.

3. Now that we have the decode_and_resize function ready, this is how we apply it to every element in our dataset object:

```
    dataset = train_all_ds.map(decode_and_resize)
    val_dataset = val_all_ds.map(decode_and_resize)
```

4. Then, we rescale or normalize the pixel values to be in a range of [0, 1] in each image so that all the images are within same pixel range for training. Let's create a normalize function:

```
def normalize(image, label):
        #Convert `image` from [0, 255] -> [0, 1.0] floats
        image = tf.cast(image, tf.float32) / 255. + 0.5
        return image, label
```

We need to prepare the training data by applying a batch operation. We use the following function to achieve this:

```
def prepare_for_training(ds, cache=True, shuffle_buffer_
size=1000):
        if cache:
            if isinstance(cache, str):
                ds = ds.cache(cache)
            else:
                ds = ds.cache()

        ds = ds.shuffle(buffer_size=shuffle_buffer_size)
        ds = ds.repeat()
        ds = ds.batch(BATCH_SIZE)

        AUTOTUNE = tf.data.experimental.AUTOTUNE
        ds = ds.prefetch(buffer_size=AUTOTUNE)

        return ds
```

The preceding function accepts a dataset, then shuffles it and batches it based on a global variable, BATCH_SIZE, and prefetches it for the training pipeline.

We use the map method again to apply the normalize operation to our training and validation datasets:

```
AUTOTUNE = tf.data.experimental.AUTOTUNE
BATCH_SIZE = flags_obj.train_batch_size
VALIDATION_BATCH_SIZE = flags_obj.validation_batch_size
train_dataset = train_dataset.map(normalize, num_
parallel_calls=AUTOTUNE)
val_dataset = val_dataset.map(normalize, num_parallel_
```

```
calls=AUTOTUNE)
val_ds = val_dataset.batch(VALIDATION_BATCH_SIZE)
train_ds = prepare_for_training(train_dataset)
```

This is the data pipeline part of the run function. We are not done with the run function yet.

5. Next, we are going to set up the model and conduct the training. We will leverage the popular transfer learning technique, where a prebuilt model is applied and trained with our own training dataset. The prebuilt model of interest here is the ResNet-50 image classification model. Remember how we already specified our TPU-based distributed strategy for training? We can simply wrap the model definition and optimizer choice here with the strategy:

```
with strategy.scope():
    base_model = tf.keras.applications.ResNet50(
        input_shape=(224,224,3), include_top=False,
        weights='imagenet')
    model = tf.keras.Sequential(
        [base_model,
         tf.keras.layers.GlobalAveragePooling2D(),
         tf.keras.layers.Dense(5,
                               activation='softmax',
                               name = 'custom_class')
        ])
    lr_schedule = \
    tf.keras.optimizers.schedules.ExponentialDecay(
        0.05, decay_steps=100000, decay_rate=0.96)
    optimizer = tf.keras.optimizers.SGD(
        learning_rate=lr_schedule)
  model.compile(optimizer=optimizer,
    loss=tf.keras.losses.CategoricalCrossentropy(
        from_logits=True, label_smoothing=0.1),
    metrics=['accuracy'])
```

The preceding code describes the model architecture, designates the optimization strategy for training, and compiles the model. We use the ResNet-50 feature vector as our base model for the classification of the five flower types.

6. Then, we set up the checkpoint and callbacks with the help of the following code:

```
checkpoint_prefix = os.path.join(flags_obj.model_dir,
                                 'ckpt_{epoch}')

callbacks = [
tf.keras.callbacks.ModelCheckpoint
        (filepath=checkpoint_prefix,
        save_weights_only=True)]
```

Callbacks will save the model weights and biases for each epoch of training separately as checkpoints.

7. Next, we need to set up sample sizes at each epoch for training and cross validation:

```
train_sample_size=0
    for raw_record in train_all_ds:
        train_sample_size += 1
    print('TRAIN_SAMPLE_SIZE = ', train_sample_size)
    validation_sample_size=0
    for raw_record in val_all_ds:
        validation_sample_size += 1
    print('VALIDATION_SAMPLE_SIZE = ',
        validation_sample_size)


    steps_per_epoch = train_sample_size // BATCH_SIZE
    validation_steps = validation_sample_size
                            // VALIDATION_BATCH_SIZE
```

8. Then, at last, this is the code for the training process:

```
hist = model.fit(
        train_ds,
        epochs=flags_obj.train_epochs,
                        steps_per_epoch=steps_per_epoch,
        validation_data=val_ds,
        validation_steps=validation_steps,
        callbacks=callbacks)


    model_save_dir = os.path.join(flags_obj.model_
dir,
```

```
        'save_model')
            model.save(model_save_dir)
```

This concludes the run function. This is a rather long function. Make sure you observe all the proper indentation demarcation. This is just a minimalist example for Google Cloud AI Platform. It includes all the necessary code and patterns for a scalable data pipeline, distributed training workflow, and TPU utilization. In your practice, you can organize and refactor your code to best suit your needs for clarity and maintainability.

Submitting the training script

Now is the time to submit our training script. We submit it from the vs_code directory according to the local directory organization mentioned in *Figure 5.11*. The TensorFlow runtime version in Cloud AI Platform is not necessarily most up to date with respect to the TensorFlow stable release in Cloud AI Notebook. As we know, the current stable release in Cloud Notebook is TFE 2.3. However, in Cloud AI Platform, the most recent release is 2.2. Therefore we use --runtime-version=2.2.

You can check this link to ascertain the latest runtime: https://cloud.google.com/ai-platform/prediction/docs/runtime-version-list.

The following is the command and terminal output:

```
vs_code % gcloud ai-platform jobs submit training
traincloudtpu_tfk_resnet50 \
--staging-bucket=gs://ai-tpu-experiment \
--package-path=python \
--module-name=python.ScriptProject.trainer \
--runtime-version=2.2 \
--python-version=3.7 \
--scale-tier=BASIC_TPU \
--region=us-central1 \
-- \
--distribution_strategy=tpu \
--model_dir=gs://ai-tpu-experiment/traincloudtpu_tfk_resnet50 \
--train_epochs=10 \
--data_dir=gs://ai-tpu-experiment/tfrecord-flowers
Job [traincloudtpu_tfk_resnet50] submitted successfully.
```

Your job is still active. You can view the status of your job with the following command:

```
$ gcloud ai-platform jobs describe traincloudtpu_tfk_resnet50
```

Or, you can continue streaming the logs with the following command:

```
$ gcloud ai-platform jobs stream-logs traincloudtpu_tfk_
resnet50
jobId: traincloudtpu_tfk_resnet50
state: QUEUED
```

The preceding command submits a piece of training code to the Cloud TPU. From the current directory (vs_code), there is a subfolder (python), which contains a ScriptProject module. In ScriptProject, there is a part of the script named trainer.py. You can see the content of trainer.py in the GitHub repo at https://github.com/PacktPublishing/learn-tensorflow-enterprise/blob/master/chapter_05/cnn_on_tpu/custom_model_on_tpu/trainer.py.

We also have to specify the following parameters, which are used in trainer.py (https://github.com/PacktPublishing/learn-tensorflow-enterprise/blob/master/chapter_05/cnn_on_tpu/custom_model_on_tpu/trainer.py):

```
Job name: traincloudtpu_tfk_resnet50
Staging bucket is gs://ai-tpu-experiment
Bucket to save the model is gs://ai-tpu-experiment/
traincloudtpu_tfk_resnet50
Training data is in gs://tfrecord-dataset/flowers
```

As soon as we submit the preceding command, it will be in the queue for execution in your Cloud AI Platform instance. To find out where we can monitor the training process, we can run gcloud ai-platform jobs describe traincloudtpu_tfk_resnet50 to retrieve a URL to the running log:

```
vs_code % gcloud ai-platform jobs describe traincloudtpu_tfk_
resnet50
createTime: ,2020-08-09T20:59:16Z'
etag: QMhh5Jz_KMU=
jobId: traincloudtpu_tfk_resnet50
state: PREPARING
trainingInput:
```

```
  args:
  - --distribution_strategy=tpu
  - --model_dir=gs://ai-tpu-experiment/traincloudtpu_tfk_
resnet50
  - --train_epochs=10
  - --data_dir=gs://ai-tpu-experiment/tfrecord-flowers
  packageUris:
  - gs://ai-tpu-experiment/traincloudtpu_tfk_resnet50/XXXXXX/
official-0.0.0.tar.gz
  pythonModule: python.ScriptProject.trainer
  pythonVersion: '3.7'
  region: us-central1
  runtimeVersion: '2.2'
  scaleTier: BASIC_TPU
trainingOutput: {}
```

You can view job in Cloud Console at `https://console.cloud.google.com/mlengine/jobs/traincloudtpu_tfk_resnet50?project=project1-190517`.

You can view the logs at `https://console.cloud.google.com/logs?resource=ml_job%2Fjob_id%2Ftraincloudtpu_tfk_resnet50&project=project1-190517`.

As per the preceding code the preceding highlighted output, we can go to the logs URL in a browser and observe the training progress. The following are some example excerpts (see *Figure 5.13* and *Figure 5.14*):

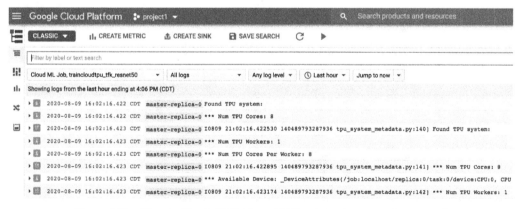

Figure 5.13 – Google Cloud AI Platform TPU training log example excerpt 1

This is a lengthy log that will run until the training job is complete. Toward the end of the training run, the log will look like this:

Figure 5.14 – Google Cloud AI Platform TPU training log example excerpt 2

In the storage bucket, we see the folder created by the training workflow (*Figure 5.15*):

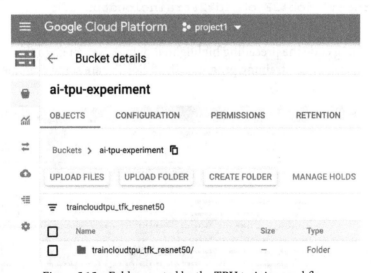

Figure 5.15 – Folder created by the TPU training workflow

Inside this bucket, we see the checkpoints and model assets (*Figure 5.16*):

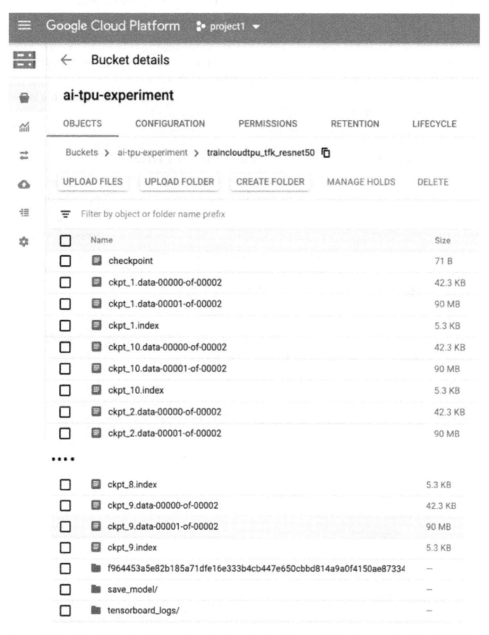

Figure 5.16 – Model checkpoints and assets after the training workflow is completed by the TPU

It is exactly the same as if the training is done on a local standalone machine. The complete `trainer.py` is available at `https://github.com/PacktPublishing/learn-tensorflow-enterprise/blob/master/chapter_05/cnn_on_tpu/custom_model_on_tpu/trainer.py`.

Next, we are going to take a look at how to reuse what we have learned here. As it turns out, if we want to use a model available in TensorFlow Hub, we can reuse the training patterns, file organization, and workflow. However, a slight change is required. This is because currently, the TPU has no direct access to TensorFlow Hub's module URL.

Working with models in TensorFlow Hub

TensorFlow Hub hosts a huge collection of pre-trained models. However, in order to use them, the user or client code must be able to connect to the hub and download the model via the RESTful API to the client's TensorFlow runtime. Currently, this cannot be done with the TPU. Therefore, we have to download the model we are interested in from TensorFlow Hub to our local computer, then upload it to cloud storage, where it can be accessed by the TPU. Typically, the following is how you would implement a pre-trained model from TensorFlow Hub using the `tf.keras` API:

```
m = tf.keras.Sequential([
    hub.KerasLayer('https://tfhub.dev/google/imagenet/resnet_
v2_50/feature_vector/4', trainable=False),
    tf.keras.layers.Dense(num_classes, activation='softmax')
])
m.build([None, 224, 224, 3])  # Batch input shape.
```

As shown in the preceding lines of code, the URL to a pre-trained model is passed into `KerasLayer`. However, currently, the TPU running in Cloud AI Platform has no direct access to TensorFlow Hub's URL. To download the model, follow the simple instructions from TensorFlow Hub's site, as shown in *Figure 5.17*:

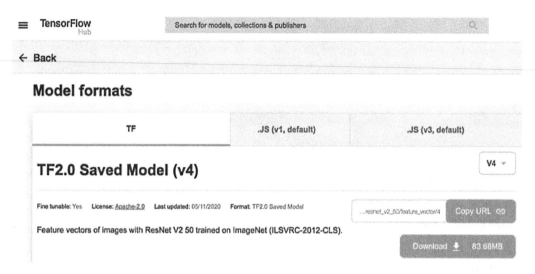

Figure 5.17 – Downloading a pre-trained model from TensorFlow Hub

The model is compressed. Once it is extracted, you will see the content, as shown in *Figure 5.18*:

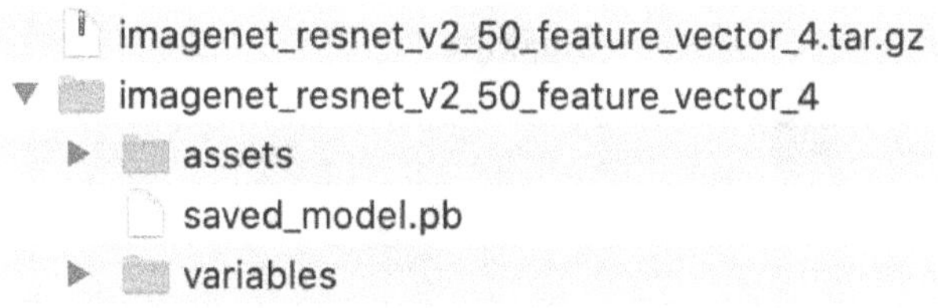

Figure 5.18 – Downloaded pre-trained model from TensorFlow Hub

Once the model is downloaded and extracted, let's upload it to a storage bucket accessible by the TPU service account, as in *Figure 5.19*:

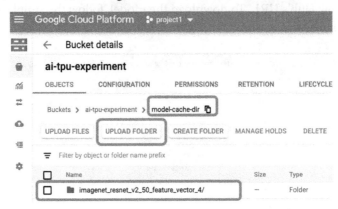

Figure 5.19 – Uploading the pre-trained model to cloud storage

Notice that we created a `model-cache-dir` folder in our storage bucket, then selected **UPLOAD FOLDER**, and the model folder is now available for the TPU to use.

Then, inside the `run` function, we need to leverage an environmental variable to tell the TPU where to find this model:

```
os.environ['TFHUB_CACHE_DIR'] = 'gs://ai-tpu-experiment/model-
cache-dir/imagenet_resnet_v2_50_feature_vector_4'
```

This line can be inserted before the model definition in the `run` function. In the model definition, we will specify the model architecture by using `hub.KerasLayer`, as usual:

```
with strategy.scope():

  model = tf.keras.Sequential([
    tf.keras.layers.InputLayer(input_shape=IMAGE_SIZE + (3,)),
    hub.KerasLayer('https://tfhub.dev/google/imagenet/resnet_
v2_50/feature_vector/4',
                trainable=flags_obj.fine_tuning_choice),
        tf.keras.layers.Dense(5, activation='softmax',
                                name = 'custom_class')
    ])
```

Because we have the `TFHUB_CACHE_DIR` environmental variable already defined with our cloud storage name and path, when the TPU executes the `hub.KerasLayer` part of the model architecture code, the TPU runtime will look for the model from `TFHUB_CACHE_DIR` first instead of attempting to go through a RESTful API call to retrieve the model. After these small modifications are made to the training script, we can rename it as `trainer_hub.py`. The training work can be launched with a similar invocation style:

```
vs_code % gcloud ai-platform jobs submit training
traincloudtpu_tfhub_resnet50 \
--staging-bucket=gs://ai-tpu-experiment \
--package-path=python \
--module-name=python.ScriptProject.trainer_hub \
--runtime-version=2.2 \
--python-version=3.7 \
--scale-tier=BASIC_TPU \
--region=us-central1 \
-- \
--distribution_strategy=tpu \
--model_dir=gs://ai-tpu-experiment/traincloudtpu_tfhub_resnet50 \
--train_epochs=10 \
--data_dir=gs://ai-tpu-experiment/tfrecord-flowers
Job [traincloudtpu_tfhub_resnet50] submitted successfully.
```

Your job is still active. You may view the status of your job with the command

```
$ gcloud ai-platform jobs describe traincloudtpu_tfhub_
resnet50
```

or continue streaming the logs with the command

```
$ gcloud ai-platform jobs stream-logs traincloudtpu_tfhub_
resnet50
jobId: traincloudtpu_tfhub_resnet50
state: QUEUED
```

The complete `trainer_hub.py` code is in `https://github.com/ PacktPublishing/learn-tensorflow-enterprise/blob/master/ chapter_05/tfhub_on_tpu/tfhub_resnet_fv_on_tpu/trainer_hub.py`.

Next, we are going to take a look at how to use the `gcloud ai-platform` command to leverage the GPU for a similar training job.

Using the Google Cloud GPU through AI Platform

Having worked through the previous section for utilizing Cloud TPU with AI Platform, we are ready to do the same with the GPU. As it turns out, the formats of training script and invocation commands are very similar. With the exception of a few more parameters and slight differences in the distributed strategy definition, everything else remains the same.

There are several distributed strategies (`https://www.tensorflow.org/guide/ distributed_training#types_of_strategies`) currently available. For a TensorFlow Enterprise distribution in Google AI Platform, `MirroredStrategy` and `TPUStrategy` are the only two that are fully supported. All the others are experimental. Therefore, in this section's example, we will use `MirroredStrategy`. This strategy creates copies of all the variables in the model on each GPU. As these variables are updated at each gradient decent step, the value updates are copied to each GPU synchronously. By default, this strategy uses an `NVIDIA NCCL` all-reduce implementation. Now, we are going to start with the following steps:

1. We can start with small modifications to the TPU training script used in the previous section. Let's implement a condition for selecting a distributed strategy based on the choice of TPU or GPU:

```
if flags_obj.distribution_strategy == 'tpu':
    resolver = tf.distribute.cluster_resolver.
TPUClusterResolver()
    tf.config.experimental_connect_to_
cluster(resolver)
    tf.tpu.experimental.initialize_tpu_
system(resolver)
    strategy = tf.distribute.experimental.
TPUStrategy(resolver)
    strategy_scope = strategy.scope()
    print('All devices: ', tf.config.list_logical_
```

```
devices('TPU'))
    elif flags_obj.distribution_strategy == 'gpu':
        devices = ['device:GPU:%d' % i for i in
range(flags_obj.num_gpus)]
        strategy = tf.distribute.
MirroredStrategy(device=devices)
        strategy_scope = strategy.scope()
```

The full implementation of the training script for using `MirroredStrategy`
with the GPU can be found at `https://github.com/PacktPublishing/`
`learn-tensorflow-enterprise/blob/master/chapter_05/tfhub_`
`on_gpu/tfhub_resnet_fv_on_gpu/trainer_hub_gpu.py`.

For `MirroredStrategy`, we will set `scale-tier` to `BASIC_GPU`. This will give
us a single worker instance with one NVIDIA Tesla K80 GPU. The command to
invoke training with `trainer_hub_gpu.py` is as follows:

```
vs_code % gcloud ai-platform jobs submit training
traincloudgpu_tfhub_resnet_gpu_1 \
--staging-bucket=gs://ai-tpu-experiment \
--package-path=python \
--module-name=python.ScriptProject.trainer_hub \
--runtime-version=2.2 \
--python-version=3.7 \
--scale-tier=BASIC_GPU \
--region=us-central1 \
-- \
--distribution_strategy=gpu \
--model_dir=gs://ai-tpu-experiment/traincloudgpu_tfhub_
resnet_gpu_1 \
--train_epochs=10 \
--data_dir=gs://ai-tpu-experiment/tfrecord-flowers
Job [traincloudtpu_tfhub_resnet_gpu_1] submitted
successfully.
```

Your job is still active. You may view the status of your job with the command

```
$ gcloud ai-platform jobs describe traincloudgpu_tfhub_
resnet_gpu_1
```

or continue streaming the logs with the command

```
$ gcloud ai-platform jobs stream-logs traincloudtpu_
tfhub_resnet_gpu_1
jobId: traincloudgpu_tfhub_resnet_gpu_1
state: QUEUED
```

Notice that we changed `scale-tier` to `BASIC_GPU`. We set our script-specific `distribution_strategy` flag to gpu. This is how we specify what compute instance we want and the distribution strategy.

Summary

From all the examples that we have covered in this chapter, we learned how to leverage a distributed training strategy with the TPU and GPU through AI Platform, which runs on TensorFlow Enterprise 2.2 distributions. AI Platform is a service that wraps around TPU or GPU accelerator hardware and manages the configuration and setup for your training job.

Currently, in Google AI Platform, the data ingestion pipeline relies on `TFRecordDataset` to stream training data in batches into the model training workflow. We also learned how to leverage a prebuilt model downloaded from TensorFlow Hub through the use of the `TFHUB_CACHE_DIR` environment variable. This is also the means to import your own saved model from an offline estate into Google AI Platform. Overall, in this platform, we used a TensorFlow Enterprise 2.2 distribution to achieve scalable data streaming and distributed training on Google Cloud's TPU or GPU and serialized all the model checkpoints and assets back to cloud storage.

In the next chapter, we will use Cloud AI Platform to submit a hyperparameter tuning job. Hyperparameter tuning is typically very time-consuming and resource-intensive. We will see how to take advantage of the compute power of the Cloud TPU for this process.

6
Hyperparameter Tuning

In this chapter, we are going to start by looking at three different hyperparameter tuning algorithms—Hyperband, Bayesian optimization, and random search. These algorithms are implemented in the `tf.keras` API, which makes them relatively easy to understand. With this API, you now have access to simplified APIs for these complex and advanced algorithms that we will encounter in this chapter. We will learn how to implement these algorithms and use the best hyperparameters we can find to build and train an image classification model. We will also learn the details of its learning process in order to know which hyperparameters to search and optimize. We will start by getting and preparing the data, and then we'll apply our algorithm to it. Along the way, we will also try to understand key principles and the logic to implement user choices for these algorithms as user inputs, and we'll look at a template to submit tuning and training jobs in GCP Cloud TPU.

In this chapter, we will cover the following topics:

- Delineating hyperparameter types
- Understanding the syntax and use of Keras Tuner
- Delineating hyperparameter search algorithms

- Submitting tuning jobs in a local environment
- Submitting tuning jobs in Google's AI Platform

Technical requirements

The entire code base for this chapter is in the following GitHub repository. Please clone it to your environment:

```
https://github.com/PacktPublishing/learn-tensorflow-
enterprise/blob/master/chapter_06/
```

This can be done through a command-line environment:

```
git clone https://github.com/PacktPublishing/learn-tensorflow-
enterprise.git
```

Delineating hyperparameter types

As we develop a model and its training process, we define variables and set their values to determine the training workflow and the model's structure. These values (such as the number of hidden nodes in a layer of a multilayer perceptron, or the selection of an optimizer and a loss function) are known as hyperparameters. These parameters are specified by the model creator. The performance of a machine learning model often depends on the model architecture and the hyperparameters selected during its training process. Finding a set of optimal hyperparameters for the model is not a trivial task. The simplest method to this task is by grid search, that is, building all possible combinations of hyperparameter values within a search space and then comparing the evaluation metrics across these combinations. While this is straightforward and thorough, it is a tedious process. We will see how the new `tf.keras` API implements three different search algorithms.

There are two types of hyperparameters in the context of model training:

- **Model hyperparameters**: These parameters are directly related to the structure of a model layer, such as the number of nodes in a layer.
- **Algorithm hyperparameters**: These parameters are required to execute the learning algorithm, such as the learning rate in the loss function used during gradient descent, or the choice of loss function.

The code modification required to scan through both types of hyperparameters would be very complicated if you want to use the grid search technique. This is where a more efficient and comprehensive framework would be very helpful for hyperparameter tuning.

In this chapter, we are going to see the latest addition in hyperparameter tuning frameworks to the TensorFlow ecosystem. This framework is Keras Tuner. As the name suggests, it is for models developed with the TensorFlow 2.x Keras API. The minimum requirement for this framework is TensorFlow 2.0+ and Python 3.6. It is released as a part of the TensorFlow 2.3 distribution. If you are not yet using TensorFlow 2.3, then as long as you are using TensorFlow 2.x, Keras Tuner can be installed with the help of the following command:

```
pip install keras-tuner
```

Once Keras Tuner is installed, you can load it in your Python code.

> **Note**
>
> You need not put a dash - between `keras-tuner` while importing it. It will be imported like this: `import kerastuner as kt`.

Keras Tuner is a distributable hyperparameter optimization framework that helps to define the search space for collections of hyperparameters. It also includes the following three built-in algorithms to help find the best hyperparameters:

- Hyperband
- Bayesian optimization
- Random search

For Keras Tuner, whether it is model hyperparameters or algorithm hyperparameters, it makes no difference to the syntax or definition style of these hyperparameters. Therefore, you have great flexibility in choosing what hyperparameters to tune without complicated coding patterns or loops.

The Keras Tuner framework makes it easy for us to modify our training script. While there are changes and refactoring involved, the API format and logical flow are very much consistent with Keras styles and implementations. Before we jump into the examples, let's spend some time understanding this framework and seeing how to extend our training code to accommodate it.

Understanding the syntax and use of Keras Tuner

For the most part, as far as Keras Tuner is concerned, hyperparameters can be described by the following three data types: integers, floating points, and choices from a list of discrete values or objects. In the following sub-sections, we will take a closer look at how to use these data types to define hyperparameters in different parts of the model architecture and training workflow.

Using hp.Int for hyperparameter definition

Keras Tuner defines a search space with a very simple and intuitive style. To define a set of possible number of nodes in a given layer, you typically would have a layer definition like the this:

```
tf.keras.layers.Dense(units = hp_units, activation = 'relu')
```

In the preceding line of code, `hp_units` is the number of nodes in this layer. If you wish to subject `hp_units` to hyperparameter search, then you simply need to define the definition for this hyperparameter's search space. Here's an example:

```
hp = kt.HyperParameters()
hp_units = hp.Int('units', min_value = 64, max_value = 256,
step = 16)
```

`hp` is the object that represents an instance of `kerastuner`.

This is simply an array of integers between `64` and `256` at an increment of `16`. When applied to the `Dense` layer, it becomes an array of possible values in the search space for `hp_units`.

Using hp.Choice for hyperparameter definition

If you have a set of values in mind and these values do not fall into incremental steps, you may specify a list of values as shown in the following line of code:

```
hp_units = hp.Choice('units', values = [64, 80, 90])
```

`hp_Choice` is a flexible type for hyperparameters. It can also be used to define algorithmic hyperparameters such as activation functions. All it needs is the name of possible activation functions. A search space for different activation functions may look like this:

```
hp_activation = hp.Choice('dense_activation', values=['relu',
'tanh', 'sigmoid'])
```

Then the definition for the layer that uses this hyperparameter would be:

```
tf.keras.layers.Dense(units = hp_units, activation = hp_
activation)
```

Another place where `hp.Choice` may be applied is when you want to try different optimizers:

```
hp_optimizer = hp.Choice('selected_optimizer', ['sgd', 'adam'])
```

Then, in the model compilation step, where an optimizer is specified in the training workflow, you would simply define `optimizer` as `hp_optimizer`:

```
model.compile(optimizer = hp_optimizer, loss = …, metrics = …)
```

In the preceding example, we pass `hp_optimizer` into the model compilation step as our selection for the optimizer to be used in the training process.

Using hp.Float for hyperparameter definition

Floating points frequently appear as parameters in the training workflow, such as the learning rate for the optimizer. Here is an example that demonstrates how it is defined in a case with the optimizer's learning rate as a hyperparameter:

```
hp_learning_rate = hp.Float('learning_rate', min_value = 1e-4,
max_value = 1e-2, step = 1e-3)
optimizer=tf.keras.optimizers.SGD(lr=hp_learning_rate,
momentum=0.5)
```

In the preceding code, we define a search space for our optimizer's learning rate. We then pass the `hp_learning_rate` object into the optimizer definition.

As an example, I created a `model_builder` function. This function accepts `hp` object, which defines the hyperparameter search space, and then passes the `hp` object into the model architecture. The function returns the completed model. Here is the `model_builder` function:

```
def model_builder(hp):

    hp_units = hp.Int('units', min_value = 64, max_value = 256,
                                                         step = 64)
    hp_activation = hp.Choice('dense_activation',
        values=['relu', 'tanh', 'sigmoid'])

    IMAGE_SIZE = (224, 224)
    model = tf.keras.Sequential([
    tf.keras.layers.InputLayer(input_shape=IMAGE_SIZE + (3,)),
    hub.KerasLayer('https://tfhub.dev/google/imagenet/resnet_
v2_50/feature_vector/4', trainable=False),
    tf.keras.layers.Flatten(),
    tf.keras.layers.Dense(units = hp_units,
                        activation = hp_activation,
                        kernel_initializer='glorot_uniform'),
    tf.keras.layers.Dense(5, activation='softmax',
                                     name = 'custom_class')
    ])

    model.build([None, 224, 224, 3])

    model.compile(
        optimizer=tf.keras.optimizers.SGD(lr=1e-2,
                                             momentum=0.5),
        loss=tf.keras.losses.CategoricalCrossentropy(
                        from_logits=True, label_smoothing=0.1),
        metrics=['accuracy'])

return model
```

With the Keras Tuner API, the search space format and the way in which the search space is referenced inside the model layer or training algorithm are straightforward and provide great flexibility. All that was done was defining a search space, then passing the object holding the search space into the model definition. It would be a daunting task to handle the conditional logic following the grid search approach.

Next, we will take a look at how to use Keras Tuner classes to specify the following three different search algorithms:

- Hyperband
- Bayesian optimization
- Random search

Delineating hyperparameter search algorithms

In this section, we will take a closer look at three algorithms that traverse the hyperparameter search space. These algorithms are implemented by the `tf.keras` API.

Hyperband

Hyperparameter search is an inherently tedious process that requires a budget B to test a finite set of possible hyperparameter configurations n. In this context, budget simply means compute time as indicated by the epoch, and the training data subsets. The hyperband algorithm takes advantage of early stopping and successive halving so that it can evaluate more hyperparameter configurations in a given time and with a given set of hardware resources. Early stopping helps eliminate underperforming configurations before too much training time is invested in them.

The successive halving method is very intuitive: for a set of hyperparameter configurations, run them through the same budget (that is, epoch, memory, and training data subset size). Then we rank the performance of these configurations, discarding the configurations in the worst half. This process is repeated until only one configuration remains. This is similar to playoff brackets in that at every bracket, half of the configurations are eliminated, until only one remains.

There are two `for` loops in the Hyperband algorithm:

- The inner loop, which performs successive halving that discards a portion of hyperparameter configurations, thereby reducing the search space
- An outer loop, which iterates over different combinations of B and n

In early iterations, there are many candidate configurations. As each candidate is given a portion of budget B to train, early stopping ensures that a fraction (that is, half) of these configurations are discarded early before too much training time is wasted. As brackets become smaller through successive halving, fewer candidate configurations remain, and therefore each candidate is more likely to get a higher portion of B. This continues until the last hyperparameter configuration remains. Therefore, you may think of the Hyperband algorithm as an approach for selecting the best hyperparameter configurations that cuts the losses early by discarding low-performing configurations.

Here is a reference for more information on the Hyperband algorithm: `https://openreview.net/pdf?id=ry18Ww5ee`.

Now let's take a look at how to define a tuner instance that uses the Hyperband algorithm (for a detailed description of the API and its parameters, see `https://keras-team.github.io/keras-tuner/documentation/tuners/`). Here is an example:

```python
import kerastuner as kt
import tensorflow_hub as hub
import tensorflow as tf
from absl import flags
flags_obj = flags.FLAGS
strategy = tf.distribute.MirroredStrategy()


tuner = kt.Hyperband(
            hypermodel = model_builder,
            objective = 'val_accuracy',
            max_epochs = 3,
            factor = 2,
            distribution_strategy=strategy,
            directory = flags_obj.model_dir,
            project_name = 'hp_tune_hb',
            overwrite = True)
```

Here is a description of the parameters shown:

- `hypermodel`: A function of the class that builds a model architecture.
- `objective`: Performance metrics for evaluation.

- `max_epoch`: The maximum number of epochs to train a model.

- `factor`: Reduction for the number of epochs and number of models for each bracket. It selects configurations ranked in the top 1/`factor` of all configurations. A higher `factor` means more pruning and therefore it's quicker for the search process to identify a top performer.

- `distribution_strategy`: This is used if hardware is available for distributed training.

- `directory`: The target directory or path to write the search results.

- `project_name`: The name used as a prefix for files saved by the tuner.

- `overwrite`: This is a Boolean. If `True`, then hyperparameter search will start from scratch. Let's explain a bit more about this API. In this case, `kt` is the tuner object. In the hyperband definition, `hypermodel` designates a function that builds the model architecture.

In this example, we will define the search space for the number of nodes (`hp_units`) in the middle `Dense` layer of the model architecture, as well as the search space for the activation function (`hp_activation`) of that layer. After these definitions, we construct the model architecture, pass these `hp` objects into the destined layer, compile the model, and return the model.

Notice hp in the function signature. It indicates this is the entry function for the model structure definition, where the hyperparameters are specified. In this example, there are two hyperparameters:

```
hp_units = hp.Int('units', min_value = 64, max_value = 256,
step = 64)
```
```
hp_activation = hp.Choice('dense_activation', values=['relu',
'tanh', 'sigmoid'])
```

Inside the model's sequential API definition, you will find these hyperparameters in one of the `Dense` layers:

```
tf.keras.layers.Dense(units = hp_units, activation = hp_
activation, kernel_initializer='glorot_uniform'),
```

Before exiting this function, you would compile the model and return the model to the tuner instance. Now let's begin with the training of the Hyperband hyperparameter:

1. Now that the tuner and its search algorithm are defined, this is how you would set up the search:

```
tuner.search(train_ds,
        steps_per_epoch=STEPS_PER_EPOCHS,
        validation_data=val_ds,
        validation_steps=VALIDATION_STEPS,
        epochs=30,
        callbacks=[tf.keras.callbacks.EarlyStopping(
                                'val_accuracy')])
```

In this example, `train_ds` is the training dataset, while `val_ds` is the cross-validation dataset. The rest of the parameters are the same as seen in a typical training routine.

2. After the search is done, you may retrieve the best hyperparameter configuration through an object:

```
best_hps = tuner.get_best_hyperparameters(num_trials = 1)
[0]
print(f'''
        The hyperparameter search is done.
        The best number of nodes in the dense layer is
{best_hps.get('units')}.
        The best activation function in mid dense layer
is {best_hps.get('dense_activation')},
        ''')
```

By default, `num_trials = 1` indicates this will return the best model. Since this is a list object, we retrieve it by the first index of a list, which is `0`. The `print` statement shows how the item in `best_hps` may be referenced.

3. It is recommended that once you have `best_hps`, you should retrain your model with these parameters. We will start with the `tuner` object initialized with `best_hps`:

```
model = tuner.hypermodel.build(best_hps)
```

4. Then we may define checkpoints and callbacks for the formal training:

```
checkpoint_prefix = os.path.join(flags_obj.model_dir,
'best_hp_train_ckpt_{epoch}')
    callbacks = [
      tf.keras.callbacks.ModelCheckpoint(
          filepath=checkpoint_prefix,
          save_weights_only=True)]
```

5. Now let's call the `fit` function to start training with the best hyperparameter configuration:

```
model.fit(
      train_ds,
      epochs=30, steps_per_epoch=STEPS_PER_EPOCHS,
      validation_data=val_ds,
      validation_steps=VALIDATION_STEPS,
      callbacks=callbacks)
```

6. Once training is completed, save the trained model:

```
model_save_dir = os.path.join(flags_obj.model_dir,
                                'best_save_model')
model.save(model_save_dir)
```

Now the model trained with the hyperband hyperparameter search is saved in the file path designated by `model_save_dir`. Next, we are going to take a look at another algorithm for hyperparameter search: Bayesian optimization.

Bayesian optimization

This method leverages what is learned from the initial training samples and nudges changes in hyperparameter values towards the favorable direction of the search space. Actually, what was learned from the initial training samples is a probabilistic function that models the value of our objective function. This **probabilistic** function, also known as a **surrogate** function, models the distribution of our objective (that is, validation loss) as a Gaussian process. With a surrogate function ready, the next hyperparameter configuration candidate is selected such that it is most likely to improve (that is, minimize, if the objective is validation loss) the surrogate function.

The `tuner` instance invokes this algorithm in a straightforward fashion. Here is an example:

```
tuner = kt.BayesianOptimization(
        hypermodel = model_builder,
        objective ='val_accuracy',
        max_trials = 50,
        directory = flags_obj.model_dir,
        project_name = 'hp_tune_bo',
        overwrite = True
        )
```

This line of code defines a `tuner` object that I set up to use the Bayesian optimization algorithm as a means for hyperparameter optimization. Similar to Hyperband, it requires a function definition for `hypermodel`. In this case, `model_builder` from Hyperband is used again. The criterion for optimization is validation accuracy. The maximum number of trials is set to `50`, and we will specify the directory in which to save the model as user input during job submission. The user input for `model_dir` is carried by `flags_obj.model_dir`.

As indicated by the `BayesianOptimization` API, there are not many differences in the function signature compared to Hyperband. `max_trials` is the maximum number of hyperparameter configurations to try. This value may be pre-empted or ignored if the search space is exhausted.

The next step is the same as seen in the *Hyperband* section when launching the search process:

```
tuner.search(train_ds,
        steps_per_epoch=STEPS_PER_EPOCHS,
        validation_data=val_ds,
        validation_steps=VALIDATION_STEPS,
        epochs=30,
        callbacks=[tf.keras.callbacks.EarlyStopping(
                                        'val_accuracy')])
```

And the rest of it, such as retrieving the best hyperparameter configuration and training the model with this configuration, is all the same as in the *Hyperband* section.

Random search

Random search is simply a random selection of the hyperparameter configuration search space. Here's an example definition:

```
tuner = kt.RandomSearch(
            hypermodel = model_builder,
            objective='val_accuracy',
            max_trials = 5,
            directory = flags_obj.model_dir,
            project_name = 'hp_tune_rs',
            overwrite = True)
```

In the `RandomSearch` API in the preceding code, we define the `model_builder` function as `hypermodel`. This function contains our hyperparameter objects that hold definitions for the hyperparameter name and search space. `hypermodel` specifies the name of our function, which will accept the best hyperparameters found by the search and use these values to build a model. Our objective is to find the best set of hyperparameters that maximizes validation accuracy, and we set `max_trials` to 5. The directory to save the model is provided as user input. The user input for `model_dir` is captured by the `flags_obj.model_dir` object.

A few words about `directory`

The `directory` argument is required in all three types of algorithm. It is the target where search results will be stored. This argument accepts a text string and is very flexible. The text string may indicate text passed by the input flag (as in the case of `flags_obj.model_dir`) when this code is run as a script. Alternatively, if you are using a notebook environment, the text string may be a file path or a cloud storage bucket path.

Submitting tuning jobs in a local environment

Since the hyperparameter tuning process is inherently time-consuming, it is more practical to run it from a script rather than in a notebook environment. Also, although in a sense, a hyperparameter tuning process consists of multiple model training jobs, the tuner API and search workflow require a certain code refactoring style. The most obvious point is that we must wrap the model structure around a function (in our example, a function named `model_builder`), whose signature indicates that hyperparameter arrays are expected to be referenced in the model structure.

You may find the code and instructions in the GitHub repository: `https://github.com/PacktPublishing/learn-tensorflow-enterprise/blob/master/chapter_06/localtuningwork`

With the help of the following code, we will set up user inputs or flags and perhaps assign default values to these flags when necessary. Let's have a quick review of how user inputs may be handled and defined in the Python `script`. `absl` library, and the APIs that are commonly used for handling user input:

1. Import the `absl` library and the relevant APIs:

    ```
    from absl import flags
    from absl import logging
    from absl import app
    ```

2. Next, we will use the following lines of code to indicate user inputs or flags:

    ```
    tf.compat.v1.flags.DEFINE_string('model_dir', 'default_
    model_dir', 'Directory or bucket for storing checkpoint
    model.')
    tf.compat.v1.flags.DEFINE_bool('fine_tuning_choice',
    False, 'Retrain base parameters')
    tf.compat.v1.flags.DEFINE_integer('train_batch_size', 32,
    'Number of samples in a training batch')
    tf.compat.v1.flags.DEFINE_integer('validation_batch_
    size', 40, 'Number of samples in a validation batch')
    tf.compat.v1.flags.DEFINE_float('learning_rate', 0.01,
    'Initial learning rate.')
    tf.compat.v1.flags.DEFINE_string('tuner_type',
    'Hyperband', 'Type of tuner. Default is hyperband')
    ```

The first argument is the name of the input flag, followed by its default value, then an explanation. The preceding examples demonstrate commonly used type casting to these flags: `string`, `Boolean`, `integer`, and `float`.

3. In the code, how do we reference and make use of these flags? It turns out we need to use a `flags.FLAGS` object in the function where the input flags are used. This function could be `main()` or any function. In many cases, for convenience and readability, we will assign this object to a variable:

```
flags_obj = flags.FLAGS
```

4. Now, to refer to `model_dir`, we just need to do the following:

```
flags_obj.model_dir
```

This effectively decodes the object the and `model_dir` attribute as a text string.

5. Now let's see an example script. We will start with the `import` statements to bring all the libraries we will need into the scope:

```
import kerastuner as kt
import tensorflow as tf
import tensorflow_hub as hub
import tensorflow_datasets as tfds
import os
import IPython
from kerastuner import HyperParameters

from absl import flags
from absl import logging
from absl import app
```

6. Define the user input argument names, default values, and short explanations:

```
tf.compat.v1.flags.DEFINE_string('model_dir', 'default_
model_dir', 'Directory or bucket for storing checkpoint
model.')
tf.compat.v1.flags.DEFINE_bool('fine_tuning_choice',
False, 'Retrain base parameters')
tf.compat.v1.flags.DEFINE_integer('train_batch_size', 32,
'Number of samples in a training batch')
tf.compat.v1.flags.DEFINE_integer('validation_batch_
size', 40, 'Number of samples in a validation batch')
```

7. Define a function for loading working data. In this case, we will load it directly from TensorFlow for convenience:

```
def get_builtin_data():
    data_dir = tf.keras.utils.get_file(
'flower_photos', 'https://storage.googleapis.com/
download.tensorflow.org/example_images/flower_photos.
tgz',
        untar=True)
    return data_dir
```

This function invokes the `tf.keras` API to retrieve the built-in image data that comes with TensorFlow. It is hosted in Google's public-facing storage. It is compressed, so we need to set `untar` to `True`.

8. We also create a function called `make_generators`. This is a function that we will use to make data generators to stream the image data into the model training process:

```
def make_generators(data_dir, flags_obj):
    BATCH_SIZE = flags_obj.train_batch_size
    IMAGE_SIZE = (224, 224)
    datagen_kwargs = dict(rescale=1./255,
                                        validation_split=.20)
    dataflow_kwargs = dict(target_size=IMAGE_SIZE,
                                batch_size=BATCH_SIZE,
                                interpolation='bilinear')

    valid_datagen = tf.keras.preprocessing.image.
ImageDataGenerator(
        **datagen_kwargs)
    valid_generator = valid_datagen.flow_from_directory(
        data_dir, subset='validation', shuffle=False,
    **dataflow_kwargs)
```

The function in the preceding code accepts a data path and user input. `train_batch_size` is one of the user inputs. This value is used to define `BATCH_SIZE` in this function. The validation generator is created first. We may have different preferences for training data, such as the options for data augmentation.

9. Let's continue with the `make_generators` function. In this example, by default we are not going to do data augmentation on the training data. At the end of this function, `train_generator` is returned alongside `valid_generator`:

```
    do_data_augmentation = False
    if do_data_augmentation:
        train_datagen = tf.keras.preprocessing.image.
ImageDataGenerator(
            rotation_range=40,
            horizontal_flip=True,
            width_shift_range=0.2,
            height_shift_range=0.2,
            shear_range=0.2, zoom_range=0.2,
            **datagen_kwargs)
    else:
        train_datagen = valid_datagen
        train_generator = train_datagen.flow_from_
directory(
            data_dir, subset='training', shuffle=True,
**dataflow_kwargs)

    return train_generator, valid_generator
```

This function will create two generators: one for training data, the other one for cross-validation data. See *Chapter 4, Reusable Models and Scalable Data Pipeline*, the *Creating a generator to feed image data at scale* section, for more details.

10. Next, we define a function to retrieve the index to label mapping. As the model outputs a prediction, the prediction is in the form of an integer between 0 and 4. Each integer corresponds to a class name of the flowers:

```
def map_labels(train_generator):
    labels_idx = (train_generator.class_indices)
    idx_labels = dict((v,k) for k,v in labels_idx.
items())
return idx_labels
```

The function in the preceding code iterates through the flower type index and the corresponding flower type name, and creates a dictionary as a lookup. Now let's proceed towards building a model architecture.

11. The following function builds the model architecture, as described in the *Hyperband* section:

```
def model_builder(hp):
os.environ['TFHUB_CACHE_DIR'] =
        '/Users/XXXXX/Downloads/imagenet_resnet_v2_50_
feature_vector_4'
    hp_units = hp.Int('units', min_value = 64,
                               max_value = 256, step = 64)
    IMAGE_SIZE = (224, 224)
    model = tf.keras.Sequential([
    tf.keras.layers.InputLayer(input_shape=IMAGE_SIZE +
(3,)),
        hub.KerasLayer('https://tfhub.dev/google/imagenet/
resnet_v2_50/feature_vector/4', trainable=False),
    tf.keras.layers.Flatten(),
    tf.keras.layers.Dense(units = hp_units,
                                 activation = 'relu',
                    kernel_initializer='glorot_uniform'),
    tf.keras.layers.Dense(5, activation='softmax',
                                name = 'custom_class')
    ])
    model.build([None, 224, 224, 3])
    hp_learning_rate = hp.Choice('learning_rate',
                                values = [1e-2, 1e-4])
    model.compile(
```

```
          optimizer=tf.keras.optimizers.SGD(
                    lr=hp_learning_rate, momentum=0.5),
          loss=tf.keras.losses.CategoricalCrossentropy(
                    from_logits=True, label_smoothing=0.1),
          metrics=['accuracy'])
    return model
```

12. Define an object to clear the screen as the hyperparameter search moves around the search space:

```
class ClearTrainingOutput(tf.keras.callbacks.Callback):
    def on_train_end(*args, **kwargs):
        IPython.display.clear_output(wait = True)
```

This will help clear some of the printed output during the search process. This is passed into a callback.

13. This is the main driver for the training script:

```
def main(_):
    flags_obj = flags.FLAGS
    strategy = tf.distribute.MirroredStrategy()

    data_dir = get_builtin_data()
    train_gtr, validation_gtr = make_generators(data_dir,
                                                flags_obj)

    idx_labels = map_labels(train_gtr)
```

In the preceding code, we set the distributed training strategy, defined the data source, and created training and validation data generators. Also, label mapping is retrieved.

In the following logical block of conditional code, we handle the choice for the hyperparameter search algorithm. All three choices are present: Bayesian optimization, random search, and Hyperband. The default choice is Hyperband. Within each choice, there is a hypermodel attribute. This attribute specifies the name of the function that will take up the best hyperparameters to build the model:

```
    '''Runs the hyperparameter search.'''

    if(flags_obj.tuner_type.lower() == 'BayesianOptimization'.
lower()):
```

```
        tuner = kt.BayesianOptimization(
            hypermodel = model_builder,
            objective ='val_accuracy',
            tune_new_entries = True,
            allow_new_entries = True,
            max_trials = 5,
            directory = flags_obj.model_dir,
            project_name = 'hp_tune_bo',
            overwrite = True
            )
    elif (flags_obj.tuner_type.lower() == 'RandomSearch'.
lower()):
        tuner = kt.RandomSearch(
            hypermodel = model_builder,
            objective='val_accuracy',
            tune_new_entries = True,
            allow_new_entries = True,
            max_trials = 5,
            directory = flags_obj.model_dir,
            project_name = 'hp_tune_rs',
            overwrite = True)
```

Unless it's specified via input to use either Bayesian optimization or random search, the default choice is Hyperband. This is indicated in the `else` block in the following code:

```
else:
    # Default choice for tuning algorithm is hyperband.
        tuner = kt.Hyperband(
            hypermodel = model_builder,
            objective = 'val_accuracy',
            max_epochs = 3,
            factor = 2,
            distribution_strategy=strategy,
            directory = flags_obj.model_dir,
            project_name = 'hp_tune_hb',
            overwrite = True)
```

Now the search algorithm is executed based on the logic of the preceding code; we need to pass the best hyperparameters. For our own information, we may use the get_gest_hyperparameters API to print out the best hyperparameters. We will get the optimal hyperparameters with the help of the following code:

```
best_hps = tuner.get_best_hyperparameters(num_trials = 1)
[0]
```

```
print(f'''
    The hyperparameter search is done.
    The best number of nodes in the dense layer is {best_
hps.get('units')}.
    The optimal learning rate for the optimizer
is     {best_hps.get('learning_rate')}.
    ''')
```

Now we can pass these best hyperparameters, best_hp, to the model and train the model with these values. The tuner.hypermodel.build API handles the passing of these values to the model.

In the following code, we will set up the training and validation data batches, create a callback object, and start the training with the fit API:

```
    # Build the model with the optimal hyperparameters and
train it on the data
    model = tuner.hypermodel.build(best_hps)
    checkpoint_prefix = os.path.join(flags_obj.model_dir,
'best_hp_train_ckpt_{epoch}')
    callbacks = [
    tf.keras.callbacks.ModelCheckpoint(filepath=checkpoint_
prefix,
                                    save_weights_only=True)]

    steps_per_epoch = train_gtr.samples // train_gtr.batch_size
    validation_steps = validation_gtr.samples // validation_
gtr.batch_size
    model.fit(
        train_gtr,
        epochs=3, steps_per_epoch=steps_per_epoch,
```

```
        validation_data=validation_gtr,
        validation_steps=validation_steps,
        callbacks=callbacks)
```

Here, we log the output of the destination directory for the saved model on screen:

```
logging.info('INSIDE MAIN FUNCTION user input model_dir %s',
                                      flags_obj.model_dir)
    # Save model trained with chosen HP in user specified
bucket location
    model_save_dir = os.path.join(flags_obj.model_dir,
                                      'best_save_model')
    model.save(model_save_dir)


if __name__ == '__main__':
    app.run(main)
```

To run this as a script (hp_kt_resnet_local.py), you could simply invoke it with the following command:

```
python3 hp_kt_resnet_local_pub.py \
--model_dir=resnet_local_hb_output  \
--train_epoch_best=2 \
--tuner_type=hyperband
```

In the preceding command, we invoke the python3 runtime to execute our training script, hp_kt_resnet_local.py. model_dir is the place we wish to save the model. Tuner_type designates the selection of the hyperparameter search algorithm. Other algorithm choices you may try are *Bayesian optimization and random search*.

Submitting tuning jobs in Google's AI Platform

Now we are ready to use Google's AI Platform to perform hyperparameter training. You may download everything you need from the GitHub repository for this chapter. For the AI Platform code in this section, you can refer to the gcptuningwork file in this chapter's folder in the GitHub repository for the book.

In the cloud, we have access to powerful machines that can speed up our search process. Overall, the approach we will leverage is very similar to what we saw in the previous section about submitting a local Python script training job. We will use the `tf.compat.v1.flag` method to handle user input or flags. The rest of the script follows a similar structure, with the exception of data handling, because we will use `TFRecord` instead of `ImageGenerator` and a conditional flag for the distributed training strategy.

Since the tuning job is submitted to AI Platform from a remote node (that is, your local compute environment), some prerequisites need to be met (see *Chapter 5, Training at Scale*):

1. In the directory where the tuning job will be invoked, `setup.py` needs to be updated to include `keras-tuner`. And while we are at it, let's also add IPython. So, edit the `setup.py` file as follows:

```
from setuptools import find_packages
from setuptools import setup

setup(
    name='official',
    install_requires=['IPython', 'keras-tuner',
'tensorflow-datasets~=3.1', 'tensorflow_hub>=0.6.0'],
    packages=find_packages()
)
```

This is the entire content of `setup.py`. In this file, we specify the libraries we need for our training job and instruct the runtime to find these libraries with the `find_packages` function.

2. You are now ready to submit a tuning job. In the following command, the job is submitted to Cloud TPU to run in the distributed training strategy:

```
gcloud ai-platform jobs submit training hp_kt_resnet_tpu_
hb_test \
--staging-bucket=gs://ai-tpu-experiment \
--package-path=tfk \
--module-name=tfk.tuner.hp_kt_resnet_tpu_act \
--runtime-version=2.2 \
--python-version=3.7 \
--scale-tier=BASIC_TPU \
```

```
--region=us-central1 \
--use-chief-in-tf-config='true' \
-- \
--distribution_strategy=tpu \
--data_dir=gs://ai-tpu-experiment/tfrecord-flowers \
--model_dir=gs://ai-tpu-experiment/hp_kt_resnet_tpu_hb_
test \
--tuner_type=hyperband
```

Notice the separator `--  \` in the preceding code, before `--  \`, they are Google Cloud-specific arguments. We submit a training script from our environment to Cloud TPU. For the training script, we need to specify the package path and module name. The Python version and TensorFlow runtime are also selected. We will use `BASIC_TPU` in the `us-central1` region.

After `--  \` are the custom arguments for training scripts. These arguments are defined for and used in the training script. We designated the value `tpu` for our choice of distribution training strategy. Further, the training data location is designated by `data_dir`. And once the training job is done, the model will be saved in `model_dir`. Finally, we select `HYPERBAND` as our `tuner_type` for the hyperparameter tuning algorithm.

And from the current directory, where the preceding command is invoked, the training script is stored in the `/python/ScriptProject/hp_kt_resnet_tpu_act.py` folder.

This training script performs a hyperparameter search for two hyperparameters: the number of units in a middle `Dense` layer of our image classification model, and the activation function. The added `tuner_type` flag lets the user select the algorithm: Hyperband, Bayesian optimization, or random search. Once the search is completed, it then trains the model with the best hyperparameter configuration and saves the model to a storage bucket.

> **Note**
>
> The code is lengthy, so you can find the entire code and instructions in the following GitHub repository: `https://github.com/PacktPublishing/learn-tensorflow-enterprise/tree/master/chapter_06/gcptuningwork`.
>
> The main driver script for training is available at `https://github.com/PacktPublishing/learn-tensorflow-enterprise/blob/master/chapter_06/gcptuningwork/tfk/tuner/hp_kt_resnet_tpu_act.py`.

Once the training is completed, you will see an output in the cloud storage specified by `model_dir` as shown in Figure 6.1:

Figure 6.1 – Hyperparameter tuning and training job output

In the storage bucket, there are the model assets saved from training using the best hyperparameter configuration in the `best_save_model` folder. Further, we can see that each trial of the hyperparameter tuning workflow is also saved in the `hp_tune_hb` folder.

Of all the search algorithms, Hyperband is the newest approach and offers an effective and efficient search experience based on an exploitation-exploration strategy. It is often the fastest algorithm to converge to a winning configuration. From the hardware choice perspective, for this example, Cloud TPU offers the shortest runtime. However, since hyperparameter search is inherently a time-consuming process, data size and data I/O also are also important factors that impact the speed of the search. Sometimes it is better to start with a smaller dataset or smaller search space to eliminate some selections from further analysis.

Summary

In this chapter, we learned how to use Keras Tuner in Google Cloud AI Platform. We learned how to run the hyperparameter search, and we learned how to train a model with the best hyperparameter configuration. We have also seen that in a typical Keras style, integrating Keras Tuner into our existing model training workflow is very easy, especially with the simple treatment of hyperparameters as just arrays of a certain data type. This really opens up the choices for hyperparameters, and we do not need to implement the search logic or complicated conditional loops to keep track of the results.

In the next chapter, we will see the latest model optimization techniques that reduce the model size. As a result, our model can be leaner and more compact.

Section 4 – Model Optimization and Deployment

This part introduces ways to improve the efficiency and speed of a model and its pipeline. We will start with the concept of model runtime, and then model optimization, followed by using TensorFlow Serving to serve models as a Docker container via a RESTful API.

This section comprises the following chapters:

- *Chapter 7, Model Optimization*
- *Chapter 8, Best Practices for Model Training and Performance*
- *Chapter 9, Serving a TensorFlow Model*

7
Model Optimization

In this chapter, we will learn about the concept of model optimization through a technique known as quantization. This is important because even though capacity, such as compute and memory, are less of an issue in a cloud environment, latency and throughput are always a factor in the quality and quantity of the model's output. Therefore, model optimization to reduce latency and maximize throughput can help reduce the compute cost. In the edge environment, many of the constraints are related to resources such as memory, compute, power consumption, and bandwidth.

In this chapter, you will learn how to make your model as lean and mean as possible, with acceptable or negligible changes in the model's accuracy. In other words, we will reduce the model size so that we can have the model running on less power and fewer compute resources without overly impacting its performance. In this chapter, we are going to take a look at recent advances and a method available for TensorFlow: TFLite Quantization.

In this chapter, we will cover the following topics:

- Understanding the quantization concept
- Preparing a full original model for scoring
- Converting a full model to a reduced float16 model
- Converting a full model to a reduced hybrid quantization model
- Converting a full model to an integer quantization model

Technical requirements

You will find all the source code in `https://github.com/PacktPublishing/learn-tensorflow-enterprise.git`.

You may clone it with a `git` command in your command terminal:

```
git clone https://github.com/PacktPublishing/learn-tensorflow-
  enterprise.git
```

All the resources for this chapter are available in the `chapter_07` folder in the GitHub link for the book.

Understanding the quantization concept

Quantization is a technique whereby the model size is reduced and its efficiency therefore improved. This technique is helpful in building models for mobile or edge deployment, where compute resources or power supply are constrained. Since our aim is to make the model run as efficiently as possible, we are also accepting the fact that the model has to become smaller and therefore less precise than the original model. This means that we are transforming the model into a lighter version of its original self, and that the transformed model is an approximation of the original one.

Quantization may be applied to a trained model. This is known as a post-training quantization API. Within this type of quantization, there are three approaches:

- **Reduced float quantization**: Convert `float 32 bits` ops to `float 16` ops.
- **Hybrid quantization**: Convert weights to `8 bits`, while keeping biases and activation as `32 bits` ops.
- **Integer quantization**: Convert everything to integer ops. Weights are converted to `8 bits`, while biases and activations may be 8 or `16 bits`.

The preceding approaches are applicable to a TensorFlow model that was built and trained using traditional means. Another approach is to train the model while performing optimization. This is known as **quantization-aware training**, in which we apply the API to emulate the quantization operations during the forward pass of the deep learning training.

The result model contains quantized values. This is relatively new and only an integer quantization API is available. Quantization-aware training currently only works for custom built models, not models from TensorFlow Hub, which are pre-trained. If you wish to use a quantized version of those famous pre-trained models, you can find these models here: `https://www.tensorflow.org/lite/guide/hosted_models`.

Training a baseline model

Let's begin start by training an image classification model with five classes of flowers. We will leverage a pre-trained ResNet feature vector hosted in TensorFlow Hub (https://tfhub.dev/google/imagenet/resnet_v2_50/feature_vector/4) and you can download the flower images in TFRecord format from here: https://dataverse.harvard.edu/dataset.xhtml?persistentId=doi:10.7910/DVN/1ECTVN.

Alternatively, if you cloned the repository for this book, the source code and TFRecord dataset for training a baseline model can be found at https://github.com/PacktPublishing/learn-tensorflow-enterprise/tree/master/chapter_07/train_base_model.

The following is a training script default_trainer.py file that trains this model with the TFRecord dataset:

1. We start this training script with an import statement for all the libraries we will require:

```
import tensorflow as tf
import tensorflow_hub as hub
import tensorflow_datasets as tfds
import os
import IPython
import time
from absl import flags
from absl import logging
from absl import app
```

A Absl is a useful library. In this library, the flags API is used to define user input. This is especially handy because we invoke this script through a user command instead of running it as a notebook.

2. Equipped with a flags API in the import statement, we will define a short-hand alias for flags.FLAGS, and then define a series of user inputs that we will pass to the script. This is accomplished with the help of the tf.compat.v1.flags API. Notice that we can define a data type for user inputs and provide a default value so that users do not have to specify every input:

```
FLAGS = flags.FLAGS
# flag name, default value, explanation/help.
tf.compat.v1.flags.DEFINE_string('model_dir', 'default_
model_dir', 'Directory or bucket for storing checkpoint
```

```
model.')
tf.compat.v1.flags.DEFINE_bool('fine_tuning_choice',
False, 'Retrain base parameters')
tf.compat.v1.flags.DEFINE_integer('train_batch_size', 32,
'Number of samples in a training batch')
tf.compat.v1.flags.DEFINE_integer('validation_batch_
size', 40, 'Number of samples in a validation batch')
tf.compat.v1.flags.DEFINE_string('distribution_strategy',
'tpu', 'Distribution strategy for training.')
tf.compat.v1.flags.DEFINE_integer('train_epochs', 3,
'Number of epochs for training')
tf.compat.v1.flags.DEFINE_string('data_dir', 'tf_
datasets/flower_photos', 'training data path')
tf.compat.v1.flags.DEFINE_integer('num_gpus', 4, 'Number
of GPU per worker')
tf.compat.v1.flags.DEFINE_string('cache_dir', '../
imagenet_resnet_v2_50_feature_vector_4' , 'Location of
cached model')
```

There are a couple of user flags that are worthy of further explanation. The `data_dir` flag defines the file path for training data. In this case, it is pointing to a folder path, `tf_datasets/flower_photos`, from the current directory, `train_base_model`. The other user flag is `cache_dir`. This is the path to our downloaded ResNet feature vector model. While we can access the TensorFlow Hub directly through the internet, there are occasions where connectivity may be an issue. Therefore, downloading the model and putting it in a local environment is a good idea.

3. We may wrap the model architecture and compilation in the following function:

```
def model_default():
    flags_obj = flags.FLAGS
    os.environ['TFHUB_CACHE_DIR'] = flags_obj.cache_dir
    IMAGE_SIZE = (224, 224)
    model = tf.keras.Sequential([
    tf.keras.layers.InputLayer(input_shape=IMAGE_SIZE +
(3,)),
    hub.KerasLayer('https://tfhub.dev/google/imagenet/
resnet_v2_50/feature_vector/4', trainable=flags_obj.fine_
tuning_choice),
    tf.keras.layers.Flatten(),
```

```
        tf.keras.layers.Dense(units = 64,
                                    activation = 'relu',
                    kernel_initializer='glorot_uniform'),
        tf.keras.layers.Dense(5, activation='softmax',
                                    name = 'custom_class')
    ])
    model.build([None, 224, 224, 3])
    model.compile(
        optimizer=tf.keras.optimizers.SGD(lr=1e-2,
                                    momentum=0.5),
        loss=tf.keras.losses.CategoricalCrossentropy(
                from_logits=True, label_smoothing=0.1),
        metrics=['accuracy'])
    return model
```

This function is responsible for building the model and compiling it with proper `optimizer` and `loss` functions. It returns a model object for training.

4. As for the image data's input pipeline, the pipeline needs to handle data parsing. This is accomplished with the following function:

```
def decode_and_resize(serialized_example):
    # resized image should be [224, 224, 3] and
normalized to value range [0, 255]
    # label is integer index of class.
        parsed_features = tf.io.parse_single_example(
    serialized_example,
    features = {
    'image/channels' :  tf.io.FixedLenFeature([],
                                    tf.int64),
    'image/class/label' :  tf.io.FixedLenFeature([],
                                    tf.int64),
    'image/class/text' : tf.io.FixedLenFeature([],
                                    tf.string),
    'image/colorspace' : tf.io.FixedLenFeature([],
                                    tf.string),
    'image/encoded' : tf.io.FixedLenFeature([],
                                    tf.string),
    'image/filename' : tf.io.FixedLenFeature([],
                                    tf.string),
```

```
        'image/format' : tf.io.FixedLenFeature([],
                                                tf.string),
        'image/height' : tf.io.FixedLenFeature([], tf.int64),
        'image/width' : tf.io.FixedLenFeature([], tf.int64)
        })
    image = tf.io.decode_jpeg(parsed_features[
                        'image/encoded'], channels=3)
    label = tf.cast(parsed_features['image/class/label'],
                                                tf.int32)
    label_txt = tf.cast(parsed_features[
                        'image/class/text'], tf.string)
    label_one_hot = tf.one_hot(label, depth = 5)
    resized_image = tf.image.resize(image, [224, 224],
                                        method='nearest')
    return resized_image, label_one_hot
```

As the function's name suggests, this function takes a sample that is stored in TFRecord. It is parsed with a feature description and the sample image (which is a byte string) decoded as a JPEG image. As for the image label, the function also parses the label name (image/class/text) and converts it into a one-hot vector. The jpeg image is resized to 224 by 224. As a result, this function returns a tuple. This tuple consists of one resized image and its label.

5. We also need to normalize the image pixel value to a range of [0, 1.0]. This is done through the following function:

```
def normalize(image, label):
    #Convert `image` from [0, 255] -> [0, 1.0] floats
    image = tf.cast(image, tf.float32) / 255.
    return image, label
```

In the normalize function, a JPEG image, represented as a NumPy array, is normalized to a range of [0, 1.0]. At the same time, although we are not doing anything with the label, it is a good idea to pass the label along with the image and return them as a tuple so that you keep track of the image and label together.

6. Then we apply shuffle and batch ops to the training data in the following function:

```
def prepare_for_training(ds, cache=True, shuffle_buffer_
size=1000):
    # This is a small dataset, only load it once, and
```

```
keep it in memory.
    # use `.cache(filename)` to cache preprocessing work
for datasets that don't
    # fit in memory.
    flags_obj = flags.FLAGS
    if cache:
        if isinstance(cache, str):
            ds = ds.cache(cache)
        else:
            ds = ds.cache()

    ds = ds.shuffle(buffer_size=shuffle_buffer_size)
    # Repeat forever
    ds = ds.repeat()
    ds = ds.batch(flags_obj.train_batch_size)
    # `prefetch` lets the dataset fetch batches in the
background while the model
    # is training.
    AUTOTUNE = tf.data.experimental.AUTOTUNE
    ds = ds.prefetch(buffer_size=AUTOTUNE)
return ds
```

This function returns a dataset with shuffle, repeat, batch, and prefetch ops attached. This is a standard approach for getting the dataset ready for training.

7. Now we come to the main driver of this code:

```
def main(_):
    flags_obj = flags.FLAGS
        if flags_obj.distribution_strategy == 'tpu':
            resolver = tf.distribute.cluster_resolver.
TPUClusterResolver()
        tf.config.experimental_connect_to_
cluster(resolver)
        tf.tpu.experimental.initialize_tpu_
system(resolver)
            strategy = tf.distribute.experimental.
TPUStrategy(resolver)
            strategy_scope = strategy.scope()
```

```
        print('All devices: ', tf.config.list_logical_
devices('TPU'))
    elif flags_obj.distribution_strategy == 'gpu':
        strategy = tf.distribute.MirroredStrategy()
        strategy_scope = strategy.scope()
        devices = ['device:GPU:%d' % i for i in
                        range(flags_obj.num_gpus)]
    else:
        strategy = tf.distribute.MirroredStrategy()
        strategy_scope = strategy.scope()
  print('NUMBER OF DEVICES: ',
                            strategy.num_replicas_in_sync)
```

In this section of the `main()` function, we provide the logic for a distributed training strategy.

8. Continuing with `main()`, the data paths are identified and handled by the `tf.data` API:

```
    ## identify data paths and sources
    root_dir = flags_obj.data_dir # this is
gs://<bucket>/folder or file path where tfrecord is found
    file_pattern = '{}/image_classification_builder-
train*.tfrecord*'.format(root_dir)
    val_file_pattern = '{}/image_classification_builder-
validation*.tfrecord*'.format(root_dir)

    file_list = tf.io.gfile.glob(file_pattern)
    all_files = tf.data.Dataset.list_files(
                        tf.io.gfile.glob(file_pattern))

    val_file_list = tf.io.gfile.glob(val_file_pattern)
    val_all_files = tf.data.Dataset.list_files(
                        tf.io.gfile.glob(val_file_pattern))

    train_all_ds = tf.data.TFRecordDataset(all_files,
        num_parallel_reads=tf.data.experimental.AUTOTUNE)
  val_all_ds = tf.data.TFRecordDataset(val_all_files,
        num_parallel_reads=tf.data.experimental.AUTOTUNE)
```

With the preceding code, all three data sources – training, validation, and testing – are identified and referenced. Recall that the wildcard symbol, *, in the filename pattern helps this pipeline to be scalable. It doesn't matter how many TFRecord data parts you have; this pipeline can handle it.

9. Continuing with `main()`, now we need to apply feature engineering and normalization functions to every sample in the training and validation datasets. This is done through the `map` function:

```
# perform data engineering
dataset = train_all_ds.map(decode_and_resize)
val_dataset = val_all_ds.map(decode_and_resize)


# Create dataset for training run
BATCH_SIZE = flags_obj.train_batch_size
VALIDATION_BATCH_SIZE =
                        flags_obj.validation_batch_size
dataset = dataset.map(normalize,
    num_parallel_calls=tf.data.experimental.AUTOTUNE)
val_dataset = val_dataset.map(normalize,
    num_parallel_calls=tf.data.experimental.AUTOTUNE)
val_ds = val_dataset.batch(VALIDATION_BATCH_SIZE)
AUTOTUNE = tf.data.experimental.AUTOTUNE
train_ds = prepare_for_training(dataset)
```

Training and validation datasets are batched according to the respective user flags. If none are given, default values are used.

10. Now we need to set up some parameters for training and validation:

```
NUM_CLASSES = 5
IMAGE_SIZE = (224, 224)
    train_sample_size=0
for raw_record in train_all_ds:
    train_sample_size += 1
print('TRAIN_SAMPLE_SIZE = ', train_sample_size)
validation_sample_size=0
for raw_record in val_all_ds:
    validation_sample_size += 1
print('VALIDATION_SAMPLE_SIZE = ',
```

```
                                    validation_sample_size)
        STEPS_PER_EPOCHS = train_sample_size // BATCH_SIZE
    VALIDATION_STEPS = validation_sample_size
                                  // VALIDATION_BATCH_SIZE
```

In the preceding code, we set the number of classes and image size in variables to be passed into the model training process. Then we determine the number of steps for each epoch of training and cross-validation.

11. Continuing with `main()`, we can now create the model by invoking the `model_default` function:

```
    model = model_default()
    checkpoint_prefix = os.path.join(flags_obj.model_dir,
                              'train_ckpt_{epoch}')
    callbacks = [
      tf.keras.callbacks.TensorBoard(log_dir=os.path.
    join(flags_obj.model_dir, 'tensorboard_logs')),
      tf.keras.callbacks.ModelCheckpoint(
                          filepath=checkpoint_prefix,
        save_weights_only=True)]
```

In the preceding code, we invoke the `model_default` function to build and compile our model. We also set up callbacks for the training checkpoint.

12. Continuing with `main()`, we can now launch the training process:

```
    model.fit(
        train_ds,
        epochs=flags_obj.train_epochs,
        steps_per_epoch=STEPS_PER_EPOCHS,
        validation_data=val_ds,
        validation_steps=VALIDATION_STEPS,
        callbacks=callbacks)
```

In the preceding code, we pass the training and validation datasets into the `fit` function. The number of epochs is determined by the user input. If none is given, then the default value is used.

13. Continuing with `main()`, we may log output as STDOUT in the terminal where this script is executed:

```
    logging.info('INSIDE MAIN FUNCTION user input model_
dir %s', flags_obj.model_dir)
        timestr = time.strftime('%Y%m%d-%H%M%S')
    output_folder = flags_obj.model_dir + '-' + timestr

    if not os.path.exists(output_folder):
        os.mkdir(output_folder)
        print('Directory ' , output_folder , ' Created ')
    else:
        print('Directory ' , output_folder , ' already
exists')
    model_save_dir = os.path.join(output_folder,
                                    'save_model')
    model.save(model_save_dir)
if __name__ == '__main__':
    app.run(main)
```

In the preceding code, we also leverage a timestamp value to build a folder name, where the models built each time may be saved according to the time of training completion.

This concludes `main()`. The model is saved in `model_save_dir`. To invoke this script, you simply have to run the following command in your Python environment:

```
python3 default_trainer.py \
--distribution_strategy=default \
--fine_tuning_choice=False \
--train_batch_size=32 \
--validation_batch_size=40 \
--train_epochs=5 \
--data_dir=tf_datasets/flower_photos \
--model_dir=trained_resnet_vector
```

From the directory where this script is stored, you will find a subfolder with the prefix name `trained_resnet_vector`, followed by a date and time stamp such as `20200910-213303`. This subfolder contains the saved model. We will use this model as our baseline model. Once training is complete, you will find the saved model in the following directory:

```
trained_resnet_vector-20200910-213303/save_model/assets
```

This saved model is in the same directory where `default_trainer.py` is stored. Now that we have a trained TensorFlow model, in the next section, we are going score our test data with the trained model.

Preparing a full original model for scoring

After training for a full model is complete, we will use a `Scoring` Jupyter notebook in this repository to demonstrate scoring with a full model. This notebook can be found in `https://github.com/PacktPublishing/learn-tensorflow-enterprise/blob/master/chapter_07/train_base_model/Scoring.ipynb`.

For the original model, it is stored in the `savedModel` Protobuf format. We need to load it as follows:

```
import tensorflow as tf
import numpy as np
import matplotlib.pyplot as plt
from PIL import Image, ImageOps
import IPython.display as display
path_saved_model = 'trained_resnet_vector-unquantized/save_
model'
trained_model = tf.saved_model.load(path_saved_model)
```

The full model we just trained is now loaded in our Jupyter notebook's runtime as `trained_model`. For scoring, a few more steps are required. We have to find the model signature for prediction:

```
signature_list = list(trained_model.signatures.keys())
signature_list
```

It shows that there is only one signature in this list:

```
['serving_default']
```

We will create an `infer` wrapper function and pass the signature into it:

```
infer = trained_model.signatures[signature_list[0]]
```

Here, `signature_list[0]` is equivalent to `serving_default`. Now let's print the output:

```
print(infer.structured_outputs)
```

Let's take a look at the output of the preceding function:

```
{'custom_class': TensorSpec(shape=(None, 5), dtype=tf.float32,
name='custom_class')}
```

The output is a NumPy array of `shape=(None, 5)`. This array will hold the probability of classes predicted by the model.

Now let's work on the test data. The test data provided in this case is in TFRecord format. We are going to convert it to a batch of images expressed as a NumPy array in the dimensions of `[None, 224, 224, 3]`.

Preparing test data

This part is very similar to what we saw in *Chapter 6, Hyperparameter Tuning*, where we used TFRecord extensively as the input format for model training. The TFRecord used here is available in `https://github.com/PacktPublishing/learn-tensorflow-enterprise/tree/master/chapter_07/train_base_model/tf_datasets/flower_photos`.

Loading test data

Let's start by loading the TFRecord data:

```
root_dir = ' tf_datasets/flower_photos'
test_pattern = '{}/image_classification_builder-test.
tfrecord*'.format(root_dir)
test_all_files = tf.data.Dataset.list_files( tf.io.gfile.
glob(test_pattern))
```

```
test_all_ds = tf.data.TFRecordDataset(test_all_files,
num_parallel_reads=tf.data.experimental.AUTOTUNE)
```

We will check the sample size of the image with the following code:

```
sample_size = 0
for raw_record in test_all_ds:
    sample_size += 1
print('Sample size: ', sample_size)
```

Here is the output:

```
Sample size:    50
```

This shows that we have 50 samples in our test data.

There are 50 images in this test dataset. We will reuse the helper function from *Chapter 6, Hyperparameter Tuning*, to decode the TFRecord and the metadata within and then normalize the pixel values:

```
def decode_and_resize(serialized_example):
    # resized image should be [224, 224, 3] and normalized to
value range [0, 255]
    # label is integer index of class.
        parsed_features = tf.io.parse_single_example(
    serialized_example,
    features = {
    'image/channels' :  tf.io.FixedLenFeature([], tf.int64),
    'image/class/label' :  tf.io.FixedLenFeature([], tf.int64),
    'image/class/text' : tf.io.FixedLenFeature([], tf.string),
    'image/colorspace' : tf.io.FixedLenFeature([], tf.string),
    'image/encoded' : tf.io.FixedLenFeature([], tf.string),
    'image/filename' : tf.io.FixedLenFeature([], tf.string),
    'image/format' : tf.io.FixedLenFeature([], tf.string),
    'image/height' : tf.io.FixedLenFeature([], tf.int64),
    'image/width' : tf.io.FixedLenFeature([], tf.int64)
    })
    image = tf.io.decode_jpeg(parsed_features['image/encoded'],
                                              channels=3)
    label = tf.cast(parsed_features['image/class/label'],
```

```
                                                    tf.int32)
    label_txt = tf.cast(parsed_features['image/class/text'],
                                                    tf.string)
    label_one_hot = tf.one_hot(label, depth = 5)
    resized_image = tf.image.resize(image, [224, 224],
                                        method='nearest')
    return resized_image, label_one_hot
def normalize(image, label):
    #Convert `image` from [0, 255] -> [0, 1.0] floats
    image = tf.cast(image, tf.float32) / 255.
    return image, label
```

The decode_and_resize function parses an image, resizes it to 224 by 224 pixels, and, at the same time, one-hot encodes the image's label. decode_and_resize then returns the image and corresponding label as a tuple, so that the image and label are always kept together.

The normalize function divides the image pixel value by 255 in order to bring the pixel range to [0, 1.0]. And even though nothing is done in relation to the label, it is necessary to keep track of the image and label as a tuple so that they are always kept together.

Now we may apply the preceding helper functions to decode, standardize, and normalize images in the TFRecord dataset:

```
decoded = test_all_ds.map(decode_and_resize)
normed = decoded.map(normalize)
```

Notice that we introduced an additional dimension as the first dimension through np.expand_dims. This extra dimension is intended for the variable batch size:

```
np_img_holder = np.empty((0, 224, 224,3), float)
np_lbl_holder = np.empty((0, 5), int)
for img, lbl in normed:
    r = img.numpy() # image value extracted
    rx = np.expand_dims(r, axis=0)
    lx = np.expand_dims(lbl, axis=0)
    np_img_holder = np.append(np_img_holder, rx, axis=0)
np_lbl_holder = np.append(np_lbl_holder, lx, axis=0)
```

The test data is now in NumPy format with standardized dimensions, pixel values between 0 and 1, and is batched, as are the labels.

We will now inspect these images. In order to do so, we may display the NumPy array, np_img_holder, as images with the following code in Figure 7.1:

```
%matplotlib inline
plt.figure()
for i in range(len(np_img_holder)):
    plt.subplot(10, 5, i+1)
    plt.axis('off')
plt.imshow(np.asarray(np_img_holder[i]))
```

In the preceding code snippet, we iterate through our image array and place each image in one of the subplots. There are 50 images (10 rows, with each row having five subplots), as can be seen in the following figure:

Figure 7.1 – 50 images within the test dataset of five flower classes

Scoring a single image with a full model

Let's now take a look at the shape of the test data, and understand what it takes to transform test data into the shape expected by the model:

1. We will first test our scoring routine with just a single image. Just like how we created an image batch by adding a new dimension as the first dimension, we will do the same to create an image batch with a sample size of 1:

```
x = np.expand_dims(np_img_holder[0], axis=0)
x.shape
(1, 224, 224, 3)
```

2. Now the dimension is correct, which is a batch of one image. Let's convert this to a tensor with a type of `float32`:

```
xf = tf.dtypes.cast(x, tf.float32)
```

Then, pass this to the `infer` function for scoring:

```
prediction = infer(xf)
```

You will recall that the last layer of our model is a dense layer named `custom_class`. With five nodes, and softmax as the activation function in each node, we will get the probability for each of the five classes.

3. We will now inspect the content of the prediction:

```
prediction.get('custom_class')
```

The output should appear similar to this:

```
<tf.Tensor: shape=(1, 5), dtype=float32, numpy=
array([[1.5271275e-04, 2.0515859e-05, 1.0230409e-06,
2.9591745e-06, 9.9982280e-01]], dtype=float32)>
```

These values in the array represent probability. Each position in the array represents a class of flower type. As you can see, the highest probability is in the very last position of the array; the index corresponding to this position is 4. We need to map 4 to the plaintext name.

Now we will convert it to a NumPy array so that we may find the index where the maximum probability is predicted:

```
predicted_prob_array = prediction.get('custom_class').
numpy()
idx = np.argmax(predicted_prob_array)
print(idx)
```

4. The fourth position index is where maximum probability is predicted. Now we need to know what this represents by mapping this index to a label. We need to create a reverse lookup dictionary to map probability back to the label. We just found the index where the maximum probability is located. The next step is to map idx to the correct flower type. In order to do this, we need to extract this information from TFRecord:

```
feature_description = {
    'image/channels' :  tf.io.FixedLenFeature([],
                                                tf.int64),
    'image/class/label' :  tf.io.FixedLenFeature([],
                                                tf.int64),
    'image/class/text' : tf.io.FixedLenFeature([],
                                                tf.string),
    'image/colorspace' : tf.io.FixedLenFeature([],
                                                tf.string),
    'image/encoded' : tf.io.FixedLenFeature([],
                                                tf.string),
    'image/filename' : tf.io.FixedLenFeature([],
                                                tf.string),
    'image/format' : tf.io.FixedLenFeature([],
                                                tf.string),
    'image/height' : tf.io.FixedLenFeature([], tf.int64),
    'image/width' : tf.io.FixedLenFeature([], tf.int64)
}

def _parse_function(example_proto):
    return tf.io.parse_single_example(example_proto,
                                        feature_description)

parsd_ds = test_all_ds.map(_parse_function)
```

```
val_label_map = {}
# getting label mapping
for image_features in parsd_ds.take(50):
    label_idx = image_features[
                            'image/class/label'].numpy()
    label_str = image_features[
                    'image/class/text'].numpy().decode()
    if label_idx not in val_label_map:
        val_label_map[label_idx] = label_str
```

In the preceding code, we used the same feature description (`feature_description`) to parse `test_all_ds`. Once it is parsed using `_parse_function`, we iterate through the entire test dataset. The information we want is in `image/class/label` and `image/class/text`.

5. We simply create a dictionary, where the key is `label_idx` and the value is `label_str`. The result is `val_label_map`. If we inspect it as follows:

```
val_label_map
```

The output is as follows:

```
{4: 'tulips', 3: 'dandelion', 1: 'sunflowers', 2:
'daisy', 0: 'roses'}
```

Then we evaluate `idx`:

```
print(val_label_map.get(idx))
```

Here is the output:

```
tulip
```

This maps our image to the `tulip` class.

Scoring batch images with a full model

In the previous section, we looked at how to score one image. Now we want to score a batch of images. In our test data, there are 50 images:

1. In the previous section, we created the image batch in the proper shape of `[50, 224, 224, 3]`. This is ready for scoring:

```
batched_input = tf.dtypes.cast(np_img_holder, tf.float32)
batch_predicted_prob_array = infer(batched_input)
```

Let's create a function that assists in looking up the label name when given a NumPy array and a lookup dictionary:

```
def lookup(np_entry, dictionary):
    class_key = np.argmax(np_entry)
    return dictionary.get(class_key)
```

This function takes a NumPy array, maps the position where the maximum value exists, and then maps that position with a dictionary.

2. This is a list holding our ground truth labels as indicated by np_lbl_holder:

```
actual = []
for i in range(len(np_lbl_holder)):
    plain_text_label = lookup(np_lbl_holder[i],
                                                val_label_map)
    actual.append(plain_text_label)
```

actual holds the actual plaintext labels of all 50 test samples.

3. This is how we can get a list holding the predicted label:

```
predicted_label = []
for i in range(sample_size):
batch_prediction = batch_predicted_prob_array.
get('custom_class').numpy()
plain_text_label = lookup(batch_prediction[i],
                                                val_label_map)
predicted_label.append(plain_text_label)
```

predicted_label holds the predictions for all 50 test samples in plaintext because we leverage the lookup function to map the probability to the flower type name.

4. We will compare predicted_label and actual to get the accuracy of the model:

```
from sklearn.metrics import accuracy_score
accuracy=accuracy_score(actual, predicted_label)
print(accuracy)
0.82
```

This shows that our full model's accuracy is 82%. This is simply done by comparing `actual` with `predicted_label` using the `accuracy_score` API from `sklearn`.

> **Note**
>
> It's expected that your model accuracy will be slightly different from the nominal value printed here. Every time a base model is trained, the model accuracy will not be identical. However, it should not be too dissimilar to the nominal value. Another factor that impacts reproducibility in terms of model accuracy is the number of epochs used in training; in this case, only five epochs for demonstration and didactic purposes. More training epochs will give you a better and tighter variance in terms of model accuracy.

Converting a full model to a reduced float16 model

In this section, we are going to load the model we just trained and quantize it into a reduced `float16` model. For the convenience of step-by-step explanations and your learning experience, it is recommended that you use JupyterLab or Jupyter Notebook to follow along with the explanation here:

1. Let's start by loading the trained model:

    ```
    import tensorflow as tf
    import pathlib
    import os
    import numpy as np
    from matplotlib.pyplot import imshow
    import matplotlib.pyplot as plt
    root_dir = '../train_base_model'
    model_dir = ' trained_resnet_vector-unquantized/save_
    model'
    saved_model_dir = os.path.join(root_dir, model_dir)
    trained_model = tf.saved_model.load(saved_model_dir)
    ```

    The `tf.saved_model.load` API helps us to load the saved model we built and trained.

2. Then we will create a `converter` object to refer to the `savedModel` directory with the following line of code:

```
converter = tf.lite.TFLiteConverter.from_saved_
model(saved_model_dir)
```

For the `converter` object, we will select the `DEFAULT` optimization strategy for the converter to best improve model size and latency:

```
converter.optimizations = [tf.lite.Optimize.DEFAULT]
```

The alternatives are `OPTIMIZE_FOR_LATENCY` or `OPTIMIZE_FOR_SIZE`. Refer to `https://www.tensorflow.org/api_docs/python/tf/lite/Optimize` for information.

3. Next, we will set `float16` as the target type for the model parameters and start the conversion process:

```
converter.target_spec.supported_types = [tf.float16]
tflite_model = converter.convert()
```

We will set up a directory designation for saving the quantized model using the following code:

```
root_dir = ''
tflite_model_dir = trained_resnet_vector-unquantized
to_save_tflite_model_dir = os.path.join(root_dir,
                                    tflite_model_dir)
```

4. Now, we will create a `pathlib` object to represent the directory where we want to save our quantized model:

```
saved_tflite_model_dir = pathlib.Path(
                            to_save_tflite_model_dir)
```

Let's create the directory for saving the quantized model:

```
saved_tflite_model_dir.mkdir(exist_ok=True, parents=True)
```

5. We will now create a `pathlib` object, `tgt`, to represent the quantized model file:

```
tgt = pathlib.Path(tflite_models_dir,
                    'converted_model_reduced.tflite')
```

We will now write the quantized model using the `pathlib` object, `tgt`:

```
tgt.write_bytes(tflite_model)
```

This will show the output in terms of the size of bytes written:

```
47487392
```

With the last command, you will see that the quantized model size is slightly more than 47 MB, at exactly 47,487,392 Bytes. Go to the following directory: `../trained_resnet_vector-unquantized/save_model/variables`.

This shows that the original model's weight and bias file is slightly more than 95 MB (results may vary and won't be exactly the same if you train it again; however, it should be very close to 95 MB) as shown in the following figure:

```
95401457 Sep 10 21:33 variables.data-00000-of-00001
   20947 Sep 10 21:33 variables.index
```

Figure 7.2 – Original model's weight and bias file size

The quantized model is about half the size of the original model. This is as expected, as the model was converted from `float32` to `float16` format. Next, we are going to score our test data with the reduced `float16` model.

Preparing the reduced float16 model for scoring

In this section, we will use the quantized model (reduced `float16`) to score the same test dataset used in the previous section. We will execute scoring (inferencing) with the TensorFlow Lite interpreter interface:

1. We will load the quantized model from the file path represented by `tflite_models_dir`. In the previous section, we created a `pathlib` object, `tgt`, to represent the quantized model file:

    ```
    tgt = pathlib.Path(tflite_models_dir,
                        'converted_model_reduced.tflite')
    ```

2. Then we need to get the `input_details` and `output_details` tensors:

    ```
    input_details = interpreter.get_input_details()
    output_details = interpreter.get_output_details()
    ```

3. From these tensors, we will inspect the shape of the NumPy arrays in both the input and output:

```
input_details[0]['shape']
array([  1, 224, 224,    3], dtype=int32)
output_details[0]['shape']
array([1, 5], dtype=int32)
```

We verified that the model input and output are expected to be a batch because there are four dimensions in these tensors. Next, we are going to see how well this model performs by scoring the test data.

Scoring a single image with a quantized model

Now we may start the scoring process with a TFLite quantized model. In the following steps, we first expand the sample to include a dimension for the batch, pass the input data to the interpreter, perform scoring of input data, and then get the output of the prediction:

```
input_data = np.array(np.expand_dims(np_img_holder[0], axis=0),
dtype=np.float32)
interpreter.set_tensor(input_details[0]['index'], input_data)
interpreter.invoke()
output_data = interpreter.get_tensor(output_details[0]
['index'])
print(output_data)
```

Here is the output:

```
[[1.5181543e-04 2.0090181e-05 1.0022727e-06 2.8991076e-06
9.9982423e-01]]
```

To map output_data back to the original labels, execute the following command:

```
lookup(output_data, val_label_map)
```

Here is the output:

```
'tulips'
```

Scoring a batch image with a quantized model

Currently, batch scoring in the TFLite model is supported through the iterative scoring process of a single image. For our example of 50 test images, we may create a helper function to encapsulate the entire single image scoring process:

1. This is a function that handles batch scoring:

```
def batch_predict(input_raw, input_tensor, output_tensor,
dictionary):
    input_data = np.array(np.expand_dims(input_raw,
                                axis=0), dtype=np.float32)
    interpreter.set_tensor(input_tensor[0]['index'],
                                input_data)
    interpreter.invoke()
    interpreter_output = interpreter.get_tensor(
                                output_tensor[0]['index'])
    plain_text_label = lookup(interpreter_output,
                                dictionary)
    return plain_text_label
```

This function expands raw image dimensions to batches, and then passes the batched image to the interpreter for scoring. The interpreter's output is then mapped to a plaintext name by means of the `lookup` function and the plaintext is returned as the predicted label.

2. Next, we will iterate through our test data to call on `batch_predict`:

```
batch_quantized_prediction = []
for i in range(sample_size):
    plain_text_label = batch_predict(np_img_holder[i],
input_details, output_details, val_label_map)
    batch_quantized_prediction.append(plain_text_label)
```

The result is stored in the `batch_quantized_prediction` list.

3. And just like how we measure the prediction accuracy of our original model, we may use `accuracy_score` to get the accuracy of the TFLite quantized model:

```
quantized_accuracy = accuracy_score(actual, batched_
quantized_prediiction)
print(quantized_accuracy)
```

The output is as follows:

```
0.82
```

The output here is shown to also be 82%. Results may vary if you retrained the model, but in my experience, it is identical to the accuracy of the base model.

> **Note**
> It's expected that your model accuracy will be slightly different from the nominal value printed here. Every time a base model is trained, the model accuracy will not be identical. However, it should not be too dissimilar to the nominal value. Another factor that impacts reproducibility in terms of model accuracy is the number of epochs used in training; in this case, only five epochs for demonstration and didactic purposes. More training epochs will give you a better and tighter variance in terms of model accuracy.

The functions, routines, and workflow developed up to this point will be used in the remaining sections of this chapter to demonstrate the process and outcome of model optimization. We have learned how to score the original model, convert the original model to the TFLite quantized model, and score the quantized model. Next, we will convert the original model to different formats using the same conversion and evaluation processes.

Converting a full model to a reduced hybrid quantization model

In the previous section, we converted a full model into a reduced `float16` TFLite model, and demonstrated its scoring and evaluation processes. Now we will try the second type of supported quantization, which is a hybrid approach.

Hybrid quantization optimizes the model by converting the model to 8-bit integer weights, 32-bit float biases, and activations. Since it contains both integer and floating-point computations, it is known as hybrid quantization. This is intended for a trade-off between accuracy and optimization.

There is only one small difference that we need to make for hybrid quantization. There is only one line of difference, as explained below. In the previous section, this is how we quantized the full model to a reduced `float16` TFLite model:

```
converter.optimizations = [tf.lite.Optimize.DEFAULT]
converter.target_spec.supported_types = [tf.float16]
tflite_model = converter.convert()
```

For hybrid quantization, we will simply remove the middle line about `supported_types`:

```
converter.optimizations = [tf.lite.Optimize.DEFAULT]
tflite_model = converter.convert()
```

Everything else remains pretty much the same. Following is the complete notebook for hybrid quantization and scoring:

1. As usual, we will specify the necessary libraries and path to the model:

```
import tensorflow as tf
import pathlib
import os
import numpy as np
from matplotlib.pyplot import imshow
import matplotlib.pyplot as plt
root_dir = ''
model_dir = 'trained_resnet_vector-unquantized/save_
model'
saved_model_dir = os.path.join(root_dir, model_dir)
```

Now, the path to the model is specified in `saved_model_dir`.

2. Then we create a `converter` object for `saved_model_dir` and use it to convert our model:

```
converter = tf.lite.TFLiteConverter.from_saved_
model(saved_model_dir)
converter.optimizations = [tf.lite.Optimize.DEFAULT]
tflite_model = converter.convert()
```

Now, the converter converts the full model to a hybrid quantization model.

3. Now we will save our hybrid quantization model:

```
root_dir = ''
tflite_models_dir = 'trained_resnet_vector-unquantized/
tflite_hybrid_model'
to_save_tflite_model_dir = os.path.join(root_dir,
tflite_models_dir)
saved_tflite_models_dir = pathlib.Path(to_save_tflite_
model_dir)
```

```
saved_tflite_models_dir.mkdir(exist_ok=True, parents=True
tgt = pathlib.Path(to_save_tflite_model_dir, 'converted_
model_reduced.tflite')
tgt.write_bytes(tflite_model)
```

The output shows the model size in bytes:

```
24050608
```

This is significantly smaller than the 95 MB of the original base model. Next, let's see how well this smaller, hybrid quantized model performs with test data.

Preparing test data for scoring

We will begin by loading the test data, as we did with the reduced `float16` model:

1. We can load TFRecord data, as we have done previously:

```
root_dir = '../train_base_model/tf_datasets/flower_
photos'
test_pattern = '{}/image_classification_builder-test.
tfrecord*'.format(root_dir)
test_all_files = tf.data.Dataset.list_files( tf.io.gfile.
glob(test_pattern))


test_all_ds = tf.data.TFRecordDataset(test_all_files,
num_parallel_reads=tf.data.experimental.AUTOTUNE)
```

Now, `test_all_ds` represents the dataset object that points to the path of our test data.

2. We may determine sample size by iterating through the dataset and keeping track of the sample count:

```
sample_size = 0
for raw_record in test_all_ds:
    sample_size += 1
print('Sample size: ', sample_size)
```

This will show the sample size as 50.

3. We use the same helper functions seen in the reduced `float16` model section to standardize the image size and pixel values:

```
def decode_and_resize(serialized_example):
    # resized image should be [224, 224, 3] and
normalized to value range [0, 255]
    # label is integer index of class.
        parsed_features = tf.io.parse_single_example(
    serialized_example,
    features = {
    'image/channels' :  tf.io.FixedLenFeature([],
                                               tf.int64),
    'image/class/label' :  tf.io.FixedLenFeature([],
                                                 tf.int64),
    'image/class/text' : tf.io.FixedLenFeature([],
                                               tf.string),
    'image/colorspace' : tf.io.FixedLenFeature([],
                                               tf.string),
    'image/encoded' : tf.io.FixedLenFeature([],
                                            tf.string),
    'image/filename' : tf.io.FixedLenFeature([],
                                             tf.string),
    'image/format' : tf.io.FixedLenFeature([],
                                           tf.string),
    'image/height' : tf.io.FixedLenFeature([], tf.int64),
    'image/width' : tf.io.FixedLenFeature([], tf.int64)
    })
    image = tf.io.decode_jpeg(parsed_features[
                       'image/encoded'], channels=3)
    label = tf.cast(parsed_features['image/class/label'],
                                                 tf.int32)
    label_txt = tf.cast(parsed_features[
                       'image/class/text'], tf.string)
    label_one_hot = tf.one_hot(label, depth = 5)
    resized_image = tf.image.resize(image, [224, 224],
                                    method='nearest')
    return resized_image, label_one_hot
def normalize(image, label):
```

```
#Convert `image` from [0, 255] -> [0, 1.0] floats
image = tf.cast(image, tf.float32) / 255.
return image, label
```

The decode_and_resize function parses an image, resizes it to 224 by 224 pixels, and, at the same time, one-hot encodes the image's label. decode_and_resize then returns the image and corresponding label as a tuple, so that the image and label are always kept together.

The normalize function divides the image pixel value by 255 in order to bring the pixel range to [0, 1.0]. And even though nothing is done in relation to the label, it is necessary to keep track of the image and label as a tuple so that they are always kept together.

4. Next, we will apply the transformation with the following helper functions:

```
decoded = test_all_ds.map(decode_and_resize)
normed = decoded.map(normalize)
```

5. Let's convert TFRecord to a NumPy array for scoring:

```
np_img_holder = np.empty((0, 224, 224,3), float)
np_lbl_holder = np.empty((0, 5), int)
for img, lbl in normed:
    r = img.numpy() # image value extracted
    rx = np.expand_dims(r, axis=0)
    lx = np.expand_dims(lbl, axis=0)
    np_img_holder = np.append(np_img_holder, rx, axis=0)
    np_lbl_holder = np.append(np_lbl_holder, lx, axis=0)
```

Now, all test images are in NumPy format with standard (224, 224, 3) dimensions, the pixel values are between 0 and 1, and images are batched. Labels are batched as well.

6. We now need to extract the ground truth labels so that we can measure our prediction accuracy:

```
actual = []
for i in range(len(np_lbl_holder)):
    class_key = np.argmax(np_lbl_holder[i])
    actual.append(val_label_map.get(class_key))
```

In the preceding code, `actual` is a list that contains class names for each test image.

7. We may inspect the NumPy array, `np_img_holder`, as images with the following code, and this will produce the images seen in *Figure 7.1*:

```
%matplotlib inline
plt.figure()
for i in range(len(np_img_holder)):
    plt.subplot(10, 5, i+1)
    plt.axis('off')
imshow(np.asarray(np_img_holder[i]))
```

In the preceding code snippet, we iterate through our image array, and place each in one of the subplots, while there are 50 images (10 rows, with each row having 5 subplots). The output images should appear in 10 rows with 5 images in each row, as seen in *Figure 7.1*.

For single test file scoring, we need to add a dimension to a sample. Since a given image is of the shape `(224, 224, 3)`, we need to make it into `(1, 224, 224, 3)` so that it will be accepted by the model for scoring. This is why we used `np.expand_dim` when we converted TFRecord to NumPy. As the model is built to handle batch scoring, it is expecting four dimensions with the first dimension being the sample size.

Mapping a prediction to a class name

From TFRecord, we need to create a reverse lookup dictionary to map probability back to the label. In other words, we need to find the index where maximum probability is positioned in the array. We will then map this position index to the flower type.

To create the lookup dictionary, we will parse the TFRecord with feature descriptions to extract the label indices and names as shown in the following code:

```
feature_description = {
    'image/channels' : tf.io.FixedLenFeature([], tf.int64),
    'image/class/label' : tf.io.FixedLenFeature([], tf.int64),
    'image/class/text' : tf.io.FixedLenFeature([], tf.string),
    'image/colorspace' : tf.io.FixedLenFeature([], tf.string),
    'image/encoded' : tf.io.FixedLenFeature([], tf.string),
    'image/filename' : tf.io.FixedLenFeature([], tf.string),
    'image/format' : tf.io.FixedLenFeature([], tf.string),
```

```
        'image/height' : tf.io.FixedLenFeature([], tf.int64),
        'image/width' : tf.io.FixedLenFeature([], tf.int64)
}
def _parse_function(example_proto):
    return tf.io.parse_single_example(example_proto,
                                        feature_description)
parsd_ds = test_all_ds.map(_parse_function)
val_label_map = {}
# getting label mapping
for image_features in parsd_ds.take(50):
    label_idx = image_features['image/class/label'].numpy()
    label_str = image_features['image/class/text'].numpy().
decode()
    if label_idx not in val_label_map:
        val_label_map[label_idx] = label_str
```

In the preceding code, we used `feature_description` to parse `test_all_ds`. Once it is parsed using `_parse_function`, we iterate through the entire test dataset. The information we want can be found in `image/class/label` and `image/class/text`.

We can also inspect `val_label_map`:

```
{4: 'tulips', 3: 'dandelion', 1: 'sunflowers', 2: 'daisy', 0:
'roses'}
```

This is the lookup table that maps the index to a plaintext name.

Scoring with a hybrid quantization model

As we did for the reduced `float16` model, we want to see how a hybrid quantization model performs with test data. Now we can start the process of scoring test images with the hybrid quantization model:

1. We will begin by loading the model and allocating tensors as usual with the help of the following lines of code:

    ```
    interpreter = tf.lite.Interpreter(model_path=str(tgt))
    interpreter.allocate_tensors()
    ```

Now the hybrid quantization model is loaded.

2. To ascertain the input and output shape of the tensors that the model operates with, we may obtain input and output tensors in the following way:

```
input_details = interpreter.get_input_details()
output_details = interpreter.get_output_details()
```

In the preceding code, the get_input_details and get_output_details methods will retrieve these tensor's details, such as name, shape, and data type, and store these in input_details and output_details, respectively.

Scoring a single image

We will score a single image by expanding its dimension, as if this is a batch of a single image, pass it to the TFLite interpreter, and then get the output:

1. We may begin by handling the image array and expanding its dimensions for batch:

```
input_data = np.array(np.expand_dims(np_img_holder[0],
axis=0), dtype=np.float32)
interpreter.set_tensor(input_details[0]['index'], input_
data)
interpreter.invoke()
output_data = interpreter.get_tensor(output_details[0]
['index'])
print(output_data)
```

The preceding code expands the image to a batch dimension, and then passes it to the interpreter for prediction. The output of the preceding code is here:

```
[[1.1874483e-04 1.3445899e-05 8.4869811e-07 2.8064751e-06
9.9986410e-01]]
```

These are probabilities for each flower type. We need to map the position of highest probability to its plaintext name. That's where we will use the lookup function again.

2. We use a helper function (`lookup`) to convert probability into the most likely class name:

```
def lookup(np_entry, dictionary):
    class_key = np.argmax(np_entry)
    return dictionary.get(class_key)
lookup(output_data, val_label_map)
```

The output is as follows:

```
'tulips'
```

In the `lookup` function, the NumPy array, `np_entry`, is the output of our model. It contains the probability for each class. We want to map the position index of the array with the highest probability to the class name. To achieve this, this function maps it to the dictionary by key. In this case, it is the last position (which corresponds to position 4) in the probability array that has the highest probability. 4 is mapped to `tulips`.

Scoring batch images

Currently, batch scoring in the TFLite model is supported through the iterative scoring process of a single image. For our example of 50 test images, we may create a helper function to encapsulate the entire single image scoring process that we just went through in the previous Scoring a single image section with the hybrid quantization model:

1. We will iterate the entire dataset to score the batch with the help of the following code:

```
def batch_predict(input_raw, input_tensor, output_tensor,
dictionary):
    input_data = np.array(np.expand_dims(input_raw,
                          axis=0), dtype=np.float32)
    interpreter.set_tensor(input_tensor[0]['index'],
                                         input_data)
    interpreter.invoke()
    interpreter_output = interpreter.get_tensor(
                             output_tensor[0]['index'])
    plain_text_label = lookup(interpreter_output,
                                         dictionary)
    return plain_text_label
```

The `batch_predict()` function expands the raw image dimensions to batches, and then passes the batched image to the interpreter for scoring. The interpreter's output is then mapped to a plaintext name by means of the `lookup` function and the plaintext is returned as the predicted label.

2.   We then need to iterate through our test data to call on `batch_predict`:

```
batch_quantized_prediction = []
for i in range(sample_size):
    plain_text_label = batch_predict(np_img_holder[i],
input_details, output_details, val_label_map)
batch_quantized_prediction.append(plain_text_label)
```

We may evaluate the model's accuracy using the `accuracy_score` function in the sklearn library:

```
accuracy=accuracy_score(actual, batch_quantized_
prediction)
print(accuracy)
```

Its output is as follows:

```
0.82
```

The output here is shown to also be 82%. Results may vary if you retrained the model, but in my experience, it is identical to the accuracy of the base model.

> **Note**
>
> It's expected that your model accuracy will be slightly different from the nominal value printed here. Every time a base model is trained, the model accuracy will not be identical. However, it should not be too dissimilar to the nominal value. Another factor that impacts reproducibility in terms of model accuracy is the number of epochs used in training; in this case, only five epochs for demonstration and didactic purposes. More training epochs will give you a better and tighter variance in terms of model accuracy.

So far, we have learned about two types of post-training quantization techniques, namely, reduced `float16` quantization and hybrid quantization. Both techniques make the TFLite model significantly smaller than the original model. This is important when deploying the model in edge devices or devices with low compute or power resources.

In these two strategies, we quantized the middle layers and left the input and output untouched. Therefore, the input and output are not quantized and keep their respective original data types. However, in some devices that are optimized for speed and being lightweight, such as an edge TPU or devices that can only handle integer ops, we need to quantize the input and output layers to an integer type.

In the next section, we are going to learn the third quantization strategy, which is integer quantization, which would do precisely this.

Converting a full model to an integer quantization model

This strategy requires **TensorFlow 2.3**. This quantization strategy is suitable for an environment where compute resources are really constrained, or where the compute node only operates in integer mode, such as edge devices or TPUs. As a result, all parameters are changed to `int8` representation. This quantization strategy will try to use `int8` representation for all ops or operations as the goal. When this is not possible, the ops are left as the original precision (in other words, `float32`).

This quantization strategy requires some representative data. This data represents the type of data that the model typically expects in terms of a range of values. In other words, we need to provide either some training or validation data to the integer quantization process. This may be the data already used, such as a subset of the training or validation data. Usually, around 100 samples are recommended. We are going to use 80 samples from the validation data because this will suffice in this case.

In this section, we will build a model with a pre-trained ResNet feature vector from TensorFlow Hub. Once the training run is complete, we will use cross-validation data again as the representative dataset. This dataset will help the model to adjust parameters in both the input and output layers to integers.

Training a full model

We are going to use the same flower dataset as in `https://github.com/`
`PacktPublishing/learn-tensorflow-enterprise/tree/master/`
`chapter_07/train_base_model/tf_datasets`.

This is the same dataset that you used for reduced `float16` and hybrid quantization Let's get started:.

1. As usual, we begin by importing libraries and loading the datasets:

```
import tensorflow as tf
import tensorflow_hub as hub
import numpy as np
import os
import pathlib
root_dir = '../train_base_model/tf_datasets/flower_
photos'
file_pattern = '{}/image_classification_builder-train*.
tfrecord*'.format(root_dir)
val_file_pattern = '{}/image_classification_builder-
validation*.tfrecord*'.format(root_dir)
file_list = tf.io.gfile.glob(file_pattern)
all_files = tf.data.Dataset.list_files( tf.io.gfile.
glob(file_pattern))
val_file_list = tf.io.gfile.glob(val_file_pattern)
val_all_files = tf.data.Dataset.list_files( tf.io.gfile.
glob(val_file_pattern))
train_all_ds = tf.data.TFRecordDataset(all_files, num_
parallel_reads=tf.data.experimental.AUTOTUNE)
val_all_ds = tf.data.TFRecordDataset(val_all_files, num_
parallel_reads=tf.data.experimental.AUTOTUNE)
```

In the preceding code, we use the `tf.io` API to encapsulate the file path and all the filenames we will use, which are training, validation, and test data. Once we have the file paths encoded, we use `tf.data.TFRecordDatasedt` to reference these files. This process is performed for the training data, which is referenced by `train_all_ds`, and for the validation data, which is referenced by `val_all_ds`.

2. Then we will require the following helper functions to decode and standardize images, normalize pixel values, and set up a training dataset:

```
def decode_and_resize(serialized_example):
    # resized image should be [224, 224, 3] and
normalized to value range [0, 255]
    # label is integer index of class.
        parsed_features = tf.io.parse_single_example(
```

```
    serialized_example,
    features = {
    'image/channels' :  tf.io.FixedLenFeature([],
                                        tf.int64),
    'image/class/label' :  tf.io.FixedLenFeature([],
                                        tf.int64),
    'image/class/text' :  tf.io.FixedLenFeature([],
                                        tf.string),
    'image/colorspace' :  tf.io.FixedLenFeature([],
                                        tf.string),
    'image/encoded' :  tf.io.FixedLenFeature([],
                                        tf.string),
    'image/filename' :  tf.io.FixedLenFeature([],
                                        tf.string),
    'image/format' :  tf.io.FixedLenFeature([],
                                        tf.string),
    'image/height' :  tf.io.FixedLenFeature([], tf.int64),
    'image/width' :  tf.io.FixedLenFeature([], tf.int64)
    })
    image = tf.io.decode_jpeg(parsed_features[
                        'image/encoded'], channels=3)
    label = tf.cast(parsed_features['image/class/label'],
                                        tf.int32)
    label_txt = tf.cast(parsed_features[
                        'image/class/text'], tf.string)
    label_one_hot = tf.one_hot(label, depth = 5)
    resized_image = tf.image.resize(image, [224, 224],
                                    method='nearest')
    return resized_image, label_one_hot


def normalize(image, label):
    #Convert `image` from [0, 255] -> [0, 1.0] floats
    image = tf.cast(image, tf.float32) / 255. + 0.5
    return image, label
```

The decode_and_resize function parses an image, resizes it to 224 by 224 pixels, and, at the same time, one-hot encodes the image's label. decode_and_resize then returns the image and corresponding label as a tuple, so that the image and label are always kept together.

The `normalize` function divides the image pixel value by 255 in order to bring the pixel range to `[0, 1.0]`. And even though nothing is done in relation to the label, it is necessary to keep track of the image and label as a tuple so that they are always kept together.

3. We now need to define a function to shuffle and fetch the training dataset. Here is the function to achieve this:

```python
def prepare_for_training(ds, cache=True, shuffle_buffer_
size=1000):
    # This is a small dataset, only load it once, and
    # keep it in memory.
    # use `.cache(filename)` to cache preprocessing work
    # for datasets that don't fit in memory.
    if cache:
        if isinstance(cache, str):
            ds = ds.cache(cache)
        else:
            ds = ds.cache()
    ds = ds.shuffle(buffer_size=shuffle_buffer_size)
    # Repeat forever
    ds = ds.repeat()
    ds = ds.batch(32)
    # `prefetch` lets the dataset fetch batches in the
    # background while the model is training.
    AUTOTUNE = tf.data.experimental.AUTOTUNE
    ds = ds.prefetch(buffer_size=AUTOTUNE)
    return ds
```

This function returns a dataset with shuffle, repeat, batch, and prefetch ops attached. This is a standard approach for getting the dataset ready for training.

4. Now we may apply the following steps to each element in the training dataset:

```python
# perform data engineering
dataset = train_all_ds.map(decode_and_resize)
val_dataset = val_all_ds.map(decode_and_resize)
```

So now, `decode_and_resize` is applied to each image in `train_all_ds` and `val_all_ds`. The resulting datasets are `dataset` and `val_dataset`, respectively.

5. We also need to normalize the validation dataset and finalize the training dataset for the training run process:

```
# Create dataset for training run
BATCH_SIZE = 32
VALIDATION_BATCH_SIZE = 40
dataset = dataset.map(normalize,
        num_parallel_calls=tf.data.experimental.AUTOTUNE)
val_dataset = val_dataset.map(normalize,
        num_parallel_calls=tf.data.experimental.AUTOTUNE)
val_ds = val_dataset.batch(VALIDATION_BATCH_SIZE)
    AUTOTUNE = tf.data.experimental.AUTOTUNE
train_ds = prepare_for_training(dataset)
```

In the preceding code, we use the `map` function to apply the `decode_and_resize` function to each image in the dataset. For the training dataset, we also apply `prepare_for_training` to prefetch the dataset and for the ingestion process.

6. Now we will set up the parameters for cross-validation:

```
NUM_CLASSES = 5
IMAGE_SIZE = (224, 224)
    train_sample_size=0
for raw_record in train_all_ds:
    train_sample_size += 1
print('TRAIN_SAMPLE_SIZE = ', train_sample_size)
validation_sample_size=0
for raw_record in val_all_ds:
    validation_sample_size += 1
print('VALIDATION_SAMPLE_SIZE = ',
                            validation_sample_size)
STEPS_PER_EPOCHS = train_sample_size // BATCH_SIZE
VALIDATION_STEPS = validation_sample_size //
                        VALIDATION_BATCH_SIZE
```

In the preceding code, we set the number of classes and the image size in variables to be passed to the model training process. Then we determine the number of steps for each epoch of training and cross-validation.

The output should be as follows:

```
TRAIN_SAMPLE_SIZE =   3540
VALIDATION_SAMPLE_SIZE =   80
```

This indicates that we have a training data sample size of 3540, while the cross-validation data sample size is 80.

7. Now we will build the model with the help of the following code:

```
model = tf.keras.Sequential([
    tf.keras.layers.InputLayer(input_shape=IMAGE_SIZE +
(3,)),
    hub.KerasLayer(
    https://tfhub.dev/google/imagenet/resnet_v1_101/
feature_vector/4',
    trainable=False),
    tf.keras.layers.Dense(NUM_CLASSES,
        activation='softmax', name = 'custom_class')
])
model.build([None, 224, 224, 3])
model.compile(
  optimizer=tf.keras.optimizers.SGD(lr=0.005,
                                    momentum=0.9),
  loss=tf.keras.losses.CategoricalCrossentropy(
                from_logits=True, label_smoothing=0.1),
  metrics=['accuracy'])
model.summary()
```

In the preceding code, we built and compiled our model using TensorFlow Hub's ResNet feature vector as the middle layer, and the output is a classification layer denoted by a dense layer with five outputs, with each output node providing a probability for one of the five flower types.

Here is the model summary, and it consists of a layer from the *resnet_v1_101* feature vector, followed by a classification head, as indicated in *Figure 7.3*:

```
Model: "sequential"
```

Layer (type)	Output Shape	Param #
keras_layer (KerasLayer)	(None, 2048)	42605504
custom_class (Dense)	(None, 5)	10245

```
Total params: 42,615,749
Trainable params: 10,245
Non-trainable params: 42,605,504
```

Figure 7.3 – Model summary for flower type classification

We will then use the `fit` API to train this model with the training and cross-validation data provided.

8. The results of the model weights and biases are saved in the `checkpoint_prefix` directory. This is how we start the training process for the model to recognize five different types of flower images:

```
checkpoint_prefix = os.path.join('trained_resnet_vector',
'train_ckpt_{epoch}')
callbacks = [
    tf.keras.callbacks.ModelCheckpoint(
                            filepath=checkpoint_prefix,
        save_weights_only=True)]
model.fit(
        train_ds,
        epochs=3,
        steps_per_epoch=STEPS_PER_EPOCHS,
        validation_data=val_ds,
        validation_steps=VALIDATION_STEPS,
        callbacks=callbacks)
```

In the preceding code, the `fit` API is called to train the model. `train_ds` and `val_ds` are the training and cross-validation data, respectively. At each epoch, the weights and biases are stored as a checkpoint. This is specified by the callbacks. To save training time, we will only train it for three epochs.

9. Next, we will save the model using the following lines of code:

```
saved_model_path = os.path.join(root_dir, 'custom_cnn/
full_resnet_vector_saved_model')
```

```
tf.saved_model.save(model, saved_model_path)
```

We can inspect the weight matrix file to get an idea of the model size using the following command:

```
!ls -lrt <YOUR-HOME-PATH>/custom_cnn/full_resnet_vector_
saved_model/variables
```

You can expect a result similar to this. The weight and biases matrix is approximately 170 MB, as shown in *Figure 7.4*:

```
-rw-r--r-- 1 root root 170682633 Sep 14 23:48 variables.data-00000-of-00001
-rw-r--r-- 1 root root     39133 Sep 14 23:48 variables.index
```

Figure 7.4 – Model file size for the ResNet feature vector-based classification model

In this section, we leveraged the transfer learning technique to reuse the pre-trained ResNet feature vector with a multiclass classification head. The model is saved as a SavedModel format.

In order to properly quantize the input and output layers, we need to provide some typical data. We will use the validation data, which contains 80 samples of 5 classes of flower images:

10. Let's standardize and normalize the validation images:

```
decoded = val_all_ds.map(decode_and_resize)
normed = decoded.map(normalize)
```

11. Next, we expand by one dimension to batch the images. This extra dimension is intended for a variable batch size:

```
np_img_holder = np.empty((0, 224, 224,3), float)
np_lbl_holder = np.empty((0, 5), int)
for img, lbl in normed:
    r = img.numpy()
    rx = np.expand_dims(r, axis=0)
    lx = np.expand_dims(lbl, axis=0)
    np_img_holder = np.append(np_img_holder, rx, axis=0)
    np_lbl_holder = np.append(np_lbl_holder, lx, axis=0)
```

The image is now expanded by one dimension to indicate that the first dimension holds the number of images, which is the size of the image batch, and the normalized images are iterated through. As we iterate through each image, we capture the image value as a NumPy array and the corresponding label, and append `np_img_holder` and `np_lbl_holder`, respectively.

12. Now that we have images as a NumPy array, we need to build a generator that feeds this representative data into the conversion process:

```
def data_generator():
   for input_tensor in tf.data.Dataset.from_tensor_
slices(np_img_holder.astype(np.float32)).batch(1).
take(sample_size):
       yield [input_tensor]
```

We need to specify a function that is a generator to stream the representative data during the conversion process. This is done through the `data_generator` function. This function invokes the generator that streams a NumPy array.

13. Let's confirm our sample size:

```
sample_size = 0
for raw_record in val_all_ds:
    sample_size += 1
print('Sample size: ', sample_size)
```

The output from the preceding `print` statement is as follows:

```
Sample size:   80
```

The preceding code iterates through a validation dataset and keeps track of the sample count as it goes over a `for` loop. For every encounter of an image, a counter (`sample_size`, which is initialized to 0) is incremented by 1. Currently this is the only way to find out about sample sizes in a dataset. We have just confirmed that there are 80 samples in our validation data.

14. Now we may start the conversion process:

```
converter = tf.lite.TFLiteConverter.from_keras_
model(model)
converter.optimizations = [tf.lite.Optimize.DEFAULT]
converter.representative_dataset = data_generator
```

In the preceding code, we set up the converter instance and optimizer as in hybrid quantization, and then we set up a data generator object for the representative dataset.

15. We also want to throw an error flag if there are any ops that failed to be quantized:

```
converter.target_spec.supported_ops = [tf.lite.OpsSet.
TFLITE_BUILTINS_INT8]
```

In the preceding code, the supported data type we want for our model is set as an 8-bit integer (INT8).

16. Now we designate the input and output tensors to be INT8:

```
converter.inference_input_type = tf.uint8
converter.inference_output_type = tf.uint8
tflite_model_quant = converter.convert()
```

Now the model is converted to an integer quantization model. The model expects an input data type of an 8-bit integer (INT8) and will output the data type of an 8-bit integer (INT8).

17. Once the preceding code finishes the execution, we may inspect and verify the data type now associated with the input and output layer as unsigned INT8:

```
interpreter = tf.lite.Interpreter(model_content=tflite_
model_quant)
input_type = interpreter.get_input_details()[0]['dtype']
print('input: ', input_type)
output_type = interpreter.get_output_details()[0]
['dtype']
print('output: ', output_type)
```

In the preceding code, we first have to get the interpreter interface to the TFLite model. An interpreter object is the component in the TFLite model that executes the inference. It has methods such as get_input_details and get_output_details, which help us to look at the data types expected by the model during inference.

The following is the output of the preceding code:

```
input:   <class 'numpy.uint8'>
output:  <class 'numpy.uint8'>
```

The model expects an input data type of an 8-bit integer (INT8) and will output the data type of an 8-bit integer (INT8).

18. Now we can save the quantized model:

```
tflite_models_dir = 'quantized_resnet_vector/tflite_int8_
model'
to_save_tflite_model_dir = os.path.join(root_dir, tflite_
models_dir)
saved_tflite_models_dir = pathlib.Path(to_save_tflite_
model_dir)
saved_tflite_models_dir.mkdir(exist_ok=True,
parents=True)
tgt = pathlib.Path(to_save_tflite_model_dir, 'converted_
model_reduced.tflite')
tgt.write_bytes(tflite_model_quant)
```

Now, with the help of the preceding code, we set up a directory path and encode the path to a string. This string represents the path where we will write our integer quantized model. Finally, the write_bytes API completes the write process and saves our integer quantized model in the path as defined by the string, tflite_models_dir.

This shows the model size to be the following:

```
44526000
```

The preceding output shows that our integer quantization model is approximately 44 MB.

Next, we are going to see how well this model performs by scoring the test data.

Scoring with an integer quantization model

For scoring, we need to prepare the test dataset and a lookup table that maps the model output to a class name. Our test dataset contains labels encoded as an index and the corresponding class name. Therefore, we will use labels and class names from the test dataset as the ground truth. This will be compared to the model predictions.

Preparing a test dataset for scoring

As we did for the reduced `float16` and hybrid quantization models, we want to see how an integer quantization model performs with test data. Now we can start the process of scoring test images with the integer quantization model:

1. We will proceed by loading the TFRecord test:

    ```
    test_pattern = '{}/image_classification_builder-test.
    tfrecord*'.format(root_dir)
    test_all_files = tf.data.Dataset.list_files( tf.io.gfile.
    glob(test_pattern))

    test_all_ds = tf.data.TFRecordDataset(test_all_files,
    num_parallel_reads=tf.data.experimental.AUTOTUNE)
    ```

    In the preceding code, we use the `tf.io` API to encapsulate the file path and all the filenames we will use, which is the test data. Once we have the file paths encoded, we use `tf.data.TFRecordDatasedt` to reference the data. This process is done for the test data, which is referenced by `test_all_ds`.

2. Next, we can verify the sample size:

    ```
    sample_size = 0
    for raw_record in test_all_ds:
        sample_size += 1
    print('Sample size: ', sample_size)
    ```

    This will show that the sample size is `50`. The preceding code iterates through the validation dataset and keeps track of the sample count as it goes over a `for` loop. For every encounter of an image, a counter (`sample_size`, which is initialized to `0`) is incremented by `1`. Currently, this is the only way to find out about sample size in a dataset. We have just confirmed that there are 80 samples in our validation data.

3. As our model was quantized to handle integer ops, we don't want to normalize pixel values into floating-point values. We only need to standardize the image size:

    ```
    decoded = test_all_ds.map(decode_and_resize)
    ```

    Then we convert TFRecord to NumPy arrays of image data and labels.

4. We also need to expand the data dimensions to handle the batch of images:

    ```
    np_img_holder = np.empty((0, 224, 224,3), float)
    np_lbl_holder = np.empty((0, 5), int)
    ```

```
for img, lbl in decoded:
    r = img.numpy()
    rx = np.expand_dims(r, axis=0)
    lx = np.expand_dims(lbl, axis=0)
    np_img_holder = np.append(np_img_holder, rx, axis=0)
    np_lbl_holder = np.append(np_lbl_holder, lx, axis=0)
```

The image is now expanded by one dimension to indicate that the first dimension holds the number of images, which is the size of the image batch, and the normalized images are iterated through. As we iterate through each image, we capture the image value as a NumPy array and the corresponding label, and append `np_img_holder` and `np_lbl_holder`, respectively.

5. To create a lookup dictionary to map the label index to the class name, we may iterate through the TFRecord dataset to create a dictionary, `val_label_map`, but first, we need to know how to parse the TFRecord dataset. This means that we need to capture the tensors in the TFRecord dataset correctly. Therefore, we need to use the following `feature_description`:

```
feature_description = {
    'image/channels' :  tf.io.FixedLenFeature([],
                                            tf.int64),
    'image/class/label' :  tf.io.FixedLenFeature([],
                                            tf.int64),
    'image/class/text' : tf.io.FixedLenFeature([],
                                            tf.string),
    'image/colorspace' : tf.io.FixedLenFeature([],
                                            tf.string),
    'image/encoded' : tf.io.FixedLenFeature([],
                                            tf.string),
    'image/filename' : tf.io.FixedLenFeature([],
                                            tf.string),
    'image/format' : tf.io.FixedLenFeature([],
                                            tf.string),
    'image/height' : tf.io.FixedLenFeature([], tf.int64),
    'image/width' : tf.io.FixedLenFeature([], tf.int64)
}
```

The feature_description in the preceding code is a collection of key-value pairs. Each pair delineates a piece of metadata represented as a tensor:

```
def _parse_function(example_proto):
  return tf.io.parse_single_example(example_proto,
                                    feature_description)
parsd_ds = test_all_ds.map(_parse_function)
```

The preceding code shows how to parse test_all_ds with the feature_description provided. The result is a parsed dataset (parsd_ds) with all the necessary tensors defined and parsed:

```
val_label_map = {}
# getting label mapping
for image_features in parsd_ds.take(30):
    label_idx = image_features[
                            'image/class/label'].numpy()
    label_str = image_features[
                    'image/class/text'].numpy().decode()
    if label_idx not in val_label_map:
        val_label_map[label_idx] = label_str
```

We now need to find out how the dataset assigns indices to class labels. One way of doing this is to iterate through the whole dataset, or a portion of it. At each iteration, we capture both the label index and the corresponding plaintext for the label, and update this as a key-value pair in a dictionary such as val_label_map. This is shown as the preceding code.

6. We may inspect the dictionary by typing val_label_map in a notebook cell:

```
val_label_map
```

You may find val_label_map to be a dictionary such as this:

```
{0: 'roses', 1: 'sunflowers', 2: 'daisy', 3: 'dandelion',
 4: 'tulips'}
```

Keys are indexes of flower classes, and the values are plaintext names of flower classes.

7. We will create a helper function to handle the lookup:

```
def lookup(np_entry, dictionary):
    class_key = np.argmax(np_entry)
    return dictionary.get(class_key)
```

In the `lookup` function, the NumPy array `np_entry` is the output of our model. It contains the probability for each class. We want to map the position index of the array with the highest probability to the class name. To achieve this, this function maps it to the dictionary by key.

8. Next, we create a list that contains the ground truth flower class names:

```
actual = []
for i in range(len(np_lbl_holder)):
    class_key = np.argmax(np_lbl_holder[i])
    actual.append(val_label_map.get(class_key))
```

We can create a table that maps the integer value of the label to the corresponding plaintext name. In the preceding code, we first set up an empty list, `actual`, and then we use a `for` loop to iterate through the entire label holder, `np_lbl_holder`. The next step is to find the position where the maximum value occurs in this record, and assign it to `class_key`. `class_key` is the index that is used for looking up `val_label_map`, which maps the key to the corresponding plaintext name. The plaintext name is then added to `actual`. Then, the `for` loop starts over again with the next record it finds in `np_lbl_holder`.

Scoring batch images

A helper function is required for batch scoring. This is similar to what we used in the hybrid and reduced `float16` quantization models. The only difference lies in the data type for the NumPy array dimension expansion. Since we are using a model built by integer quantization, we need to cast the data type to an unsigned 8-bit integer (`uint8`):

1. This is a `batch_predict` function that treats the input NumPy array as an unsigned 8-bit integer (`uint8`):

```
def batch_predict(input_raw, input_tensor, output_tensor,
dictionary):
    input_data = np.array(np.expand_dims(input_raw,
                                axis=0), dtype=np.uint8)
    interpreter.set_tensor(input_tensor['index'],
```

```
                                        input_data)
    interpreter.invoke()
    interpreter_output = interpreter.get_tensor(
                            output_tensor['index'])
    plain_text_label = lookup(interpreter_output,
                                dictionary)
    return plain_text_label
```

This concludes the batch_predict function. This function takes the input_ raw array and scores it using our interpreter. The interpreter's output is then mapped to a plaintext label with the lookup function.

2. Let's now load the integer quantization model and set up the input and output tensors:

```
interpreter = tf.lite.Interpreter(model_path=str(tgt))
interpreter.allocate_tensors()
# Get input and output tensors.
input_details = interpreter.get_input_details()[0]
output_details = interpreter.get_output_details()[0]
```

In the preceding code, we initialized our quantization model and allocated memory for input tensors as per this model. The get_input_details and get_ output_details methods will then retrieve these tensors' details, such as the name, shape, and data type.

3. Then we may perform batched prediction:

```
batch_quantized_prediction = []
for i in range(sample_size):
    plain_text_label = batch_predict(np_img_holder[i],
            input_details, output_details, val_label_map)
    batch_quantized_prediction.append(plain_text_label)
```

In the preceding code, we iterate through the test images, score them, and then store the results in a list defined as batch_quantized_prediction.

4. We can calculate accuracy using accuracy_score from sklearn:

```
from sklearn.metrics import accuracy_score
accuracy_score(actual, batch_quantized_prediction)
```

The preceding function basically compares the `actual` list with the `batch_quantized_prediciton` list.

In this particular case, the accuracy is as follows:

```
0.86
```

> **Note**
>
> It's expected that your model accuracy will be slightly different from the nominal value printed here. Every time a base model is trained, the model accuracy will not be identical. However, it should not be too dissimilar to the nominal value. Another factor that impacts reproducibility in terms of model accuracy is the number of epochs used in training; in this case, only five epochs for demonstration and didactic purposes. More training epochs will give you a better and tighter variance in terms of model accuracy.

This result may vary if you retrained the full model over again, but it shouldn't be too dissimilar to this value. Furthermore, based on my experience with this data, integer quantized model performance is on a par with that of the original full model. The preceding code shows that our TFLite model performed just as well as the original model. As we reduce the model size through quantization, we are still able to preserve the model's accuracy. In this example, the accuracy is not impacted just because the model is now more compact.

Summary

In this chapter, we learned to optimize a trained model by making it smaller and therefore more compact. Therefore, we have more flexibility when it comes to deploying these models in various hardware or resource constrained conditions. Optimization is important for model deployment in a resource constrained environment such as edge devices with limited compute, memory, or power resources. We achieved model optimization by means of quantization, where we reduced the model footprint by altering the weight, biases, and activation levels' data type.

We learned about three quantization strategies: reduced `float16`, hybrid quantization, and integer quantization. Of these three strategies, integer quantization currently requires an upgrade to TensorFlow 2.3.

Choosing a quantization strategy depends on factors such as target compute, resource, model size limit, and model accuracy. Furthermore, you have to consider whether or not the target hardware requires integer ops only (in other words, TPU). If so, then integer quantization is the obvious choice. With all the examples, we learned that model accuracy is not impacted by model optimization strategies. After quantization, model size is a fraction of the original. This demonstrates the value of model optimization, especially when the deployment scenarios require efficient use of the compute and power resources.

In the next chapter, we are going to take a closer look at some common practices in the model building process. This practice involves data ingestion pipeline design and how to avoid model overfitting.

8
Best Practices for Model Training and Performance

In order for a supervised machine learning model to be well trained, it requires large volumes of training data. In this chapter, we are going to look at a few common examples and patterns for handling input data. We will specifically learn how to access training data regardless of its size and train the model with it. After that, we will look at regularization techniques that help to prevent overfitting. Having large volumes of training data is no guarantee of a well-trained model. In order to prevent overfitting, we may need to apply various regularization techniques in our training processes. We will take a look at a number of such techniques, starting with the typical Lasso (**L1**), Ridge (**L2**), and elastic net regularizations, before moving on to a modern regularization technique known as adversarial regularization. With these techniques at our disposal, we put ourselves in a good position vis-à-vis reducing overfitting as a result of training.

When it comes to regularization, there is no straightforward way to determine which method works best. It certainly depends on other factors, such as the distribution or sparsity of features and the volume of data. The purpose of this chapter is to provide various examples and give you several choices to try during your own model training process. In this chapter, we will cover the following topics:

- Input handling for loading data
- Regularization to reduce overfitting

Input handling for loading data

Many common examples that we typically see tend to focus on the modeling aspect, such as how to build a deep learning model using TensorFlow with various layers and patterns. In these examples, the data used is almost always loaded into the runtime memory directly. This is fine as long as the training data is sufficiently small. But what if it is much larger than your runtime memory can handle? The solution is data streaming. We have been using this technique to feed data into our model in the previous chapters, and we are going to take a closer look at data streaming and generalize it to more data types.

The streaming data technique is very similar to a Python generator. Data is ingested into the model training process in batches, meaning that all the data is not sent at one time. In this chapter, we are going to use an example of flower image data. Even though this data is not big by any means, it is a convenient tool for our teaching and learning purposes in this regard. It is multiclass and contains images of different sizes. This reflects what we usually have to deal with in reality, where available training images may be crowdsourced or provided at different scales or dimensions. In addition, an efficient data ingestion workflow is needed as the frontend to the model training process.

Working with the generator

When it comes to the generator, TensorFlow now has a very convenient `ImageDataGenerator` API that greatly simplifies and speeds up the code development process. From our experience in using pretrained models for image classification, we have seen that it is often necessary to standardize image dimensions (height and width as measured by the number of pixels) and normalize image pixel values to within a certain range (from [0, 255] to [0, 1]).

The `ImageDataGenerator` API provides optional input parameters to make these tasks almost routine and reduce the work of writing your own functions to perform standardization and normalization. So, let's take a look at how to use this API:

1. Organize raw images. Let's begin by setting up our image collection. For convenience, we are going to use the flower images directly from the `tf.keras` API:

```
import tensorflow as tf
import tensorflow_hub as hub
data_dir = tf.keras.utils.get_file(
    'flower_photos', 'https://storage.googleapis.com/
download.tensorflow.org/example_images/flower_photos.
tgz',
    untar=True)
```

In the preceding code, we use the `tf.keras` API to download the images of five flower types.

2. Next, we will set up `ImageDataGenerator` and streaming objects with `flow_from_directory`. In this step, several operations are defined:

a. Image pixel intensity is scaled to a range of [0, 255], along with a cross-validation fraction. The `ImageDataGenerator` API comes with optional input argument rescaling and `validation_split`. These arguments have to be in a dictionary format. Therefore, we can organize the rescale (normalization) factor and fraction for cross-validation together in `datagen_kwargs`.

b. The image height and width are both reformatted to 224 pixels. The `flow_from_directory` API contains the optional `target_size`, `batch_size`, and `interpolation` arguments. These arguments are designed in a dictionary format. We may use these input arguments to set image size standardization, batch size, and the resampling interpolation algorithm in `dataflow_kwargs`.

c. The preceding settings are passed to the generator instance. We then pass these into `ImageDataGenerator` and `flow_from_directory`:

```
pixels =224
BATCH_SIZE = 32
IMAGE_SIZE = (pixels, pixels)
NUM_CLASSES = 5
datagen_kwargs = dict(rescale=1./255, validation_
split=.20)
```

```
dataflow_kwargs = dict(target_size=IMAGE_SIZE,
                       batch_size=BATCH_SIZE,
                       interpolation="bilinear")
valid_datagen = tf.keras.preprocessing.image.
ImageDataGenerator(
    **datagen_kwargs)
valid_generator = valid_datagen.flow_from_directory(
    data_dir, subset="validation", shuffle=False,
**dataflow_kwargs)
train_datagen = valid_datagen
train_generator = train_datagen.flow_from_directory(
data_dir, subset="training", shuffle=True, **dataflow_
kwargs)
```

The preceding code demonstrates a typical workflow for creating image generators as a means of ingesting training data in to a model. Two dictionaries are defined and hold the arguments we need. Then, the `ImageDataGenerator` API is invoked, followed by the `flow_from_directory` API. The process is repeated for training data as well. For the results, we have set up an ingestion workflow for training and cross-validation data through `train_generator` and `valid_generator`.

3. Retrieve mapping for labels. Since we use `ImageDataGenerator` to create a data pipeline for training, we may use it to retrieve image labels as well:

```
labels_idx = (train_generator.class_indices)
idx_labels = dict((v,k) for k,v in labels_idx.items())
print(idx_labels)
```

In the preceding code, `idx_labels` is a dictionary that maps the classification model output, which is an index, to the `flower` class. This is `idx_labels`:

```
{0: 'daisy', 1: 'dandelion', 2: 'roses', 3: 'sunflowers',
4: 'tulips'}
```

Since this is a multiclass classification problem, our model prediction will be an array of five probabilities. Therefore, we want the position of the class with the highest probability, and then we will map the position to the name of the corresponding class using `idx_labels`.

4. Build and train the model. This step is the same as we performed in the previous chapter, *Chapter 7, Model Optimization*, where we will build a model by means of transfer learning. The model of choice is a ResNet feature vector, and the final classification layer is a dense layer with five nodes (NUM_CLASSES is defined to be 5, as indicated in *step 2*), and these five nodes output probabilities for each of the five classes:

```
mdl = tf.keras.Sequential([
    tf.keras.layers.InputLayer(input_shape=IMAGE_SIZE +
(3,)),
hub.KerasLayer("https://tfhub.dev/google/imagenet/resnet_
v1_101/feature_vector/4", trainable=False),
    tf.keras.layers.Dense(NUM_CLASSES,
            activation='softmax', name = 'custom_class')
])
mdl.build([None, 224, 224, 3])
mdl.compile(
  optimizer=tf.keras.optimizers.SGD(lr=0.005,
                                          momentum=0.9),
  loss=tf.keras.losses.CategoricalCrossentropy(from_
logits=True, label_smoothing=0.1),
  metrics=['accuracy'])
steps_per_epoch = train_generator.samples
                        // train_generator.batch_size
validation_steps = valid_generator.samples
                        // valid_generator.batch_size
mdl.fit(
    train_generator,
    epochs=5, steps_per_epoch=steps_per_epoch,
    validation_data=valid_generator,
    validation_steps=validation_steps)
```

The preceding code shows the general flow of setting up a model's architecture through training. We started by building an `mdl` model using the `tf.keras` sequential API. Once the `loss` function and optimizer were designated, we compiled the model. Since we want to include cross-validation as part of the training routine, we need to set up `step_per_epoch`, which is the total number of data batches for the generator to yield as one epoch. This process is repeated for cross-validation data. Then we call the Fit API to launch the training process for five epochs.

The preceding steps demonstrate how to start with `ImageDataGenerator` to build a pipeline that flows image data from the image directory via `flow_from_directory`, and we are also able to handle image normalization and standardization routines as input arguments.

TFRecord dataset – ingestion pipeline

Another means of streaming training data into the model during the training process is through the TFRecord dataset. TFRecord is a protocol buffer format. Data stored in this format may be used in **Python**, **Java**, and **C++**. In enterprise or production systems, this format may provide versatility and promote reusability of data across different applications. Another caveat for TFRecord is that if you wish to use TPU as your compute target, and you wish to use a pipeline to ingest training data, then TFRecord is the means to achieve it. Currently, TPU does not work with generators. Therefore, the only way to stream data through a pipeline approach is by means of TFRecord. Again, the size of this dataset does not require TFRecord in reality. This is only used for learning purposes.

We are going to start with a TFRecord dataset already prepared. It contains the same flower images and classes as seen in the previous section. In addition, this TFRecord dataset is partitioned into training, validation, and test datasets. This TFRecord dataset is available in this book's GitHub repository. You may clone this repository with the following command:

```
git clone https://github.com/PacktPublishing/learn-tensorflow-
enterprise.git
```

Once this command is complete, get in the following path:

```
 learn-tensorflow-enterprise/tree/master/chapter_07/train_base_
model/tf_datasets/flower_photos
```

You will see the following TFRecord datasets:

```
image_classification_builder-train.tfrecord-00000-of-00002
image_classification_builder-train.tfrecord-00001-of-00002
image_classification_builder-validation.tfrecord-00000-of-00001
image_classification_builder-test.tfrecord-00000-of-00001
```

Make a note of the file path where these datasets are stored.

We will refer to this path as `<PATH_TO_TFRECORD>`. This could be the path in your local system or any cloud notebook environment where you uploaded and mounted these TFRecord files:

1. Set up the file path. As you can see, in this TFRecord collection, there are multiple parts (two) of `train.tfrecord`. We will use the wildcard (`*`) symbol to denote multiple filenames that follow the same naming pattern. We may use `glob` to keep track of the pattern, pass it to `list_files` to create a list of files, and then let `TFRecordDataset` create a dataset object.

2. Recognize and encode the filename convention. We want to have a pipeline that can handle the data ingestion process. Therefore, we have to create variables to hold the file path and naming convention:

```python
import tensorflow as tf
import tensorflow_hub as hub
import tensorflow_datasets as tfds
root_dir = '<PATH_TO_TFRECORD>'
train_file_pattern = "{}/image_classification_builder-
train*.tfrecord*".format(root_dir)
val_file_pattern = "{}/image_classification_builder-
validation*.tfrecord*".format(root_dir)
test_file_pattern = "{}/image_classification_builder-
test*.tfrecord*".format(root_dir)
```

Here, we encoded text string representations of the file path to training, validation, and test data in the `train_file_pattern`, `val_file_pattern`, and `test_file_pattern` variables. Notice that we used the wildcard operator `*` to handle multiple file parts, if any. This is an important way to achieve scalability in data ingestion pipelines. It doesn't matter how many files there are, because now you have a way to find all of them by means of the path pattern.

3. Create a file list. To create an object that can handle multiple parts of TFRecord files, we will use `list_files` to keep track of these files:

    ```
    train_all_files = tf.data.Dataset.list_files( tf.io.
    gfile.glob(train_file_pattern))
    ```

    ```
    val_all_files = tf.data.Dataset.list_files( tf.io.gfile.
    glob(val_file_pattern))
    ```

    ```
    test_all_files = tf.data.Dataset.list_files( tf.io.gfile.
    glob(test_file_pattern))
    ```

    In the preceding code, we use the `tf.io` API to make a reference to the training, validation, and test files. The path to these files is defined by `train_file_pattern`, `val_file_pattern`, and `test_file_pattern`.

4. Create a dataset object. We will use `TFRecordDataset` to create dataset objects from training, validation, and test list objects:

    ```
    train_all_ds = tf.data.TFRecordDataset(train_all_files,
    num_parallel_reads = AUTOTUNE)
    ```

    ```
    val_all_ds = tf.data.TFRecordDataset(val_all_files, num_
    parallel_reads = AUTOTUNE)
    ```

    ```
    test_all_ds = tf.data.TFRecordDataset(test_all_files,
    num_parallel_reads = AUTOTUNE)
    ```

    The `TFRecordDataset` API reads the `TFRecord` file referenced by the file path variables.

5. Inspect the sample size. So far, there is no quick way to establish the sample size in each TFRecord. The only way to do so is by iterating it:

    ```
    print("Sample size for training: {0}".format(sum(1 for _
    in tf.data.TFRecordDataset(train_all_files)))
    ```

    ```
         ,'\n', "Sample size for validation: {0}".
    format(sum(1 for _ in tf.data.TFRecordDataset(val_all_
    files)))
    ```

    ```
         ,'\n', "Sample size for test: {0}".format(sum(1 for
    _ in tf.data.TFRecordDataset(test_all_files))))
    ```

    The preceding code prints and verifies the sample sizes in each of our TFRecord datasets.

The output should be as follows:

```
Sample size for training: 3540
Sample size for validation: 80
Sample size for test: 50
```

Since we are able to count samples in TFRecord datasets, we know that our data pipeline for TFRecord is set up correctly.

TFRecord dataset – feature engineering and training

When we used a generator as the ingestion pipeline, the generator took care of batching and matching data and labels during the training process. However, unlike the generator, in order to use the TFRecord dataset, we have to parse it and perform some necessary feature engineering tasks, such as normalization and standardization, ourselves. The creator of TFRecord has to provide a feature description dictionary as a **template** for parsing the samples. In this case, the following feature dictionary is provided:

```
features = {
    'image/channels' :  tf.io.FixedLenFeature([], tf.int64),
    'image/class/label' :  tf.io.FixedLenFeature([], tf.int64),
    'image/class/text' : tf.io.FixedLenFeature([], tf.string),
    'image/colorspace' : tf.io.FixedLenFeature([], tf.string),
    'image/encoded' : tf.io.FixedLenFeature([], tf.string),
    'image/filename' : tf.io.FixedLenFeature([], tf.string),
    'image/format' : tf.io.FixedLenFeature([], tf.string),
    'image/height' : tf.io.FixedLenFeature([], tf.int64),
    'image/width' : tf.io.FixedLenFeature([], tf.int64)
    })
```

We will go through the following steps to parse the dataset, perform feature engineering tasks, and submit the dataset for training. These steps follow the completion of the *TFRecord dataset – ingestion pipeline* section:

1. Parse TFRecord and resize the images. We will use the preceding dictionary to parse TFRecord in order to extract a single image as a NumPy array and its corresponding label. We will define a decode_and_resize function that should be used:

    ```
    def decode_and_resize(serialized_example):
        # resized image should be [224, 224, 3] and
        # normalized to value range [0, 255]
        # label is integer index of class.
    ```

```
      parsed_features = tf.io.parse_single_example(
        serialized_example,
        features = {
      'image/channels' :  tf.io.FixedLenFeature([],
                                                    tf.
  int64),
          'image/class/label' :  tf.io.FixedLenFeature([],
                                                    tf.
  int64),
          'image/class/text' : tf.io.FixedLenFeature([],
                                              tf.string),
          'image/colorspace' : tf.io.FixedLenFeature([],
                                              tf.string),
          'image/encoded' : tf.io.FixedLenFeature([],
                                              tf.string),
          'image/filename' : tf.io.FixedLenFeature([],
                                              tf.string),
          'image/format' : tf.io.FixedLenFeature([],
                                              tf.string),
          'image/height' : tf.io.FixedLenFeature([], tf.int64),
          'image/width' : tf.io.FixedLenFeature([], tf.int64)
          })
      image = tf.io.decode_jpeg(parsed_features[
                          'image/encoded'], channels=3)
      label = tf.cast(parsed_features[
                          'image/class/label'], tf.int32)
      label_txt = tf.cast(parsed_features
                          ['image/class/text'], tf.string)
      label_one_hot = tf.one_hot(label, depth = 5)
      resized_image = tf.image.resize(image, [224, 224],
                                      method='nearest')
  return resized_image, label_one_hot
```

The decode_and_resize function takes a dataset in TFRecord format, parses it, extracts the metadata and actual image, and then returns the image and its label.

At a more detailed level inside this function, the TFRecord dataset is parsed with `parsed_feature`. This is how we extract different metadata from the dataset. The image is decoded by the `decode_jpeg` API, and is resized to 224 x 224 pixels. As for the label, it is extracted and one-hot encoded. Finally, the function returns the resized image and the corresponding one-hot label.

2. Normalize the pixel value. We also need to normalize pixel values within the range $[0, 255]$. Here, we define a `normalize` function to do this:

```
def normalize(image, label):
    #Convert `image` from [0, 255] -> [0, 1.0] floats
    image = tf.cast(image, tf.float32) / 255.
    return image, label
```

Here, the image is rescaled, pixel-wise, to a range of $[0, 1.0]$ by dividing each pixel by `255`. The results are cast to `float32` to represent floating-point values. This function returns the rescaled image with its label.

3. Execute these functions. These functions (`decode_and_resize` and `normalize`) are designed to be applied to each sample within TFRecord. We use a map to accomplish this:

```
resized_train_ds = train_all_ds.map(decode_and_resize,
num_parallel_calls=AUTOTUNE)
resized_val_ds = val_all_ds.map(decode_and_resize, num_
parallel_calls=AUTOTUNE)
resized_test_ds = test_all_ds.map(decode_and_resize, num_
parallel_calls=AUTOTUNE)


resized_normalized_train_ds = resized_train_
ds.map(normalize, num_parallel_calls=AUTOTUNE)
resized_normalized_val_ds = resized_val_ds.map(normalize,
num_parallel_calls=AUTOTUNE)
resized_normalized_test_ds = resized_test_
ds.map(normalize, num_parallel_calls=AUTOTUNE)
```

Here, we apply `decode_and_resize` to all the datasets, and then normalize the dataset at a pixel-wise level.

4. Batch datasets for training processes. The final step to be performed on the TFRecord dataset is batching. We will define a few variables for this purpose, and define a function, `prepare_for_model`, for batching:

```
pixels =224
IMAGE_SIZE = (pixels, pixels)
TRAIN_BATCH_SIZE = 32
# Validation and test data are small. Use all in a batch.
VAL_BATCH_SIZE = sum(1 for _ in tf.data.
TFRecordDataset(val_all_files))
TEST_BATCH_SIZE = sum(1 for _ in tf.data.
TFRecordDataset(test_all_files))
def prepare_for_model(ds, BATCH_SIZE, cache=True,
TRAINING_DATA=True, shuffle_buffer_size=1000):
  if cache:
    if isinstance(cache, str):
      ds = ds.cache(cache)
    else:
      ds = ds.cache()
  ds = ds.shuffle(buffer_size=shuffle_buffer_size)
  if TRAINING_DATA:
    # Repeat forever
    ds = ds.repeat()
  ds = ds.batch(BATCH_SIZE)
  ds = ds.prefetch(buffer_size=AUTOTUNE)
  return ds
```

Cross-validation and test data are not separated into batches. Therefore, the entire cross-validation data is a single batch, and likewise for test data.

The `prepare_for_model` function takes a dataset and then caches it in memory and prefetches it. If this function is applied to the training data, it also repeats it infinitely to make sure you don't run out of data during the training process.

5. Execute batching. Use the `map` function to apply the `batching` function:

```
NUM_EPOCHS = 5
SHUFFLE_BUFFER_SIZE = 1000
prepped_test_ds = prepare_for_model(resized_normalized_
test_ds, TEST_BATCH_SIZE, False, False)
```

```
prepped_train_ds = resized_normalized_train_
ds.repeat(100).shuffle(buffer_size=SHUFFLE_BUFFER_SIZE)

prepped_train_ds = prepped_train_ds.batch(TRAIN_BATCH_
SIZE)

prepped_train_ds = prepped_train_ds.prefetch(buffer_size
= AUTOTUNE)

prepped_val_ds = resized_normalized_val_ds.repeat(NUM_
EPOCHS).shuffle(buffer_size=SHUFFLE_BUFFER_SIZE)

prepped_val_ds = prepped_val_ds.batch(80)

prepped_val_ds = prepped_val_ds.prefetch(buffer_size =
AUTOTUNE)
```

The preceding code sets up batches of training, validation, and test data. These are ready to be fed into the training routine. We have now completed the data ingestion pipeline.

6. Build and train the model. This part does not vary from the previous section. We will build and train a model with the same architecture as seen in the generator:

```
FINE_TUNING_CHOICE = False
NUM_CLASSES = 5
IMAGE_SIZE = (224, 224)
mdl = tf.keras.Sequential([
    tf.keras.layers.InputLayer(input_shape=IMAGE_SIZE +
                                (3,), name='input_layer'),
    hub.KerasLayer("https://tfhub.dev/google/imagenet/
resnet_v1_101/feature_vector/4", trainable=FINE_TUNING_
CHOICE, name = 'resnet_fv'),
    tf.keras.layers.Dense(NUM_CLASSES,
            activation='softmax', name = 'custom_class')
])
mdl.build([None, 224, 224, 3])
mdl.compile(
   optimizer=tf.keras.optimizers.SGD(lr=0.005,
                                        momentum=0.9),
   loss=tf.keras.losses.CategoricalCrossentropy(
                    from_logits=True, label_smoothing=0.1),
   metrics=['accuracy'])
mdl.fit(
    prepped_train_ds,
```

```
      epochs=5, steps_per_epoch=100,
      validation_data=prepped_val_ds,
      validation_steps=1)
```

Notice that the training and validation datasets are passed into the model as `prepped_train_ds` and `prepped_val_ds`, respectively. In this regard, it is no different to how we passed generators into the model for training. However, the extra work we had to do in terms of parsing, standardizing, and normalizing these datasets is substantially more complex compared to generators.

The benefit of TFRecord is that if you have a large dataset, then breaking it up and storing it as TFRecord in multiple parts will help you stream the data into the model faster than using a generator. Also, if your compute target is TPU, then you cannot stream training data using a generator; you will have to use the TFRecord dataset to stream training data into the model for training.

Regularization

During the training process, the model is learning to find the best set of weights and biases that minimize the `loss` function. As the model architecture becomes more complex, or simply starts to take on more layers, the model is being fitted with more parameters. Although this may help to produce a better fit during training, having to use more parameters may also lead to overfitting.

In this section, we will dive into some regularization techniques that can be implemented in a straightforward fashion in the `tf.keras` API.

L1 and L2 regularization

Traditional methods to address the concern of overfitting involve introducing a penalty term in the `loss` function. This is known as regularization. The penalty term is directly related to model complexity, which is largely determined by the number of non-zero weights. To be more specific, there are three traditional types of regularization used in machine learning:

- **L1 regularization** (also known as Lasso): Here is the `loss` function with L1 regularization:

$$Loss = Error(y, \hat{y}) + \lambda \sum_{i=1}^{N} |w_i|$$

It uses the sum of the absolute values of the weights, w, multiplied by a user-defined penalty value, λ, to measure complexity (that is, the number of parameters that are fitted to the model indicate how complex it is). The idea is that the more parameters, or weights, that are used, the higher the penalty applied. We want the best model with the fewest parameters.

- **L2 regularization** (also known as Ridge): Here is the `loss` function with L2 regularization:

$$Loss = Error(y, \hat{y}) + \lambda \sum_{i=1}^{N} w_i^2$$

It uses the sum of the squares of the weights, w, multiplied by a user-defined penalty value, λ, to measure complexity.

- **Elastic net regularization**: Here is the `loss` function with L1 and L2 regularization:

$$Loss = Error(y, \hat{y}) + \lambda_{L1} \sum_{i=1}^{N} |w_i| + \lambda_{L2} \sum_{i=1}^{N} w_i^2$$

It uses a combination of L1 and L2 to measure complexity. Each regularization term has its own penalty factor.

(Reference: *pp. 38-39, Antonio Gulli and Sujit Pal, Deep Learning with Keras, Packt 2017*, https://www.tensorflow.org/api_docs/python/tf/keras/regularizers/)

These are the keyword input parameters available for model layer definition, including dense or convolutional layers, such as Conv1D, Conv2D, and Conv3D:

- `kernel_regularizer`: A regularizer applied to the weight matrix
- `bias_regularizer`: A regularizer applied to the bias vector
- `activity_regularizer`: A regularizer applied to the output of the layer

(Reference: *p. 63, Antonio Gulli and Sujit Pal, Deep Learning with Keras, Packt 2017*, https://www.tensorflow.org/api_docs/python/tf/keras/regularizers/Regularizer)

Now we will take a look at how to implement some of these parameters. As an example, we will leverage the model architecture built in the previous section, namely, a ResNet feature vector layer followed by a dense layer as the classification head:

```
KERNEL_REGULARIZER = tf.keras.regularizers.l2(l=0.1)
ACTIVITY_REGULARIZER = tf.keras.regularizers.
```

```
L1L2(l1=0.1,l2=0.1)
```

```
mdl = tf.keras.Sequential([
    tf.keras.layers.InputLayer(input_shape=IMAGE_SIZE + (3,)),
    hub.KerasLayer("https://tfhub.dev/google/imagenet/resnet_
v2_50/feature_vector/4",trainable=FINE_TUNING_CHOICE),
    tf.keras.layers.Dense(NUM_CLASSES
                        ,activation='softmax'
                        ,kernel_regularizer=KERNEL_REGULARIZER
                        ,activity_regularizer =
                        ACTIVITY_REGULARIZER
                        ,name = 'custom_class')
])
mdl.build([None, 224, 224, 3])
```

Notice that we are using an alias to define regularizers of interest to us outside the layer. This will make it easy to adjust the hyperparameters (l1, l2) that determine how strongly we want the regularization term to penalize the loss function for potential overfit:

```
KERNEL_REGULARIZER = tf.keras.regularizers.l2(l=0.1)
ACTIVITY_REGULARIZER = tf.keras.regularizers.
L1L2(l1=0.1,l2=0.1)
```

This is followed by the addition of these regularizer definitions in the dense layer definition:

```
tf.keras.layers.Dense(NUM_CLASSES
                    ,activation='softmax'
                    ,kernel_regularizer=KERNEL_REGULARIZER
                    ,activity_regularizer =
                                        ACTIVITY_REGULARIZER
                    ,name = 'custom_class')
```

These are the only changes that are required to the code used in the previous section.

Adversarial regularization

An interesting technique known as adversarial learning emerged in 2014 (if interested, read the seminal paper published by *Goodfellow et al., 2014*). This idea stems from the fact that a machine learning model's accuracy can be greatly compromised, and will produce incorrect predictions, if the inputs are slightly noisier than expected. Such noise is known as adversarial perturbation. Therefore, if the training dataset is augmented with some random variation in the data, then we can use this technique to make our model more robust.

TensorFlow's `AdversarialRegularization` API is designed to complement the `tf.keras` API and simplify model building and training processes. We are going to reuse the TFRecord dataset downloaded as the original training data. Then we will apply a data augmentation technique to this dataset, and finally we will train the model. To do so follow the given steps:

1. Download and unzip the training data (if you didn't do so at the start of this chapter). You need to download flower_tfrecords.zip, the TFRecord dataset that we will use from Harvard Dataverse (`https://dataverse.harvard.edu/dataset.xhtml?persistentId=doi:10.7910/DVN/1ECTVN`). Put it in the compute node you intend to use. It may be your local compute environment or a cloud-based environment such as JupyterLab in Google AI Platform, or Google Colab. Unzip the file once you have downloaded it, and make a note of its path. We will refer to this path as `<PATH_TO_TFRECORD>`. In this path, you will see these TFRecord datasets:

    ```
    image_classification_builder-train.tfrecord-
    00000-of-00002
    ```

    ```
    image_classification_builder-train.tfrecord-
    00001-of-00002
    ```

    ```
    image_classification_builder-validation.tfrecord-
    00000-of-00001
    ```

    ```
    image_classification_builder-test.tfrecord-00000-of-00001
    ```

2. Install the library. We need to make sure that the neural structured learning module is available in our environment. If you haven't done so yet, you should install this module using the following `pip` command:

```
!pip install --quiet neural-structured-learning
```

3. Create a file pattern object for the data pipeline. There are multiple files (two). Therefore, we may leverage the file naming convention and wildcard * qualifier during the data ingestion process:

```
import tensorflow as tf
import neural_structured_learning as nsl
import tensorflow_hub as hub
import tensorflow_datasets as tfds
AUTOTUNE = tf.data.experimental.AUTOTUNE
root_dir = './tfrecord-dataset/flowers'
train_file_pattern = "{}/image_classification_builder-
train*.tfrecord*".format(root_dir)
val_file_pattern = "{}/image_classification_builder-
validation*.tfrecord*".format(root_dir)
test_file_pattern = "{}/image_classification_builder-
test*.tfrecord*".format(root_dir)
```

For convenience, the path to these TFRecord files is designated as the following variables: `train_file_pattern`, `val_file_pattern`, and `test_file_pattern`. These paths are represented as text strings. The wildcard symbol * is used to handle multiple file parts, in case there are any.

4. Take an inventory of all the filenames. We may use the `glob` API to create a dataset object that tracks all parts of the file:

```
train_all_files = tf.data.Dataset.list_files( tf.io.
gfile.glob(train_file_pattern))
val_all_files = tf.data.Dataset.list_files( tf.io.gfile.
glob(val_file_pattern))
test_all_files = tf.data.Dataset.list_files( tf.io.gfile.
glob(test_file_pattern))
```

Here, we use the `tf.io` API to refer to the file paths indicated in the previous step. The filenames referred to by the `glob` API of `tf.io` are then encoded in a list of filenames by the `list_files` API of `tf.data`.

5. Establish the loading pipeline. Now we may establish the reference to our data
    source via TFRecordDataset:

```
train_all_ds = tf.data.TFRecordDataset(train_all_files,
num_parallel_reads = AUTOTUNE)

val_all_ds = tf.data.TFRecordDataset(val_all_files, num_
parallel_reads = AUTOTUNE)

test_all_ds = tf.data.TFRecordDataset(test_all_files,
num_parallel_reads = AUTOTUNE)
```

Here, we use the TFRecordDataset API to create respective datasets from
our source.

6. To check whether we have total visibility of the data, we will count the sample sizes
    in each dataset:

```
train_sample_size = sum(1 for _ in tf.data.
TFRecordDataset(train_all_files))

validation_sample_size = sum(1 for _ in tf.data.
TFRecordDataset(val_all_files))

test_sample_size = sum(1 for _ in tf.data.
TFRecordDataset(test_all_files))

print("Sample size for training: {0}".format(train_
sample_size)

      ,'\n', "Sample size for validation: {0}".
format(validation_sample_size)

       ,'\n', "Sample size for test: {0}".format(test_
sample_size))
```

Currently, the way to find out how many samples are in a TFRecord file is by
iterating through it. In the code:

```
sum(1 for _ in tf.data.TFRecordDataset(train_all_files))
```

We use the for loop to iterate through the dataset, and sum up the iteration count
to obtain the final count as the sample size. This coding pattern is also used to
determine validation and test dataset sample sizes. The sizes of these datasets are
then stored as variables.

The output of the preceding code will look like this:

```
Sample size for training: 3540
Sample size for validation: 80
Sample size for test: 50
```

7. As regards data transformation, we need to transform all images to the same size, which is 224 pixels in height and 224 pixels in width. The intensity level of each pixel should be in the range [0, 1]. Therefore, we need to divide each pixel's value by 255. We need these two functions for these transformation operations:

```
def decode_and_resize(serialized_example):
    # resized image should be [224, 224, 3] and
    # normalized to value range [0, 255]
    # label is integer index of class.

    parsed_features = tf.io.parse_single_example(
      serialized_example,
      features = {
      'image/channels' :  tf.io.FixedLenFeature([],
                                                  tf.
int64),
        'image/class/label' :  tf.io.FixedLenFeature([],
                                                  tf.
int64),
        'image/class/text' : tf.io.FixedLenFeature([],
                                              tf.string),
        'image/colorspace' : tf.io.FixedLenFeature([],
                                              tf.string),
        'image/encoded' : tf.io.FixedLenFeature([],
                                              tf.string),
        'image/filename' : tf.io.FixedLenFeature([],
                                              tf.string),
        'image/format' : tf.io.FixedLenFeature([],
                                              tf.string),
        'image/height' : tf.io.FixedLenFeature([], tf.int64),
        'image/width' : tf.io.FixedLenFeature([], tf.int64)
      })
    image = tf.io.decode_jpeg(parsed_features[
                          'image/encoded'], channels=3)
```

```
    label = tf.cast(parsed_features['image/class/label'],
                                                    tf.int32)
    label_txt = tf.cast(parsed_features[
                            'image/class/text'], tf.string)
    label_one_hot = tf.one_hot(label, depth = 5)
    resized_image = tf.image.resize(image, [224, 224],
                                        method='nearest')
return resized_image, label_one_hot
```

The decode_and_resize function takes a dataset in TFRecord format, parses it, extracts the metadata and actual image, and returns the image and its label. At a more detailed level, inside this function, the TFRecord dataset is parsed with parsed_feature. This is how we extract different metadata from the dataset. The image is decoded by the decode_jpeg API, and it is resized to 224 by 224 pixels. As for the label, it is extracted and one-hot encoded.

8. Finally, the function returns the resized image and the corresponding one-hot label.

```
def normalize(image, label):
    #Convert `image` from [0, 255] -> [0, 1.0] floats
    image = tf.cast(image, tf.float32) / 255.
    return image, label
```

This function takes a JPEG image and normalizes pixel values (dividing each pixel by 255) in the range of [0, 1.0], and casts it to tf.float32 to represent floating-point values. It returns the normalized image with its corresponding label.

9. Execute data transformation. We will use the map function to apply the preceding transformation routines to each element in our dataset:

```
resized_train_ds = train_all_ds.map(decode_and_resize,
num_parallel_calls=AUTOTUNE)
resized_val_ds = val_all_ds.map(decode_and_resize, num_
parallel_calls=AUTOTUNE)
resized_test_ds = test_all_ds.map(decode_and_resize, num_
parallel_calls=AUTOTUNE)
resized_normalized_train_ds = resized_train_
ds.map(normalize, num_parallel_calls=AUTOTUNE)
resized_normalized_val_ds = resized_val_ds.map(normalize,
num_parallel_calls=AUTOTUNE)
resized_normalized_test_ds = resized_test_
ds.map(normalize, num_parallel_calls=AUTOTUNE)
```

In the preceding code, we apply `decode_and_resize` to each dataset, and then we rescale it by applying the `normalize` function to each pixel in the dataset.

10. Define the parameters for training. We need to specify the batch size for our dataset, as well as the parameters that define the epochs:

```
pixels =224
IMAGE_SIZE = (pixels, pixels)
TRAIN_BATCH_SIZE = 32
VAL_BATCH_SIZE = validation_sample_size
TEST_BATCH_SIZE = test_sample_size
NUM_EPOCHS = 5
SHUFFLE_BUFFER_SIZE = 1000
FINE_TUNING_CHOICE = False
NUM_CLASSES = 5
prepped_test_ds = resized_normalized_test_ds.batch(TEST_
BATCH_SIZE).prefetch(buffer_size = AUTOTUNE)
prepped_train_ds = resized_normalized_train_
ds.repeat(100).shuffle(buffer_size=SHUFFLE_BUFFER_SIZE)
prepped_train_ds = prepped_train_ds.batch(TRAIN_BATCH_
SIZE)
prepped_train_ds = prepped_train_ds.prefetch(buffer_size
= AUTOTUNE)
prepped_val_ds = resized_normalized_val_ds.repeat(NUM_
EPOCHS).shuffle(buffer_size=SHUFFLE_BUFFER_SIZE)
prepped_val_ds = prepped_val_ds.batch(80)
prepped_val_ds = prepped_val_ds.prefetch(buffer_size =
AUTOTUNE)
```

In the preceding code, we defined the parameters required to set up the training process. Datasets are also batched and fetched for consumption.

Now we have built our dataset pipeline that will fetch a batch of data at a time to ingest into the model training process.

11. Build your model. We will build an image classification model using the ResNet feature vector:

```
mdl = tf.keras.Sequential([
    tf.keras.layers.InputLayer(input_shape=IMAGE_SIZE +
(3,)),
    hub.KerasLayer("https://tfhub.dev/google/imagenet/
```

```
resnet_v2_50/feature_vector/4",trainable=FINE_TUNING_
CHOICE),
    tf.keras.layers.Dense(NUM_CLASSES,
activation='softmax', name = 'custom_class')
])
mdl.build([None, 224, 224, 3])
```

We use the `tf.keras` sequential API to build an image classification model. It first uses the input layer to accept the training data as 224 by 224 by 3 pixels. Then we leverage the feature vector of `ResNet_V2_50` as the middle layer. We will use it as is (`trainable` = `FINE_TUNING_CHOICE`. `FINE_TUNING_CHOICE` is set to `False` in the previous step. If you wish, you may set it to `True`. However, this would increase your training time significantly). Finally, the output layer is represented by a dense layer with five nodes (`NUM_CLASSES` = 5). Each node represents a probability value for the respective flower type.

So far, there is nothing specific to adversarial regularization. Starting with the next step, we will begin by building a configuration object that specifies adversarial training data and launch the training process.

12. Convert the training samples to a dictionary. A particular requirement for adversarial regularization is to have training data and labels combined as a dictionary and then streamed into the training process. This can easily be accomplished with the following function:

```
def examples_to_dict(image, label):
    return {'image_input': image, 'label_output': label}
```

This function accepts the image and corresponding label, and then reformats these as key-value pairs in a dictionary.

13. Convert the data and label collection into a dictionary. For the batched dataset, we may use the `map` function again to apply `examples_to_dict` to each element in the dataset:

```
train_set_for_adv_model = prepped_train_ds.map(examples_
to_dict)
val_set_for_adv_model = prepped_val_ds.map(examples_to_
dict)
test_set_for_adv_model = prepped_test_ds.map(examples_to_
dict)
```

In this code, each sample in the dataset is also converted to a dictionary. This is done via the map function. The map function applies the examples_to_dict function to each element (sample) in the dataset.

14. Create an adversarial regularization object. Now we are ready to create an adv_config object that specifies adversarial configuration. Then we wrap the mdl base model we created in a previous step with adv_config:

```
adv_config = nsl.configs.make_adv_reg_config()
adv_mdl = nsl.keras.AdversarialRegularization(mdl,
label_keys=['label_output'],
adv_config=adv_config)
```

Now we have a model, adv_mdl, that contains the base model structure as defined by mdl. adv_mdl includes knowledge of the adversarial configuration, adv_config, which will be used to create adversarial images during the training process.

15. Compile and train the model. This part is similar to what we did previously. It is no different to training the base model, except for the input dataset:

```
adv_mdl.compile(optimizer=tf.keras.optimizers.
SGD(lr=0.005, momentum=0.9),
    loss=tf.keras.losses.CategoricalCrossentropy(
                  from_logits=True, label_smoothing=0.1),
    metrics=['accuracy'])
adv_mdl.fit(
    train_set_for_adv_model,
    epochs=5, steps_per_epoch=100,
    validation_data=val_set_for_adv_model,
    validation_steps=1)
```

Notice now the input to the fit function for training is train_set_for_adv_model and val_set_for_adv_model, which is a dataset that streams each sample as a dictionary into the training process.

It doesn't take a lot of work to set up adversarial regularization with tf.keras and adversarial regularization APIs. Basically, an extra step is required to reformat the sample and label into a dictionary. Then, we wrap our model using the nsl.keras.AdversarialRegularization API, which encapsulates the model architecture and adversarial regularization object. This makes it very easy to implement this type of regularization.

Summary

This chapter presented some common practices for enhancing and improving your model building and training processes. One of the most common issues in dealing with training data handling is to stream or fetch training data in an efficient and scalable manner. In this chapter, you have seen two methods to help you build such an ingestion pipeline: generators and datasets. Each has its strengths and purposes. Generators manage data transformation and batching quite well, while a dataset API is designed where a TPU is the target.

We also learned how to implement various regularization techniques using the traditional L1 and L2 regularization, as well as a modern regularization technique known as adversarial regularization, which is applicable to image classification. Adversarial regularization also manages data transformation and augmentation on your behalf to save you the effort of generating noisy images. These new APIs and capabilities enhance TensorFlow Enterprise's user experience and help save on development time.

In the next chapter, we are going to see how to serve a TensorFlow model with TensorFlow Serving.

9
Serving a TensorFlow Model

By now, after learning all the previous chapters, you have seen many facets of a model building process in **TensorFlow Enterprise (TFE)**. Now it is time to wrap up what we have done and look at how we can serve the model we have built. In this chapter, we are going to look at the fundamentals of serving a TensorFlow model, which is through a RESTful API in localhost. The easiest way to get started is by using **TensorFlow Serving (TFS)**. Out of the box, TFS is a system for serving machine learning models built with TensorFlow. Although it is not yet officially supported by TFE, you will see that it works with models built by TFE 2. It can run as either a server or as a Docker container. For our ease, we are going to use a Docker container, as it is really the easiest way to start using TFS, regardless of your local environment, as long as you have a Docker engine available. In this chapter, we will cover the following topics:

- Running Local Serving
- Understanding TFS with Docker
- Downloading TFS Docker images

Technical requirements

To follow along with this chapter, and for trying the example code here: `https://github.com/PacktPublishing/learn-tensorflow-enterprise`, you will need to clone the GitHub repository for this book, and navigate to the folder in `chapter_09`. You may clone the repository with the following command:

```
git clone https://github.com/PacktPublishing/learn-tensorflow-
enterprise.git
```

We will work from the folder named `chapter_09`. Inside this folder, there is a Jupyter notebook containing source code. You will also find the `flowerclassifier/001` directory, which contains a `saved_model.pb` file ready for your use. In the `raw_images` directory, you will find a few raw JPG images for testing.

Running Local Serving

A prerequisite to serving the model is serialization of the model structure and its assets, such as weights and biases matrices. A trained TensorFlow model is typically saved in a `SavedModel` format. A `SavedModel` format consists of the complete TensorFlow program with weights, biases, and computation ops. This is done through the low-level `tf.saved_model` API.

Typically, when you execute a model training process using Fit, you end up with something like this:

```
mdl.fit(
    train_dataset,
    epochs=5, steps_per_epoch=steps_per_epoch,
    validation_data=valid_dataset,
    validation_steps=validation_steps)
```

After you've executed the preceding code, you have a model object, `mdl`, that can be saved via the following syntax:

```
saved_model_path = ''
tf.saved_model.save(mdl, saved_model_path)
```

If you take a look at the current directory, you will find a `saved_model.pb` file there.

For your convenience, a `saved_model` file is provided for this exercise. In the `flowerclassifier/001` directory, you will find the following output:

```
-rw-r--r--  1 2405393 Oct 12 22:02 saved_model.pb
drwxr-xr-x@ 2      64 Oct 12 22:02 assets
drwxr-xr-x@ 4     128 Oct 12 22:02 variables
```

Notice that `save_model_path` is defined as `null`. This indicates that the model is to be saved in the current directory. If you have another directory that you want to use, you need to specify the full or relative path for that directory.

`saved_model.pb` is the Protobuf format of the model structure. The `assets` folder contains objects such as a vocabulary list or any lookup table, which are necessary for model execution. It may be empty if no such objects are created or required. The `variables` folder contains the weights and bias values as the result of training. These items constitute `SavedModel`. We are going to take a look at how to invoke `SavedModel` for scoring test data. Now let's turn our attention to the Jupyter notebook in this chapter's GitHub repository:

1. If you simply want to use a Python script to invoke `SavedModel`, it is very simple. All you need to do is load the model as follows:

    ```
    path_saved_model =  'flowerclassifier/001'
    working_model = tf.saved_model.load(path_saved_model)
    ```

2. Each `SavedModel` has a default model signature that describes model inputs and outputs structures. This signature also has a name associated with it. We need to find out what this name is:

    ```
    print(list(working_model.signatures.keys()))
    ```

    Since the signature name is not specified during the save process, the output of the signature name is as follows:

    ```
    ['serving_default']
    ```

3. Next, we need to create an inference object, `infer`, and then find the name for the model output as well as its shape, which are required when using this model to score test data:

    ```
    infer = working_model.signatures['serving_default']
    print(infer.structured_outputs)
    ```

This will output the following:

```
{'custom_class': TensorSpec(shape=(None, 5), dtype=tf.
float32, name='custom_class')}
```

The output is named `custom_class`, and it is a tensor with a floating-point NumPy array of `shape=(None, 5)`. This indicates that the output is an array of probabilities for each of the five flower types. And the position index of the array with the highest probability is what we need to map to the flower type. We have seen this map in *Chapter 7*, *Model Optimization*, where we learned how to process TFRecord to build and train this model. This is the map:

```
{4: 'tulips', 3: 'dandelion', 1: 'sunflowers', 2:
'daisy', 0: 'roses'}
```

If the highest probability is in the first position in the `custom_class` output's array, then the prediction is mapped to `roses`. If it is in the fifth position, then the prediction is mapped to `tulips`.

4. Another thing we need to confirm is the shape of the input expected by the model. We may use `save_model_cli` to give us this information. We may execute this inline command in the Jupyter notebook cell:

    ```
    !saved_model_cli show --dir {path_saved_model} --all
    ```

    You will observe that the output of this command includes the following:

    ```
    signature_def['serving_default']:
      The given SavedModel SignatureDef contains the
    following input(s):
        inputs['input_4'] tensor_info:
          dtype: DT_FLOAT
          shape: (-1, 224, 224, 3)
    ```

    Notice the `shape` requirement. We know that (224, 224, 3) refers to the image dimensions. -1 in the first dimension indicates this input is set up to handle multiple (batches) of (224, 224, 3) image arrays. Therefore, if we want to score one image, we need to expand that image by a dimension.

5. Let's use a test image in the `raw_image` directory and read the image with the `nvision` library's `imread`:

```
jpg1 = 'raw_images2440874162_27a7030402_n.jpg'
img1_np = nv.imread(jpg1, resize=(224,224),normalize=True)
img1_np = nv.expand_dims(img1_np,axis=0)
```

Notice that we only need to provide the height and width for resizing images to the correct pixel count in each dimension.

6. Use the `infer` object to score this image:

```
prediction = infer(tf.constant(img1_np))
```

This produces the prediction for each of the five flower types, given `img1_np`:

```
prediction['custom_class'].numpy()
```

This generates the following output:

```
array([[2.4262092e-06, 5.6151916e-06, 1.8000206e-05,
1.4342861e-05, 9.9995959e-01]], dtype=float32)
```

The highest probability occurs in the fifth position with a value of $9.9995959e-01$. Therefore, based on the aforementioned map in *step 3*, this image is mapped to `tulips`.

We have seen how to use `SavedModel` for inference. This requires us to work in a Python runtime to load the model, read the image, and pass it to the model for scoring. In a production or application environment, however, the call to model is usually through TFS. In the next section, we are going to see how to make this model work with this approach.

Understanding TensorFlow Serving with Docker

At the core of TFS is actually a TensorFlow model server that runs a model Protobuf file. Installing the model server is not straightforward, as there are many dependencies. As a convenience, the TensorFlow team also provides this model server in a Docker container, which is a platform that uses virtualization at the operating system level, and it is self-contained with all the necessary dependencies (that is, libraries or modules) to run in an isolated environment.

Therefore, the easiest way to deploy a TensorFlow `SavedModel` is by means of TFS with a Docker container. To install Docker, you can refer to the Docker site (`https://docs.docker.com/install/`), along with the instructions for Mac, Windows, or Linux installations. For our chapter, a community version will suffice. We will be using Docker Desktop 2.4 running in macOS Catalina 10.15.6 with specs as indicated in *Figure 9.1*:

Figure 9.1 – The Docker version used for this chapter

It is assumed that you have installed Docker Desktop properly and that it is running. At a high level, we are going to download a TFS Docker image, add our model to it, and build a new Docker image on top of the base image, which is TFS. The final image is exposed through a TCP/IP port, which handles a RESTful API call from a client.

Downloading TensorFlow Serving Docker images

Once the Docker engine is up and running, you are ready to perform the following steps:

1. You may pull the latest TFS Docker image with this Docker command:

    ```
    docker pull tensorflow/serving
    ```

2. This is now our base image. In order to add our model on top of this image, we need to run this base image first:

    ```
    docker run -d --name serv_base_img tensorflow/serving
    ```

In the preceding command, we invoked the `tensorflow/serving` image and now it is running as a Docker container. We also name this container `serv_base_img`.

Creating a new image with the model and serving it

Let's now take a look at the file directory here. For this example, the directory structure is as shown in the following figure:

Figure 9.2 – Directory structure for creating a custom Docker container

We will execute the following commands from the same directory as `Tensorflow_Serving.ipynb`.

After we have the TFS base Docker image up and running as a container, we are ready to put our own `SavedModel` into this container:

1. Basically, we have to copy our model into the TFS container's `model` folder:

    ```
    docker cp ${PWD}/flowerclassifier serv_base_img:/models/
    flowerclassifier
    ```

    `flowerclassifier` is the directory name two levels up from the `saved_model.pb` file. In between the two, you will notice that there is a directory, `001`. This hierarchy is required by TFS, and so is the naming convention for the middle directory, which has to be an integer. It doesn't have to be `001`, as long as it is all integers.

The preceding command copies our model into the base image's `/model` directory.

2. Now we commit our change to the base image and give the container a name that matches our model directory:

```
docker commit --change "ENV MODEL_NAME flowermodel" serv_
base_img flowermodel
```

3. We no longer require the base image to be running. Now we can just kill it:

```
docker kill serv_base_img
```

What we have done so far is create a Docker image of our model, `flowermodel`, which is deployed in a TFS container. Once we launch the TFS container, it brings our model up for serving.

4. To serve the image and score on our test image, we will run the following command:

```
docker run -p 8501:8501 \
    --mount type=bind,\
source=$PWD/flowerclassifier,\
target=/models/flowerclassifier \
    -e MODEL_NAME=flowerclassifier -t tensorflow/serving &
```

We first open a local TC/PIP port, `8501`, and map it to the Docker container's port, `8501`. If your local port `8501` is not available, you may try another local port, say `8502`. Then the command would take on `-p 8502:8501`.

The source of our model is in the current directory (as indicated by the inline `$PWD` command) and followed by `flowerclassifier`. This folder also defines an environment variable, `MODEL_NAME`. `-t tensorflow/serving` indicates we want the container to be ready for `STDIN` from `tensorflow/serving`.

At your command terminal, you will observe output such as that shown in the following figure:

```
                         model_works — -zsh • com.docker.cli — 139×45
(tf23) (base) mbp16@casablancas-MacBook-Pro model_works % docker run -p 8501:8501 \
  --mount type=bind,\
source=$PWD/flowerclassifier,\
target=/models/flowerclassifier \
  -e MODEL_NAME=flowerclassifier -t tensorflow/serving &
[1] 4610
(tf23) (base) mbp16@casablancas-MacBook-Pro model_works % 2020-10-19 21:14:18.983925: I tensorflow_serving/model_servers/server.cc:87] Buil
ding single TensorFlow model file config:  model_name: flowerclassifier model_base_path: /models/flowerclassifier
2020-10-19 21:14:18.984146: I tensorflow_serving/model_servers/server_core.cc:464] Adding/updating models.
2020-10-19 21:14:18.984181: I tensorflow_serving/model_servers/server_core.cc:575]  (Re-)adding model: flowerclassifier
2020-10-19 21:14:19.098190: I tensorflow_serving/core/basic_manager.cc:739] Successfully reserved resources to load servable (name: flowerc
lassifier version: 1}
2020-10-19 21:14:19.098271: I tensorflow_serving/core/loader_harness.cc:66] Approving load for servable version (name: flowerclassifier ver
sion: 1}
2020-10-19 21:14:19.098315: I tensorflow_serving/core/loader_harness.cc:74] Loading servable version (name: flowerclassifier version: 1}
2020-10-19 21:14:19.099343: I external/org_tensorflow/tensorflow/cc/saved_model/reader.cc:31] Reading SavedModel from: /models/flowerclassi
fier/001
2020-10-19 21:14:19.150111: I external/org_tensorflow/tensorflow/cc/saved_model/reader.cc:54] Reading meta graph with tags { serve }
2020-10-19 21:14:19.150301: I external/org_tensorflow/tensorflow/cc/saved_model/loader.cc:234] Reading SavedModel debug info (if present) f
rom: /models/flowerclassifier/001
2020-10-19 21:14:19.152103: I external/org_tensorflow/tensorflow/core/platform/cpu_feature_guard.cc:142] This TensorFlow binary is optimize
d with oneAPI Deep Neural Network Library (oneDNN)to use the following CPU instructions in performance-critical operations:  AVX2 FMA
To enable them in other operations, rebuild TensorFlow with the appropriate compiler flags.
2020-10-19 21:14:19.234844: I external/org_tensorflow/tensorflow/cc/saved_model/loader.cc:199] Restoring SavedModel bundle.
2020-10-19 21:14:19.766939: W external/org_tensorflow/tensorflow/core/framework/cpu_allocator_impl.cc:81] Allocation of 9437184 exceeds 10%
 of free system memory.
2020-10-19 21:14:19.827168: W external/org_tensorflow/tensorflow/core/framework/cpu_allocator_impl.cc:81] Allocation of 8388608 exceeds 10%
 of free system memory.
2020-10-19 21:14:19.891709: W external/org_tensorflow/tensorflow/core/framework/cpu_allocator_impl.cc:81] Allocation of 9437184 exceeds 10%
 of free system memory.
2020-10-19 21:14:19.964423: W external/org_tensorflow/tensorflow/core/framework/cpu_allocator_impl.cc:81] Allocation of 9437184 exceeds 10%
 of free system memory.
2020-10-19 21:14:20.032284: I external/org_tensorflow/tensorflow/cc/saved_model/loader.cc:183] Running initialization op on SavedModel bund
le at path: /models/flowerclassifier/001
2020-10-19 21:14:20.106305: I external/org_tensorflow/tensorflow/cc/saved_model/loader.cc:303] SavedModel load for tags { serve }; Status:
success: OK. Took 1006981 microseconds.
2020-10-19 21:14:20.117126: I tensorflow_serving/servables/tensorflow/saved_model_warmup_util.cc:59] No warmup data file found at /models/f
lowerclassifier/001/assets.extra/tf_serving_warmup_requests
2020-10-19 21:14:20.124194: I tensorflow_serving/core/loader_harness.cc:87] Successfully loaded servable version (name: flowerclassifier ve
rsion: 1}
2020-10-19 21:14:20.127435: I tensorflow_serving/model_servers/server.cc:367] Running gRPC ModelServer at 0.0.0.0:8500 ...
[warn] getaddrinfo: address family for nodename not supported
2020-10-19 21:14:20.129379: I tensorflow_serving/model_servers/server.cc:387] Exporting HTTP/REST API at:localhost:8501 ...
[evhttp_server.cc : 238] NET_LOG: Entering the event loop ...
```

Figure 9.3 – Docker container running with a custom-built model

Notice the following in the preceding screenshot: **Successfully loaded servable version {name: flowerclassifier version: 1}**.

This line indicates that the container successfully found our model, flowerclassifier, and the next directory in the naming hierarchy, 001. This is a general pattern that TFS needs in order to make TFS work with a custom model that you have built.

Now the model is served. In the next section, we will see how to build our client that calls this model using the Python JSON library.

Scoring through the RESTful API

Now let's return to our Jupyter environment. We will see how to pick up from what we did in Local Serving and continue from there. Recall that we used the `nvision` library to normalize and standardize our test image. We also need to expand the image dimension because the model expects to have a batch dimension in our input. After we have performed these steps as in Local Serving, we will have `img1_np` as the properly shaped NumPy array. Let's build this array into a JSON payload, and pass the payload to our model through the RESTful API with the help of the following steps:

1. We will build the JSON payload with the following command:

   ```
   data = json.dumps({
       "instances": img1_np.tolist()
   })
   headers = {"content-type": "application/json"}
   ```

   In the preceding code, we converted the test image into a JSON payload format and we defined a header for our RESTful API call to indicate that the payload is in JSON format for the application to consume.

   As per TFS, the payload must encode the scoring data with a key-value pair by the key name of the instances and the NumPy array to be converted to a list as the input. We also need a header to be defined for the JSON payload as well.

2. We will score our test image, `img1_np`, for this data with the following command:

   ```
   response = requests.post('http://localhost:8501/
   v1/models/flowerclassifier:predict', data=data,
   headers=headers)
   ```

   The preceding command will produce a `response` payload back from our TFS container.

3. We will examine the `response` payload by using the following command:

   ```
   response.json()
   ```

   The following is the output of the preceding command:

   ```
   {'predictions': [[2.42621149e-06,
       5.61519164e-06,
       1.80002226e-05,
       1.43428879e-05,
       0.999959588]]}
   ```

This is a dictionary containing the key prediction and the probability values for each of the five flower types. These values are identical to what we saw in Local Serving. Therefore, we know that the model is correctly served via TFS using a Docker container.

Summary

In this chapter, you learned how to deploy a TensorFlow `SavedModel`. This is by no means the most common method to use in enterprise deployment. In an enterprise deployment scenario, many factors determine how the deployment pipeline should be built, and depending on the use cases, it can quickly diverge in terms of deployment patterns and choices from there. For example, some organizations use AirFlow as their orchestration tool, and some may prefer KubeFlow, while many others still use Jenkins.

The goal of this book is to show you how to leverage the latest and most reliable implementation of TensorFlow Enterprise from a data scientist/machine learning model builder's perspective.

From here, depending on your interests or priorities, you may take up what you learned in this book and pursue many other topics, such as MLOps, model orchestration, drift monitoring, and redeployment. These are some of the important topics in any enterprise machine learning discussions from a use case perspective. Use cases, IT infrastructure, and business considerations typically determine how a model is actually served. Further considerations include what kind of service-level agreement the serving pipeline has to meet, and the security and compliance issues related to authentication and model safety.

Other Books You May Enjoy

If you enjoyed this book, you may be interested in these other books by Packt:

Advanced Deep Learning with TensorFlow 2 and Keras

Rowel Atienza

ISBN: 978-1-83882-165-4

- Use mutual information maximization techniques to perform unsupervised learning

- Use segmentation to identify the pixel-wise class of each object in an image

- Identify both the bounding box and class of objects in an image using object detection

- Learn the building blocks for advanced techniques - MLPss, CNN, and RNNs
  Understand deep neural networks - including ResNet and DenseNet

- Understand and build autoregressive models – autoencoders, VAEs, and GANs

- Discover and implement deep reinforcement learning methods

Hands-On Artificial Intelligence on Google Cloud Platform

Anand Deshpande, Manish Kumar and Vikram Chaudhari

ISBN: 978-1-78953-846-5

- Understand the basics of cloud computing and explore GCP components
- Work with the data ingestion and preprocessing techniques in GCP for machine learning
- Implement machine learning algorithms with Google Cloud AutoML
- Optimize TensorFlow machine learning with Google Cloud TPUs
- Get to grips with operationalizing AI on GCP
- Build an end-to-end machine learning pipeline using Cloud Storage, Cloud Dataflow, and Cloud Datalab
- Build models from petabytes of structured and semi-structured data using BigQuery ML

Leave a review - let other readers know what you think

Please share your thoughts on this book with others by leaving a review on the site that you bought it from. If you purchased the book from Amazon, please leave us an honest review on this book's Amazon page. This is vital so that other potential readers can see and use your unbiased opinion to make purchasing decisions, we can understand what our customers think about our products, and our authors can see your feedback on the title that they have worked with Packt to create. It will only take a few minutes of your time, but is valuable to other potential customers, our authors, and Packt. Thank you!

Leave a review - let other readers know what you think

Index

W